Generalized Linear Models

An Applied Approach

John P. Hoffmann

Brigham Young University

PEARSON

Boston   New York   San Francisco
Mexico City   Montreal   Toronto   London   Madrid   Munich   Paris
Hong Kong   Singapore   Tokyo   Cape Town   Sydney

To Richard C. Hoffmann, Father, Mentor, and Writer "Extraordinaire"

Senior Editor: *Jeff Lasser*
Editorial Assistant: *Andrea Christie*
Marketing Manager: *Krista Groshong*
Production Editor: *Paul Mihailidis*
Manufacturing Buyer: *JoAnne Sweeney*
Cover Administrator: *Joel Gendron*
Editorial Production Service: *Matrix Productions*
Electronic Composition: *Peggy Cabot, Cabot Computer Services*

For related titles and support materials, visit our online catalog at www.ablongman.com.

Library of Congress Cataloging-in-Publication Data

Hoffmann, John P. (John Patrick).
    Generalized linear models : an applied approach / John P. Hoffmann.
        p.   cm.
    Includes bibliographical references and index.
    ISBN 0-205-37793-9
        1. Linear models (Statistics).   I. Title.

QA276.H574 2004
519.5--dc21

                                                                2003048642

Printed in the United States of America

10   9   8   7   6   5   4   3   2   1   07   06   05   04   03

Contents

8 *Where Do We Go from Here?* *149*

Appendix

Preface

The analysis of data using statistical methods has become a mainstay for many academic disciplines, from sociology, psychology, and economics to ecology, engineering, and physics. Computer software designed for statistical analysis has grown much more powerful in recent years. Empirical models that took a group of statisticians several days to analyze three or four decades ago can now be estimated in a few seconds using an off-the-shelf computer and some modestly priced software. Models that were considered highly complex a few decades ago are now routine in almost any discipline that collects and analyzes numeric data. The increasing breadth of models available has been accompanied by more sophisticated research questions; there is (or perhaps there should be) a reciprocal interplay between the statistical tools available and the complexity of research questions.

It is difficult to find contemporary journal articles or conference presentations that stop at presenting simple statistics such as percentages, means, *t*-tests, and the like. Much of the empirical research in the social and behavioral sciences, in business research, in education, and in many other fields is conducted using some type of regression model. Regression models are designed to predict (some prefer the term *explain*) one variable based on a set of one or more other variables. The most common of these models is easily the linear regression model. Dozens of books and articles have been written on this one type of model. Most students who take at least a couple of semesters of applied statistics learn, often in painful detail, about this model before they are exposed to any other type of regression model. An assumption of this model that is usually drilled into the heads of many an overwhelmed student is that the dependent variable (also termed the *response* or *outcome* variable) is *continuous* and *normally distributed*. The linear regression model is powerful enough that this assumption may be relaxed somewhat (see Chapter 1). Nevertheless, even a cursory examination of the literature in the just-mentioned fields, as well as in many others, shows that a large number of dependent variables are not normally distributed; in fact, many, if not most, are not even continuous!

Measurement in numerous applied fields is often so imprecise that even the best tools can return only what are labeled *categorical* or *discrete* variables. Even when continuity seems assured (think about measuring education), the resulting variable is frequently categorical. For example, survey research is a huge industry in the United States and elsewhere. Examine any daily newspaper or monthly magazine and you are bound to come across a survey of one kind or another. The social and behavioral sciences, business research, and several other disciplines rely heavily on surveys to gather data about numerous issues, and these data form the basis for empirical research. However, only rarely (at least in my experience) do we find variables from these surveys that are measured in a continuous fashion. It is much more common to find variables that are measured using categories. Experimental studies in fields such as medicine and social psychology also are replete with categorical variables. Even when researchers have the luxury of designing their own surveys or questionnaires, it is often difficult to determine ways to measure concepts continuously. How does one measure concepts such as happiness, religious beliefs, customer satisfaction, depression, voting behavior, number of friends, passage of legislation, graduating from high school, first sexual experience, or attitudes toward the death penalty using a continuous scale? It is not easy and, in most cases, requires an artificial approach.

We are most fortunate to be living in a time when the statistical tools for analyzing regression models no longer require that dependent variables follow a continuous, normal distribution. The regression models that relax this requirement fall under such headings as *categorical data analysis*, *limited dependent variable analysis*, and *generalized linear models*. Specific examples of these models that may be familiar are logistic regression, multinomial logistic regression, and Poisson regression. Moreover, a class of regression techniques known as survival or event history models is designed for continuous variables that measure the time until some event occurs. Time span variables are usually not normally distributed and tend to have other peculiarities that make the linear regression model inappropriate as a modeling tool (see Chapter 7). Although the various regression models designed for categorical or nonnormal variables share some of the characteristics that have made linear regression such a popular statistical tool, there are many nuances and assumptions that are often overlooked by those using these models.

The purpose of this book is to provide readers with an elementary introduction to a class of regression techniques known as generalized linear models. Generalized linear models include the popular linear regression approach, but they also encompass several techniques that are appropriate for categorical dependent variables (e.g., logistic regression) and for variables that assess the time until some event occurs (e.g., event history models). A more specific set of objectives involves demonstrating the ease with which these models may be estimated, interpreted, and checked for appropriateness. These goals are not pursued at the expense of comprehensiveness or the need to understand the underlying assumptions we must make in order to use these models wisely. However, comprehensiveness and understanding do not demand a highly developed grasp of statistical theory or programming. It seems more important, at least in my experience, that the student learning these techniques have experience with statistical reasoning. The statistical methods then become much more intuitive (Bradstreet 1996).

But why should someone write yet another book about these methods? After all, there are many reference books and textbooks that address statistical models for categorical and non-normally distributed dependent variables. Go to virtually any university library and search for books on generalized linear models, categorical data analysis, regression analysis, or some synonym and you will be flooded with choices. In teaching undergraduate and graduate courses about generalized linear models over the last several years, I have used several of these books with the hope that they would complement the in-and-out-of-classroom work. Unfortunately, I was often frustrated by these books because they assume a high level of mathematical and statistical knowledge among their readers. As many applied statistics instructors know, most students enter applied scientific disciplines with little mathematical background (at least those outside of mathematically rigorous disciplines such as statistics, engineering, or physics). Moreover, given the rapid advances in statistical software, the models described in this book are now available to users who do not have strong mathematical skills. Hence this book assumes little knowledge on the part of the reader beyond a solid understanding of algebraic manipulations, some exposure to mathematical transformations such as logarithms, a basic understanding of elementary statistics, and a bit of experience with the linear regression model.

The path to comprehension will also be somewhat smoother if the reader is familiar with some type of statistical software. These modest requirements will hopefully benefit not only the student, but also the instructor. Instructors who teach courses about these models will not have to either assume that students have a strong mathematical background or spend valuable course time teaching them the mathematics necessary to work through the presently available books on this topic. This is not to say that difficult work is not often necessary to understand when and why one is using these models; it is simply my contention that a rigorous theoretical and mathematical approach is not the *sine qua non* of applied statistical research.

Another goal of this book is to present the regression models using data from real data sets. The data sets used in the examples and in the exercises that follow the chapters are all available on the publisher's website: www.ablongman.com/hoffmann1e. They are the results of real research. They are not "massaged" so that they strictly meet the assumptions of the regression models; real-world experience shows that most hypothesized models do not cooperate in this way. Data are messy, residuals are ugly, and graphs almost never display the desired straight line. But this is an unavoidable part of life for the modeler. Although the how-to descriptions of the models in this book are followed by "now let's check this" sections, the results are rarely exact. Keep in mind that this is the nature of statistics, the "science of uncertainty" (Stigler 1986). Or, as Morris Kline once defined statistics, "[It is] the mathematical theory of ignorance" (Rose 1988).

The chapters are also designed as stand-alone "where do I go next" resources. Each chapter contains abundant references to articles and books that illustrate the regression techniques further and that show actual research applications from several specialty areas. I have not written this book with any particular academic field in mind, so I have attempted to draw widely from the many disciplines that use generalized linear models. Hence this book is suitable for advanced undergraduate students and graduate students from a number of disciplines such as sociology, psychology, political science, anthropology, history, marketing, management, finance, agronomy, ecology, family studies, geography, health sciences, education, and other related academic areas. It is also appropriate as a self-teaching tool, as a supplement for courses that cover other statistical topics, or as a reference book for those who find themselves using various types of regression models. The availability of the data sets and the focus on real-world applications should allow virtually any reader with a modest statistical background to learn how to construct and interpret generalized linear models. If you have access to the data sets via the website and some type of statistical software package, the learning will be all the more efficient.

A Note on Software

A growing number of statistical software packages are designed to estimate many if not all of the models presented in this book. To name a few, there is SAS, SPSS, Stata, S-Plus, Systat, Minitab, LIMDEP, Statistica, BMDP, EasyReg, XLStat, NCSS, Shazam, CDAS,

MLLSA, ResMod, TDA, GLIM, and Gauss. Each of these products includes numerous regression routines, but all have strengths and weaknesses. Nevertheless, we shall rely primarily on Stata in this book, with the occasional use of SPSS and SAS. Although the examples are shown primarily in Stata, Appendix A provides code, when available, for running the models in all three packages. Moreover, the data sets used in the examples and the exercises are all available in Stata, SPSS, and SAS.

The choice of software was not arbitrary. The software packages used in this book had to satisfy a few requirements. First, we needed software that not only would estimate the models in a straightforward manner, but also have good and easy-to-use data management capabilities. Second, the software had to be relatively comprehensive, in the sense that elementary statistics, graphical capabilities, and post-regression commands were available and simple to access. Third, the software needed to be current, with frequent updates from the developers, to keep up with the rapid advances in the field. Fourth, the software had to be widely available, given the assumption that many readers will either be taking a course or be affiliated with an academic institution or a research organization. Finally, the software needed to be familiar to a wide variety of academic disciplines.

Considering these requirements and reflecting on my own learning and teaching experiences, especially in the social sciences, it seemed that Stata best met all of the requirements, with SAS and SPSS a close second and third. Although I find that students in the social and behavioral sciences seem to prefer SPSS's Windows interface, they tend to learn Stata quickly and are very impressed by its wide-ranging capabilities. Moreover, the current version of SPSS, at least at the time I am typing this sentence, does not estimate a few of the models described in the following chapters. SAS is perhaps the best known and most widely used of the software mentioned, but, as a teaching tool, I have come to rely on Stata over SAS for a variety of reasons (even though I must admit that I still use SAS a majority of the time in my own research).

I apologize for this rather long-winded discussion of software, and conclude by saying that we will use Stata most of the time, SPSS and SAS occasionally. Hopefully, though, this will not deter readers who employ other types of statistical software from using this book. I find that other software packages (at least those I have used), such as S-Plus, LIMDEP, or Minitab, are similar enough to Stata, SPSS, and SAS in terms of organization and practical use to be frequently interchangeable. Moreover, the availability of file transfer software such as DBMS and Stat/Transfer offers the analyst simple tools for transferring data sets so they may be used with various statistical software packages. Readers who wish additional information about estimating many of the generalized linear models described in this book using Stata, SAS, or SPSS should consult Long and Freese (2001), Hardin and Hilbe (2001), Stokes, Davis, and Koch (2000), or SPSS (2002).

Organization of the Book

This book is divided into seven chapters that focus on the various regression models and a final chapter that is aptly titled "Where Do We Go from Here?" The first chapter covers the linear regression model in a concise way. Because this book begins with the assumption that readers have had some exposure to linear regression, this chapter is designed as a review. It covers the goals of the regression model, how to estimate a linear (OLS) model, the assumptions that underlie the model, and the use of interaction terms in a regression context.

Chapter 2 introduces the fundamental aspects of generalized linear models. It begins with a discussion of the link function. It then provides a primer on the most common probability distributions used by generalized linear models, followed by a brief discussion of maximum likelihood estimation. Chapter 2 concludes with a description of how to check the overall fit of models estimated with maximum likelihood and uses a Stata example of a linear regression model to demonstrate some of these fit statistics.

Chapter 3 discusses perhaps the most common generalized linear models: Logistic and probit regression. These are designed for binary or dichotomous dependent variables. The chapter describes the two models using both SPSS and Stata and includes a discussion of odds ratios and predicted probabilities that form the basis of interpretation for these models. It presents both bivariable and multivariable models and shows how to interpret coefficients and other model output. The chapter concludes with a section on diagnostic tests for the logistic regression model.

Chapter 4 describes a couple of generalized linear models that are appropriate for ordinal dependent variables: Ordered logistic and ordered probit. Following the design of Chapter 3, this chapter shows how a simple cross-tabulation of variables translates into a regression model. It then demonstrates how to estimate the models and describes an important assumption—known as the proportional odds assumption—and how to test this assumption after fitting the models. The chapter concludes with a brief description of other models that may be used with ordinal dependent variables.

Chapter 5 discusses the multinomial logistic regression model. This generalized linear model is appropriate for nominal dependent variables, or those categorical variables that have no natural ordering. It begins by revisiting the multinomial distribution. Then, after showing how to estimate these models with both single and multiple independent variables, the chapter describes several alternatives to the multinomial logistic model. It concludes with a description of diagnostic tools.

Chapter 6 shifts attention away from binary, ordinal, or multinomial variables and focuses on variables that count something, such as the number of traffic accidents, earthquakes, or volunteer activities. Although, strictly speaking, count variables are categorical, they have historically been treated as continuous. After discussing why treating them as continuous is not wise, the chapter describes three models for count variables: Poisson regression, overdispersed Poisson regression, and negative binomial regression. It includes a discussion of diagnostic approaches for the Poisson model. The chapter concludes with a discussion of alternatives to these count models.

Chapter 7 addresses another class of variables: Those that measure the time until some event occurs (e.g., death, birth, marriage). Although discussions of regression models designed to assess these types of variables, specifically event history or survival models, are often divorced from discussions of generalized linear models, several of these models actually fall under the rubric of generalized linear models. The chapter describes some peculiar issues that must be addressed when faced with these variables, in particular censoring and time-dependent covariates. It then discusses survivor and hazard functions before showing how to estimate three common parametric event history models. The final sections of the chapter address discrete-time event history models. Chapter 7 concludes with a section on problems that pertain especially, but not uniquely, to event history models, such as unobserved heterogeneity.

The final chapter briefly describes a special set of issues about which regression modelers should be aware, if not relentlessly concerned. Although each of these issues is probably important enough to warrant its own chapter, we will discuss only a few aspects of each. These issues include sample selection bias, endogeneity, longitudinal data, multi-level models, and nonparametric regression. Of course, there are many important issues that are left unaddressed, but we have to stop somewhere.

Acknowledgments

Numerous people encouraged me in one way or another to write this book. The initial seed was planted by Katherine Bell of Allyn and Bacon, who encouraged me to submit a proposal when the ideas for this book were just emerging. Jeff Lasser, also of Allyn and Bacon, took on the encouragement mantle from there and has been a been a fine editor ever since. My colleagues at Brigham Young University have provided a supportive environment for research and writing ever since my arrival a few years ago. I would especially like to thank Steve Bahr, who initially assigned me to teach a course titled "Intermediate Statistics" that provided the bed upon which the notes for this book began to take shape. A large number of students who have taken that course have taught me much about how to present statistical models so that they are intelligible in a large number of contexts. In particular, I'd like to single out Scott Baldwin and Colter Mitchell, two former students who helped me polish this book, ensured that the examples followed the actual analyses, and helped write the solutions manual. And I can't forget several colleagues with whom I worked for several years at the National Opinion Research Center (NORC). It was there that I was forced to better understand applied statistics, with all their marvelous imperfections. These colleagues include Bob Johnson, Dean Gerstein, Felicia Cerbone, Mike Pergamit, Lynn Huang, and the late Susan Su. I also wish to thank the reviewers: Yoshinori Kamo, Louisiana State University; Raymond V. Liedka, University of New Mexico; Timothy Ireland, Niagara University; and Thomas Rotolo, Washington State University. Finally, this work would not have been possible without the support and love I receive every day from my family: The amazing Lynn and our four wonderful boys, Brian, Christopher, Brandon, and Curtis.

1

A Review of the Linear Regression Model

Perhaps the most commonly used technique in statistical analysis is the linear regression model. Its long history and broad use are due to both its simplicity and its wide-ranging applicability. The linear regression model is often the first technique taught to students in a second-semester applied statistics course. Although the material in this book presumes that readers have already learned how to use the linear regression model, the present chapter is designed to review the model and set the stage for more sophisticated material in subsequent chapters. For readers who wish a more thorough review of linear regression, there are many useful books available (e.g., Allison 1999; Chatterjee and Price 1991; Graybill and Iyer 1994; Kleinbaum et al. 1998; Montgomery, Peck, and Vining 2001).

To begin, recall that the goal of regression analysis in general is to examine the association between one or more independent variables, usually denoted as X's, and a single dependent variable, denoted as Y. The *linear* regression analysis further specifies this presumed association as occurring between some set of X's and a single, continuous dependent variable, Y. Note that the term *continuous* implies that the dependent variable is measured continuously; that is, its values can conceivably be any real number, negative or positive. As later chapters will reveal, this is often an unrealistic requirement in most areas of applied statistics, mainly because the tools we use to measure variables are not precise enough to provide us with *any* real number. Even relatively sensitive instruments, such as thermometers, furnish only approximate values (e.g., 98.6 degrees F.). Now, imagine measuring something more commonly used in the social and behavioral sciences, such as the amount of formal education. Normally, we only approximate this value with something like years of formal education.

Getting back to the particular labels of variables used in the linear regression model, some researchers call the independent variables *exogenous*, *predictor*, or *explanatory* variables. To distinguish the independent variables, they are usually labeled with numeric subscripts, such as X_1, X_2, X_3, and so forth. The dependent variable is often called the *outcome*, *response*, or *endogenous* variable. There is rarely any reason to use a subscript when labeling the dependent variable because, in most applications that are of interest to us, there is only one. Occasionally you may run across E(Y) to indicate the dependent variable. This simply means the expected value of Y (sometimes known as the adjusted mean). You may also see the notation Y_i or y_i to denote the dependent variable. The subscript i is placed after the Y to indicate that there are different values of the dependent variable for each observation in the sample. Some statisticians prefer to use the lowercase y to distinguish the sample regression model from the population regression model (Graybill and Iyer 1994). We shall not make this distinction explicit in this presentation, so the uppercase Y is used throughout.

A key question is what purpose does the linear regression model, or any regression model for that matter, serve? It actually may serve a number of different purposes, but, in a basic sense, it is designed to either (1) explain differences in the dependent variable that may depend on the independent variables; or (2) predict when a specific value of the dependent variable might occur based on values of the independent variables. Oftentimes this distinction is labeled *explanation* versus *prediction*. Although the same statistical techniques apply, researchers sometimes emphasize one goal over the other.

Issues of Interest

Although *explanation* and *prediction* are labels used to identify of the general goals of the regression model, we may further specify particular issues that are of interest. These include the following:

1. *The form of the relationship.* This involves what the regression equation looks like, or how we depict the specific mathematical function that represents the association between the independent and dependent variables. You may recall that the linear regression equation is typically written as

$$Y = \alpha + \beta_1 X_1 + \beta_2 X_2 + \beta_3 X_3 + \dots + \beta_k X_k + \varepsilon \qquad (1.1)$$

where α (the Greek letter *alpha*, sometimes instead shown as β_0) is the intercept, the β's (the Greek letter *beta*) are regression or slope coefficients, the ε (the Greek letter *epsilon*) is the error term, and there are k independent variables (hence the k subscript that follows the final β and X in the equation). Note that the regression model represented in this equation is additive: The independent variables multiplied by their coefficients add up to determine the expected value of the dependent variable. Here we are assuming that the independent variables *independently* add up in some fashion to predict (or explain) the value of the dependent variable. As we shall see later in the chapter, we may relax this requirement of additivity by introducing interaction terms in the model. The error term, which is occasionally called the disturbance term, is a random variable that captures what is not explained by the set of independent variables and their coefficients. Much of the basis for linear regression analysis focuses on the assumptions made about the error term. Some of these assumptions are described subsequently.

There are many other possible forms of the relationship between the independent and dependent variables. For example, perhaps the form of the relationship is thought to follow the pattern shown in Equation 1.2.

$$Y = \alpha + \beta_1 X_1 + \beta_2 X_1^2 + \beta_3 X_2 + \varepsilon \qquad (1.2)$$

Note that we have included not only X_1, but also X_1^2, or the squared value of variable X_1, in the equation. This is often a useful step when we think that Y and X_1 have a relationship that is not linear. We'll return to this issue later in the chapter.

2. *The direction and strength of the associations.* We are frequently interested in whether there is a positive or negative association between the independent variables and the dependent variable. For example, it is safe to hypothesize that there is a positive association between educational attainment, measured as number of years of formal schooling, and personal income. In brief, we reasonably expect that, in a sample of adults in the United States, as education increases, personal income also increases. Meanwhile, there is usually a negative relationship between measures of self-esteem and depression: As self-esteem increases among a sample of, say, adolescents, we typically find that symptoms of depression such as sadness or melancholy decrease. How is this represented in our linear regression model? We simply look at the valence of the regression coefficient. If it is a negative number then we say there is a negative association; if it is a positive number we say there is a positive association.

To determine the strength of the associations, we look at the size of the regression coefficients. Assume that two independent variables are measured in the same way (e.g., in years). If we wish to ascertain which variable has a stronger association with the dependent variable, then we may examine the size of the respective coefficients. The larger coefficient, in an absolute sense, is associated with the variable that has the stronger association with the dependent variable. Unfortunately, making such determinations is often fraught with difficulties. First, the independent variables must be measured in the same way. More often than not, independent variables are measured differently. For instance, age is not measured in the same way as income. Second, making such a determination assumes that neither independent variable is contaminated by measurement error, or, if both variables are measured with error, then the amount of error is identical for both variables. This is an unlikely scenario. Some researchers argue that the use of standardized regression coefficients (also known as *beta weights*) solves the first problem because these coefficients adjust the measurement of the variables so they are in the same units (typically standard deviations). However, this approach assumes that standard deviations are an equally meaningful unit of measurement for both independent variables (see Fox (1997) and Goldberger and Manski (1995) for a general discussion of this issue). This is often not the case.

3. *Which independent variables are important and which are not.* Although this is related to the size and strength of the association issue, there are subtle differences. A standard approach is to evaluate the importance of a variable in a regression model by examining its *p*-value. As you may remember, a large majority of empirical studies use $p < 0.05$ as the cut-off level. The interpretation of this *p*-value is often ill-defined, however. Recall that one of the null hypotheses in a linear regression model is that the regression coefficient is equal to zero in the population. Put simply, a *p*-value in a regression analysis indicates how often we expect to get the coefficient observed this far from zero if the actual coefficient was zero in the population. Suppose, for example, that our estimated model provides a regression coefficient of 2.5 with a p-value of 0.03. One interpretation is the following: If we were to take thousands of samples from the population from which the sample was drawn, and the actual regression coefficient was zero in the population, we would expect, on average, to get a coefficient of 2.5 *or something further from zero* only three times out of one hundred samples. Note that we use the term *something further from zero* to denote that we are using a two-tailed significance test. In other words, we are not assuming, *a priori*, a positive or negative association.

You may by now be wondering what p-values have to do with the importance of the independent variables. One simple rule of thumb is that an independent variable is not "important" in some qualitative sense unless its coefficient is significantly different from zero. After deciding which threshold you wish to use to make this assessment, such as $p <$ 0.05 or $p < 0.01$, it is easy to conclude whether or not a coefficient, and its associated independent variable, may be important. For example, $p < 0.05$ (two-tailed test) is a commonly accepted threshold for demarcating whether or not a coefficient is statistically significant. If we decide to accept this threshold as our decision rule, then any coefficient with a p-value above 0.05 is not important, but any that is below 0.05 may be important. You should remember, however, that statistical significance tests, of which p-values are a type, are based not just on the size of the coefficient, but also on its standard error. And standard errors are based partly on sample size. All else being equal, a coefficient from an analysis is likely to have a smaller standard error (hence a smaller p-value) if it is based on a larger sample size. Given a very large sample, you will often find that many, if not all, the p-values are below 0.05, even when regression coefficients seem close to zero . If this is the case, you should fall back on the relative size of the coefficient and your conceptualization of the associations to decide which independent variables are truly important.

Other approaches recommended by applied statisticians to compare independent variables include commonality analysis, which attempts to decompose the explained variance of the dependent variable into specific components that are associated with each independent variable (see Rowell (1996) for details), and criticality analysis, a recently developed method that combines information about overall model fit with information about the importance of particular variables for the best fitting model (Azen, Budescu, and Reiser 2001). Finally, there are some who argue that coefficients and their p-values provide only a partial view of the associations in the data. Statistics is an inexact science and so presentations of associations should reflect this uncertainty. Hence some recommend that analysts provide confidence intervals (CIs) in addition to or in place of p-values (Woolson and Kleinman 1989; Poole 1987). Many statistical software packages provide CIs as part of their regression output.

4. *Is the association between an independent variable and the dependent variable confounded by other independent variables?* Answering this inquiry is one of the main reasons for including control variables in the regression model. For instance, suppose we determine that there is a statistical association between gender and blood pressure (e.g., males tend to have higher blood pressure than females), perhaps by estimating a linear regression model with data from a sample of adults. We might then ask: Is there something about "maleness" that "causes" high blood pressure? However, suppose we then re-estimated the regression model, but this time included independent variables that gauged lifestyle factors such as smoking, nutrition, and exercise. If the association between gender and high blood pressure decreased, perhaps so that it was no longer statistically significant, then we could conclude that the presumed association was confounded by these other variables. Males may have higher blood pressure than females partly because they smoke more or eat poorly. "Maleness" does not cause high blood pressure; rather, males, for some reason, are more likely than females to engage in riskier lifestyles that lead to higher blood pressure.

In order to determine the association between a particular independent variable and the dependent variable, it is necessary to include other independent variables that may be associated with both the independent variable of interest and the dependent variable. We often do not know, *a priori*, which additional variables have this effect, so we must rely on our knowledge of the processes involved in the etiology of our dependent variable to determine which variables to include in the regression model. In fact, it is not an exaggeration to claim that intimate knowledge of these processes—through reviewing the literature, conducting background research, and thinking deeply about the issues involved in your study—is necessary before estimating any regression model.

5. *Predicting a value of* Y *for a given set of* X*'s.* As mentioned previously, one general goal of estimating a regression model is to predict values of the dependent variable. An intricately related goal is to determine how well we predict values of the dependent variable based on values of the independent variables. This latter issue falls under the term goodness-of-fit. Prediction and goodness-of-fit are based on the entire regression model, not just the coefficients and *p*-values for particular variables.

Predicting a value of the dependent variable based on values of the independent variables is a simple exercise after we have estimated the linear regression model. Let's assume that we wish to estimate annual incomes (in $1,000) among a sample of adults from the United states. We think that formal education and mother's education (both measured in years) are the key determinants of one's annual income. Therefore, we estimate a linear regression model and come up with Equation 1.3.

$$\text{Annual income} = 20 + 0.8(\text{education}) + 0.5(\text{mother's education}) \qquad (1.3)$$

For those with 18 years of education and whose mothers have 12 years of education, we predict that their annual income is [20 + {0.8*18} + {0.5*12}] = 40.4, or $40,400 annually. Of course, there will likely be deviations from this predicted amount among particular observations in our data set. Hence $40,400 is the average (mean) annual income among those with 18 years of education and whose mothers have 12 years of education in our data set. As we will see in later chapters, most statistical software that estimates regression models has an option for producing predicted values.

There is an important issue to keep in mind about predicted values, however. That is, it is unwise to attempt to predict values that fall outside the range of data used in the analysis (Manski 1995). For instance, assume that, in our preceding annual income exercise, the sample includes income data that range from $10,000 to $120,000, education data that range from 8 to 20 years, and mother's education data that range from 6 to 18 years. It would be unwise, based on the regression model, to try to predict the income of someone who has only 6 years of education and whose mother has only 4 years of education; these values fall outside the range of data and are not in the sample. Any results from such a prediction can be highly misleading.

How to Estimate a Linear Regression Model

As mentioned in the opening paragraph of this chapter, one of the reasons for the widespread use of the linear regression model is its relative simplicity. Part of this is due to the simplicity of interpretation, but perhaps more important is the simplicity of estimation. The linear regression model may be estimated through various procedures (e.g., maximum likelihood; see Chapter 2), but the most common approach is ordinary least squares (OLS), also known as the method of least squares. The simplest example of OLS is when there is only one independent variable.

Consider Figure 1.1, which shows a scatterplot of annual income in $1,000s by education in years. The diagonal line is the least squares line, or the line that most closely fits the data points. In other words, the line minimizes the sum of squares of the distances from the data points to the line. The distance from the data points to the line is known as the error or residual. By summing the squared values of these distances, we may estimate the sum of squared errors (SSE). An OLS regression model minimizes this SSE, as shown in Equation 1.4.

$$\text{SSE} = \sum_{i=1}^{n}\left(Y_i - \hat{Y}_i\right)^2 \qquad (1.4)$$

where Y_i is the observed value and $\hat{Y}_i$ is the predicted value. Recall from the previous discussion that predicted values may be computed by the regression equation. Using this

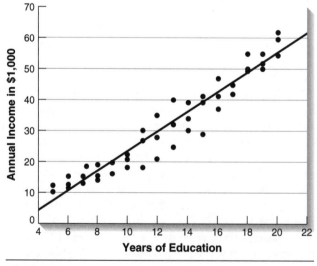

FIGURE 1.1

formula, we may compute the quantity SSE for any linear regression model. A nice property of the OLS approach to estimating a linear regression model is that the SSE from it will be the smallest of any alternative approach if the assumptions discussed in the next section are met.

Another nice property of OLS is that it leads to simple formulas for computing the regression coefficients and the intercept. The formula for the regression coefficient, or slope, if there is only one independent variable is

$$\hat{\beta}_1 = \frac{\sum\limits_{i=1}^{n}(X_i - \overline{X})(Y_i - \overline{Y})}{\sum\limits_{i=1}^{n}(X_i - \overline{X})^2} \qquad (1.5)$$

After computing the regression coefficient, it is a simple matter to compute the intercept.

$$\hat{\alpha} = \overline{Y} - \hat{\beta}_1 \overline{X} \qquad (1.6)$$

Extending the OLS (linear) regression model to accommodate more than one independent variable is relatively simple, but it requires some algebraic manipulations that are cumbersome and are therefore left to the more mathematically astute reader. The most efficient formulas are often presented using matrix notation. These formulas and their derivations are found in almost any introductory mathematical statistics textbook or book that focuses on linear regression analysis (e.g., Draper and Smith 1998). Equations for computing the standard errors of regression coefficients and the goodness-of-fit measures (e.g., R^2) may also be found in these types of books.

A Detailed Example of an OLS Regression Model

In order to bring these various issues together and introduce additional topics, the following presents a simple example of an OLS regression model. The data are from the 1996 General Social Survey (GSS), a nationally representative sample of adults in the United States. The GSS asks numerous questions about education, income, attitudes, behaviors, and many other issues. It is conducted every two years by the National Opinion Research Center of the University of Chicago. Data from all but the most recent surveys are freely available from the GSS website (http://www.icpsr.umich.edu/GSS).

In Example 1.1, we'll use data from more than 1,500 respondents to estimate the associations among annual personal income (*income*) and the following independent variables: *educate* (years of formal education), *gender* (measured as 0 = male, 1 = female), race/ethnicity (*race,* measured as 0 = white, 1 = non-white), and parent's socioeconomic status (*pasei*). For simplicity's sake, we'll assume that income is a continuous, normally distributed variable and that the model meets the assumptions described later in this chapter. The data set is labeled *GSS96.dta*; hence it is a Stata data file. SPSS and SAS versions of the data file are also available for downloading. We'll use Stata's *regress* command to estimate the OLS regression model. The term *beta* is placed after the comma at the end of the line so that Stata will also compute standardized regression coefficients.

EXAMPLE 1.1   *An OLS Regression Model of Personal Income*

regress income educate gender race pasei, beta   *This appears on the command line*

Source	SS	df	MS		
				Number of obs	= 1565
				$F(4, 1560)$	= 47.41
Model	1516.458	4	379.114478	Prob > F	= 0.0000
Residual	12475.137	1560	7.996883	R-squared	= 0.1084
				Adj R-squared	= 0.1061
Total	13991.595	1564	8.946033	Root MSE	= 2.8279

income	Coef.	Std. Err.	t	P > |t|	Beta
educate	.301480	.028860	10.45	0.000	.268143
gender	−1.324165	.143502	−9.23	0.000	−.221272
race	−.177464	.201304	−0.88	0.378	−.021276
pasei	−.009150	.004039	−2.27	0.024	−.058479
_cons	6.842638	.396127	17.27	0.000	.

The output is relatively standard across statistical software. The first part of the output shows the ANOVA table, which is designed to decompose the variability of the dependent variable into two terms: The amount of variability explained by the model (the regression sum of squares, shown in the row labeled *Model*) and the amount of variability remaining after estimating the model (the residual sum of squares, shown in the row labeled *Residual*). It also displays the total variability, or total sum of squares, which is simply the sum of squares of the dependent variable $\left(\sum_{i=1}^{n} (Y_i - \overline{Y}_i)^2 \right)$. Recall that dividing this quantity by $n - 1$ yields the sample variance.

The R-squared (R^2 for short; it is also known as the *coefficient of determination*) shows the proportion of variability in the dependent variable that is explained by the model. Its positive square root is termed the *multiple correlation coefficient*. The R^2 is simply the regression sum of squares divided by the total sum of squares. In the above model, this is 1,516.458 / 13,991.595 = 0.108. The adj(usted) R-squared is designed to adjust for the number of independent variables in the model. The R^2 increases as we add independent variables to the model, whether or not they are important. The adjusted R^2 penalizes the analyst for simply adding superfluous variables to the model. The adjusted R^2 is computed as

$$\overline{R}_2 = \left(R_2 - \frac{k}{n-1} \right) \left(\frac{n-1}{n-k-1} \right) \tag{1.7}$$

The *F*-value and its associated *p*-value (labeled *Prob > F* in the Example) tests statistically the hypothesis that all the regression coefficients are equal to zero against the alternative hypothesis that at least one coefficient is not equal to zero. Alternatively, they may be thought of as testing whether the model is explaining any of the variability in the dependent variable. A significant F-value therefore tells us that we are explaining a statistically significant amount of the variability in the dependent variable. If the independent variables were not explaining any of the dependent variable's variability, we would expect the R^2 to be statistically indistinct from zero. The F-value is computed as the mean square from the regression model divided by the mean square due to error (MSR/MSE). In the preceding table, this is 379.11 / 7.997 = 47.41. Recall that F-values have two degrees of freedom, labeled *numerator* and *denominator* degrees of freedom. The numerator degrees of freedom is simply the number of independent variables in the model, k. The denominator degrees of freedom is the sample size minus the number of coefficients estimated in the model, $n - k - 1$ (the 1 is included to denote the intercept). Note that the p-value associated with the F-value is listed as 0.000 in the printout. This implies that the p-value is actually less than 0.001. Recall from basic statistics that a p-value cannot be zero. This would imply no possibility of the null hypothesis; an untenable outcome if ever there was one. It is important to remember that significance tests depend partly on the sample size of your data set. Simply because an F-value is statistically significant or the R^2 is relatively large does not mean that the equation is valuable as a predictive tool (see Draper and Smith (1998) for a discussion of this issue).

Finally, let's discuss what for many analysts is the most consequential part of the regression output: The coefficients, standard errors, and p-values. Although goodness-of-fit measures are clearly useful, many of the applied sciences are often more interested in determining whether particular independent variables are helpful in predicting the dependent variable. A quick glance at the results suggests that education and gender may be particularly useful for predicting personal income, yet race/ethnicity (as gauged by the variable *race*) is not. Recalling the way these two independent variables are measured, the interpretation of their coefficients follows:

> Controlling for the effects of the other independent variables, we expect a one-year increase in education to be associated with a 0.30-unit increase in personal income.

> Controlling for the effects of the other variables in the model, we expect females to earn annual incomes about 1.32 units less than males.

Note that both of these coefficients are highly significant, with p-values less than 0.001. The intercept (labeled _cons in the printout) indicates the expected value of the dependent variable when all the independent variables are zero. This may be a meaningless number if the data set does not include zero values for some of the independent variables. In our example, we do not observe anyone in the data set with an *educate* value of zero, so the intercept of 6.84 is not useful.

As mentioned previously, the *Beta*'s listed in the last column of the table are standardized regression coefficients. Although there is some debate in the literature about their usefulness, their interpretation for continuously distributed independent variables is straightforward. For example, controlling for the effects of the other variables in the model, we expect a one standard deviation unit increase in education to be associated with a 0.268 standard deviation unit increase in personal income. Notice that this coefficient is fairly close in magnitude to its unstandardized counterpart. Readers who have access to the *GSS96* data set may wish to evaluate the respective standard deviations of *educate* and *income* to determine why these coefficients are similar. This simple exercise provides valuable experience with unstandardized and standardized coefficients.

Researchers often wish to utilize standardized regression coefficients to compare the predictive power of independent variables. For instance, the standardized coefficient for *educate* is much larger—in absolute value—than the standardized coefficient for parent's socioeconomic status (*pasei*). It therefore seems reasonable to conclude that *educate* has a stronger effect on income than *pasei*. Although this may be a sensible conclusion, standardized regression coefficients should be used cautiously. For dummy variables, such as *gender* in the preceding model, they are not very useful. After all, what does a one standard deviation unit change in *gender* mean? It has little meaning when independent variables take on only two possible values. Equally important is the fact that the magnitude of standardized regression coefficients depends on the variability of the independent variables, and this may shift from sample to sample (Montgomery, Peck, and Vining 2001). Hence analysts should be careful when using standardized regression coefficients.

The Assumptions of the OLS (Linear) Regression Model

As mentioned previously, the OLS regression model is a widely used and valuable statistical tool. However, there are a number of assumptions about the model that should be met if we are to use it well. This is particularly important because one goal of the analysis is to make inferences from the model to larger processes that exist in the "real" world. Many courses on linear regression analysis spend the bulk of their time discussing these assumptions and learning what to do when they are violated (Berry 1993; Fox 1991). In the interests of brevity, we shall quickly review the assumptions, discuss how to test them, and mention alternative approaches when they are violated.

1. *Independence.* A key assumption that is often violated is that the observations from which the dependent variable are measured are independent of one another. This is primarily an issue of sampling. That is, when collecting data it is best to take steps to ensure that the observations are independent. For instance, when doing survey research, perhaps on attitudes toward various political issues, it is best to collect data from respondents who do not influence one another. This is often a difficult goal in some types of studies, such as research where data are collected from family members. In this situation, it is likely that respondents within families are more similar in many ways than respondents who are not in the same family.

The key problem that arises when observations are not independent is that the standard errors of the coefficients are likely biased. Therefore, significance tests are not accurate. In many studies this problem of dependence is unavoidable. Fortunately, there are many techniques available that adjust standard errors for non-independence. Stata, for example, will adjust standard errors for clustering, a particular type of non-independence. Both Stata and SAS also have a set of regression techniques appropriate to use when observations are dependent in some way. See the SAS documentation on the *SURVEYREG* procedure or the Stata documentation on *svyreg* for regression models that are designed for survey data. These procedures are fashioned to provide the analyst with a variety of approaches when faced with non-independent data obtained from a survey.

2. *Linearity.* OLS regression assumes that the mean value of the dependent variable at each specific combination of the independent variables is a linear function of those variables. For example, this assumption implies that, in three dimensions, the regression surface is flat. The OLS regression approach is termed *linear* because we assume that the model is linear in its coefficients (e.g., β_1), not necessarily because there is a linear relationship between the independent and dependent variables. Simply including interaction $(X_1 * X_2)$ or quadratic (X_1^2) terms in the model implies that the association between the independent and dependent variables is not linear.

Nevertheless, there are situations, most of which are difficult to detect without a strong theory, where the variables are related through a nonlinear function. For example, we may find a situation where the functional relationship is

$$Y = \alpha + \beta_1 \ln[\beta_2 X_1] + \beta_3 X_3 + \varepsilon \tag{1.8}$$

where ln indicates the natural logarithm. If this is the case, and OLS regression is used, both the regression coefficients and their standard errors are biased. In some situations, it is possible to transform the equation so it may be estimated with linear methods (see Cleveland 1993).

One diagnostic check that may reveal nonlinearities in the associations is to examine the bivariate associations between the independent and dependent variables with scatterplots before estimating the regression model. After estimating the model, the analyst should always observe the distribution of the error terms with a normal probability plot. Another useful technique is to graph partial residual plots for each independent variable, where the *y*-axes are the residuals (the standardized or studentized residuals are often used; see Fox 1991) and the *x*-axes are the independent variables. These graphical approaches may reveal nonlinearities, but experience suggests that they are most useful for showing nonlinearities only in the associations among the variables, rather than nonlinearities in the functional form of the relationships. Hence, one may come across situations where nonlinear regression techniques are required. An introduction to nonlinear regression techniques is provided in Draper and Smith (1998) and Montgomery, Peck, and Vining (2001). A more comprehensive overview is available in Fox (2000) or Huet et al. (1996).

Fortunately, the regression techniques described in subsequent chapters allow a variety of nonlinear relationships to be estimated. This will become apparent as we move through this material.

3. *Homoscedasticity ("same scatter").* The OLS regression model assumes that the variance of the error term is constant for all combinations of independent variables. A common situation, especially when dealing with survey data, is that the variability of the error term increases with larger values of the independent variables. A well-known example involves wealth (measured as income plus assets) and spending patterns. Families with little wealth tend to have similar spending patterns, perhaps because after meeting basic needs there is little money left over to spend on leisure items. But, as we move up the wealth ladder, we often see highly diverse spending patterns; some wealthy families spend a lot but others save a lot. Hence when regressing wealth on spending, we often will see that the variability in the errors increases at higher values of wealth. This is an example of heteroscedastic errors.

When faced with heteroscedastic errors, one typically finds biased standard errors of the coefficients. Thus, the significance tests are incorrect and the ability to make inferences from the model is attenuated. Detection of heteroscedastic errors is accomplished through post-model scatterplots that plot the residuals against the predicted values.

A fan-shaped pattern reveals the presence of heteroscedastic errors. Figure 1.2 shows an example of this pattern based on the residuals and predicted values from a model that regresses spending on family income. Note that the y-axis involves studentized residuals (see Fox 1991). There are also some numeric tests for heteroscedastic errors, such as White's test or Glejser's test. A description of these and how to implement them is provided in Greene (2000).

There are several approaches for correcting a model with heteroscedastic errors. First, transforming the dependent variable, such as taking its natural logarithm, and then re-estimating the OLS regression model often solves heteroscedasticity problems. Second, if we can determine that one of the variables is leading to heteroscedastic errors, then re-estimating the model with weighted least squares (WLS) using some transformation of the variable may solve the problem. Third, several statistical software packages, including Stata, have specialized regression routines that are designed to correct standard errors for heteroscedasticity. Two examples are the Newey-West routine and White's correction. Long and Erwin (2000) provide an extended discussion of correction approaches for linear regression models. Finally, heteroscedastic errors are often caused by the omission of a key independent variable. Therefore, correct model specification often solves the problem.

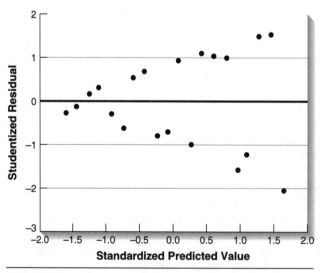

FIGURE 1.2

4. *There is no autocorrelation (serial correlation) among the error terms.* Recall that the OLS regression model assumes that the errors are random; there is no systematic pattern to them after considering the association between the independent variables and the dependent variable. Yet, data are often collected over time or across spatial units such as counties or states. Errors that occur closer together in time or space tend to be more highly correlated than errors that are more distant. These autocorrelated errors lead to biased standard errors. Time series models, in particular, are almost always plagued with autocorrelation.

The most common test for autocorrelated errors is the Durbin-Watson test (see Greene 2000 for a thorough description). Values of this test close to two indicate a lack of autocorrelation, but usually one must check tables of Durbin-Watson values to determine the likelihood of autocorrelated errors.

There are several ways to correct a model for autocorrelated errors. First, there are specialized estimation routines that fall under the class of time series models that are appropriate when data are collected over time. Second, Cochran-Orcutt or Prais-Winsten regression are designed for models with autocorrelated errors and are available in select software packages such as Stata. Third, generalized estimating equations (GEEs) are designed to model data that have been collected over time among individual respondents (i.e., longitudinal or panel data). GEEs allow a variety of error structures to be estimated, including autocorrelation. Diggle, Liang, and Zeger (1994) provide a detailed overview of GEEs and other approaches for analyzing longitudinal data. Chapter 8 includes a brief discussion of GEEs.

5. *Multicollinearity.* This assumption implies that there is not perfect collinearity between any combination of the independent variables. In other words, there is not a perfect relationship between any subset of the X's. Assume, for a moment, that two of the independent variables in the proposed model are perfectly correlated (Pearson's $r = 1.0$). Then imagine attempting to estimate the covariance between one of these variables and the dependent variable after considering the association with the other variable. It could not be done; there would be no variance left over in the independent variable once we considered its overlap with its twin.

Although most descriptions are careful to point out that the assumption describes the lack of a *perfect association* among independent variables, experience indicates that even a high correlation between subsets of independent variables may lead to problems, including biased standard errors and unusual regression coefficients.

Tests for multicollinearity include a review of variance inflation factors (VIFs) and condition indices. Rules of thumb vary, but many observers argue that a VIF above 9 or 10 should make the analyst suspicious of multicollinearity problems. After estimating the condition indices from a model, variance proportions greater than 0.5 associated with eigenvalues greater than 30 should be checked. These are useful for identifying the particular source of the problem. Kleinbaum et al. (1998) have a concise discussion of VIFs and condition indices.

If the model is contaminated by multicollinearity, there are several solutions. First, one may collect more data—all else being equal, variables based on more observations have more variability to be explained and thus are less likely to be perfectly collinear with other variables in the data set. Of course, in many research projects collecting more data is not practical. Second, if the collinearity problem involves variables that are measuring a similar phenomenon (e.g., sadness and exhaustion may be symptoms of depression), then variables can be combined in some manner, such as through factor analysis or some other latent variable technique. Third, if the collinearity problem is caused by interaction terms among the independent variables or higher-order terms (e.g., quadratic or cubic terms), then centering the independent variable(s) prior to computing the terms usually attenuates collinearity problems (Aiken and West 1991).

6. *For each independent variable, the correlation with the error term is zero.* This implies that we have not left out any important variables that may be associated with one or more of the independent variables. Suppose, for example, that an OLS regression model is designed to predict personal income and includes as independent variables gender, race, and parents' socioeconomic status. As we saw in the analysis earlier in the chapter, education is also an important determinant of income. Moreover, it is likely that one's education is associated with one's parents' status. By leaving education out of our regression model, not only have we left out an important predictor of income, but we've also not considered how education affects the association between parents' status and income. But, if we leave education out of the model, where does its effect on income go? Recall that the error term contains all the influences that are left out of the regression model. So the education effect appears under the error term, but the effect is undeterminable.

Now think about what this means for our model. By excluding education we have introduced two problems (at least). First, the error term is no longer simple random noise because it includes an important predictor of income. Second, because we have not explicitly controlled for the association between education and parents' status, the regression coefficient associated with parents' status will be incorrect. Moreover, its standard error will also be biased. Parents' status is now correlated with the error term. Leaving important variables out of regression models is known generally as *specification error*.

The best way to guard against this problem is to have a strong theory about what influences the dependent variable. Absent strong theory, partial residual plots, which were described previously, are useful to examine the association between the error term and the independent variables. Assuming no association, the partial residual plot should show a random pattern.

7. *The error term is normally distributed with mean = 0 and constant variance.* This is an important assumption for making inferences about the population from which the sample was drawn. If the error term does not have constant variance, as we learned when discussing heteroscedasticity, the standard errors of the regression coefficients are biased. If the mean of the error term does not equal zero, then the estimated intercept is incorrect.

The simplest way to determine whether the error term from the model is normally distributed is to estimate a normal probability plot after running the OLS regression model. As a preliminary measure, it is often useful to estimate a Q-Q plot of the dependent variable before model estimation because this often demonstrates non-normality that may be cured early in the modeling process. Assuming non-normality is found, an appropriate transformation of the dependent variable is often all that is needed. Cleveland (1993) describes a number of these transformations and shows when each is most useful.

8. *The dependent and independent variables are measured without error.* This is often a strong assumption to make. It involves the problem of *measurement error*. Unfortunately, given the tools presently available for measuring variables of interest in the social and behavioral sciences, measurement error is a realistic problem in many studies. One reason structural equation models (SEMs) such as LISREL and AMOS became so popular is that they purportedly corrected regression models for measurement error (Kline 1998).

If measurement error is present, then the regression coefficients and their standard errors tend to be biased. If only the dependent variable is measured with error, then only the standard errors tend to be affected. Because this is a measurement issue, the best approach for guarding against measurement error is to have good measuring instruments, whether they are mechanical, survey questions, or something else. This implies that we enter the study with a strong theory about how something should be measured. If one assumes that multiple measures are needed to gauge some phenomena, then latent variable analysis, such as SEMs, may provide a way to combine the measures into one unobserved construct. Additional information on this approach is available in many books (e.g., Kline 1998; Loehlin 1992).

9. *Outliers and influential observations do not affect the regression model.* Consider the three graphs in Figure 1.3. Each may be thought of as representing a linear regression model. The first graph shows an outlier, an observation that is far from other values of the dependent variable. It will tend to pull the regression line up in an effort to minimize the sum of squared errors (SSE). The second graph shows a high leverage point, an observation that is far from other values of the independent variable. Because it falls on the linear regression line it will not have much influence on the regression coefficient, but it will reduce its associated standard error (see a formula for the standard error of a regression coefficient to see why this occurs). The third graph shows an observation that is both an outlier and a high leverage point. These types of observations have a large impact on regression equations.

There are several procedures for detecting outliers and influential observations. Most programs allow you to save residuals, leverage values, and Cook's D values. Graphing these values with a box-and-whisker plot or simply checking their maximum absolute values is often sufficient for indicating whether there are influential points in the model.

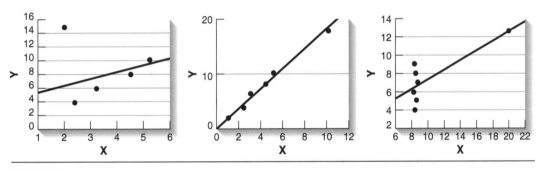

FIGURE 1.3

Studentized or standardized residuals are frequently used in this type of analysis. A rule of thumb is that only about five percent of the residuals should lie two standard deviations or further from the mean of the residuals, which is zero. Another rule of thumb involves Cook's D values, which are useful for determining the presence of both outliers and leverage points. This rule suggests looking for Cook's D values that exceed $4 / (n - k - 1)$, where n is the sample size and k is the number of independent variables in the model.

Assuming these steps do reveal outliers or influential observations, what should one do about them? The simplest step is to ignore them and accept the potential biases that they may introduce. However, a common source of these types of observations is coding error. Perhaps the person who entered the data forgot to punch a decimal point so that 30.6 became 306. Carefully reviewing the distribution of the data and locating extreme or unusual values before running a regression model is important. Or these observations may be deleted. However, care should be taken if one is considering deleting observations because they may be indicative of an interesting pattern in the statistical relationships. Finally, robust regression is a useful tool for reducing the influence of outliers and influential observations. Robust regression is an iterative procedure that reweights the observations so that highly influential ones are down-weighted. Therefore, they have less influence on the regression line.

For instance, Example 1.2 presents an OLS regression analysis that examines the association between the unemployment rate (*unemprat*), the gross state product (*gsprod*, a measure of economic productivity), and the violent crime rate per 100,000 population (*violrate*) in 1995 in the 50 states of the United States. The data set is *USdata.dta*. Stata is used to estimate the model.

Although the model appears reasonable, I discovered, after saving the Cook's D values and exploring them in detail, that one value was much larger than the others. This value was 0.597 and came from California. Using the rule of thumb previously described, we may determine whether we should be concerned about this value. The rule of thumb implies that any value above $4 / (50 - 2 - 1) = 0.085$ might be of concern. Clearly, 0.597 is

EXAMPLE 1.2   *An OLS Regression Model of Violent Crime Rates with an Influential Observation*

regress violrate unemprat gsprod, beta   *This appears on the command line*

Source	SS	df	MS		Number of obs	=	50
					F(2, 47)	=	12.08
Model	120621.62	2	603102.81		Prob > F	=	0.0001
Residual	234568.84	47	49908.17		R-squared	=	0.3396
					Adj R-squared	=	0.3115
Total	3551889.46	49	72487.54		Root MSE	=	223.40

violrate	Coef.	Std. Err.	t	P > |t|	Beta
unemprat	72.80565	25.88679	2.81	0.007	.338793
gsprod	.00067	.00019	3.47	0.001	.417660
_cons	63.51354	136.52744	0.47	0.644	.

EXAMPLE 1.3   *A Robust Linear Regression Model of Violent Crime Rates*

rreg violrate unemprat gsprod   *This appears on the command line*

Robust regression estimates

Number of obs	= 50
$F(2, 47)$	= 10.41
Prob > F	= 0.0002

violrate	Coef.	Std. Err.	t	P >	t		[95% Conf. Interval]	
unemprat	74.47831	27.6025	2.70	0.010	18.94925	130.0074
gsprod	.00065	.0002	3.14	0.003	.00023	.0011
_cons	48.80922	145.5761	0.34	0.739	−244.05210	341.6705

much larger than 0.085, so we may conclude that California is an influential observation. Its presence also suggests that we may wish to re-estimate the model using robust regression. This model, estimated using Stata's *rreg* routine, is shown in Example 1.3.

Note that the results change only slightly. The regression coefficient associated with the unemployment rate increases a bit and the intercept is smaller in the robust regression model. But conclusions drawn from the models would be similar.

Interaction Terms in the OLS (Linear) Regression Model

The final topic in this review of OLS regression involves interaction terms. Interaction terms involve the product of values from two or more independent variables. The motivation behind using interaction terms is that one's conceptual model suggests that the association between a particular independent variable and the dependent variable depends on some third variable. An example is perhaps the best way to demonstrate a statistical interaction and how it applies to the OLS regression model.

We saw earlier in the chapter that education and income are positively associated. But a question that occupies the minds of many sociologists, economists, and public policy experts is whether the relationship between education and income differs for males and female. Recent data indicate that females are now more likely than males to graduate from high school and from college. This is a relatively recent phenomenon. However, females continue to earn less than men, even when they are employed in comparable occupations. One question is whether education acts as an equalizer, closing the earnings gap, or whether it is at higher levels of education that the earnings gap is larger. Example 1.4 presents an analysis, using data from the 1996 GSS, that is designed to answer this question, albeit in a crude manner.

The dependent variable is annual personal income (*income*) and the independent variables are *gender* (0 = male, 1 = female), education (*educate*, measured in years), and an interaction term that is the product of gender and education (*gen_educ*).

In order to make use of these results, it is helpful to compute the expected differences between males and females in terms of their predicted incomes. Taking as our repre-

EXAMPLE 1.4   *An OLS Regression Model of Income with an Interaction Term*

regress income gender educate gen_educ, beta   *This appears on the command line*

Source	SS	df	MS			
Model	1948.1589	3	649.386329			
Residual	15271.1575	1939	7.875790			
Total	17219.3165	1942	8.86679532			

Number of obs	=	1943
F(3, 1939)	=	82.45
Prob > F	=	0.0000
R-squared	=	0.1131
Adj R-squared	=	0.1118
Root MSE	=	2.8064

income	Coef.	Std. Err.	t	P > | t |	Beta
gender	−3.561609	.679363	−5.24	0.000	−.5981975
educate	.198399	.033155	5.98	0.000	.1767363
gen_educ	.159355	.048092	3.31	0.001	.3858014
_cons	7.787530	.466356	16.70	0.000	.

vif   *This appears on the command line after estimating the model*

Variable	VIF	1/VIF
gen_educ	29.64	0.033740
gender	28.47	0.035130
educate	1.91	0.524334
Mean VIF	20.00	

sentative groups those who graduated from high school only (*educate* = 12) and those who graduated from college (*educate* = 16), the predicted income values are shown in Table 1.1.

The results of the OLS regression model with the interaction term suggest that, although females earn less than males on average, this gap is smaller at higher education levels. This supports the hypothesis that education acts as an equalizer in terms of gender differences in personal income. The model also demonstrates the utility of interaction terms for testing interesting and important hypotheses.

TABLE 1.1   *Predicted Annual Personal Income*

	Gender		
	Male	*Female*	*Percent Difference*
12 years of education	10.16	8.52	19.2%
16 years of education	10.96	9.96	10.0%

However, notice that below the model results in Example 1.4 we asked Stata to present the VIFs. It is important to check for collinearity when estimating models with interaction terms. It should come as no surprise that constituent variables are strongly associated with their interaction terms. The VIFs associated with *gender* and *gen_educ* both exceed even the most stringent threshold. This provides strong evidence that multicollinearity is present in the model. As mentioned in the section on multicollinearity, one approach for attenuating this type of problem, when it is caused by interaction terms, is to center the constituent variables before computing the interaction term (Aiken and West 1991). Because gender is a dummy variable it makes no sense to center it. So only *educate* is centered (i.e., *educate* – mean(*educate*) = *c_educate*) and then the interaction term is recomputed (*gen_ceducate*). The results of the OLS regression model are as follows.

EXAMPLE 1.4   *(continued)*

regress income gender c_educate gen_ceduc, beta   *This appears on the command line*

Source	SS	df	MS			
				Number of obs	=	1943
				F(3, 1939)	=	82.45
Model	1948.1589	3	649.386326	Prob > F	=	0.0000
Residual	15271.1575	1939	7.875790	R-squared	=	0.1131
				Adj R-squared	=	0.1118
Total	17219.3165	1942	8.86679532	Root MSE	=	2.8064

income	Coef.	Std. Err.	t	P>|t|	Beta
gender	−1.428919	.129563	−11.03	0.000	−.239997
c_educate	.198399	.033155	5.98	0.000	.176736
gen_ceduc	.159355	.048092	3.31	0.001	.098973
_cons	10.442750	.091076	114.66	0.000	.

vif   *This appears on the command line*

Variable	VIF	1/VIF
gen_ceduc	1.95	0.512672
c_educate	1.91	0.524334
gender	1.04	0.965870
Mean VIF	1.63	

Note that the results do not change much. The direction of effects is the same in both models. However, because *educate* is now rescaled, the intercept is different. The *gender* coefficient also changes. Nevertheless, the results continue to demonstrate that the gender gap in income dissipates at higher levels of education. And the VIFs now indicate little problem with multicollinearity in the model. It appears we have successfully solved this problem.

Conclusion

The OLS regression model continues to enjoy widespread use. When faced with the task of analyzing or predicting a dependent variable that is continuous and normally distributed, this model is highly appropriate. Moreover, if the assumptions described in this chapter are met, in particular assumptions (3), (4), (6), and (7), then the OLS results are the best linear unbiased estimators (BLUE). In other words, among any unbiased estimators that describe a linear relationship between the independent and dependent variables, the OLS coefficients have the smallest variance. This is an important property when considering the frequent goal of making inferences from a sample to the population from which it was drawn.

Moreover, even when some of the assumptions are violated, OLS regression results are fairly robust. This means that if we violate the assumptions to a modest degree, the OLS results are still pretty accurate. In certain situations, such as when an assumption is grossly violated or the sample size is small, OLS regression breaks down and provides poor results. Nevertheless, the robustness of OLS regression was amply demonstrated in the models that predicted state-level violent crime rates (Examples 1.2 and 1.3). Even in the presence of what appeared to be a substantial influential observation and a relatively small sample size, the OLS regression results were very similar to the robust regression results.

There are many other issues involving OLS regression. In fact, as mentioned early in the chapter, there are numerous book-length treatments of linear regression (e.g., Chatterjee and Price 1991; Draper and Smith 1998; Montgomery, Peck, and Vining 2001). This chapter provides what hopefully is an adequate review of the basics of this regression model. But the bulk of this book involves situations where the assumptions of OLS regression are so glaringly violated that other approaches are needed. Fortunately, these alternative approaches have become widely used in their own right and are therefore available to us as we seek to explore the intricate statistical associations among a host of variables.

Exercises

1. The following data are from a sample of college students who completed their first year shortly before the information was collected. The data set includes variables gauging first-year college grade point average (GPA) and incoming scholastic aptitude test (SAT) scores for the verbal and quantitative portions of the test. The SAT scores are divided by 100. Our goal is to analyze the linear associations among these variables. We'll begin with a subset of these data.

GPA	SAT-Quant.	SAT-Verbal
1.97	3.21	2.47
2.74	7.18	4.36
2.19	3.58	5.78
2.60	4.03	4.47
2.98	6.40	5.63
1.65	2.37	3.42
1.89	2.70	4.72
2.38	4.18	3.56

a. Construct a scatterplot with GPA on the *y*-axis and SAT-Quant. on the *x*-axis. Fit by hand (and straight edge) the estimated linear regression line. Comment on the relationship between these two variables.

b. Using the formulas for a two-variable OLS regression model, compute the slope and intercept for the following model: GPA = $\alpha + \beta_1$(SAT-Quant.).

c. Compute the predicted values, the residuals, the Sum of Squared Errors (SSE), and the R^2 for the model.

d. Plot the residuals (*y*-axis) by the predicted values (*x*-axis) and comment about what you see.

2. The data set GPA is available in SPSS, Stata, and SAS formats. It contains all 20 observations from the sample of college students. We'll use it to conduct the remaining exercises.

a. Estimate an OLS regression model with *gpa* as the dependent variable and *sat_quan* as the independent variable. Compare this model to the model you estimated in Exercise 1. In what ways are they similar or different?

3. Estimate the following three OLS regression models, all of which use *gpa* as the dependent variable:

a. Use only *hs_engl* as the independent variable.

b. Use *hs_engl* and *sat_verb* as the independent variables.

c. Use *hs_engl*, *sat_verb*, and *sat_quan* as the independent variables.

4. a. Interpret the unstandardized coefficient associated with *hs_engl* from model 3(a).

b. Interpret the unstandardized coefficient associated with *sat_quan* from model 3(c).

c. Interpret the R^2 from model (c).

5. Something happened to the association between *hs_engl* and *gpa* as we moved from model (a) to model (c). Please describe what might have happened. Remember to provide statistical evidence to support your answer. Speculate in a conceptual way why this may have happened.

6. Using model (c) from Exercise 3, check the following regression diagnostics and comment about any problems with the model:

a. A normal probability plot of the residuals.

b. A plot of the residuals by the predicted values. As some analysts recommend (Fox 1991), you may wish to use studentized residuals and standardized predicted values in your plot.

c. A distribution of the standardized (or studentized) residuals, the leverage values, and the Cook's D values.

2

Introduction to Generalized Linear Models

Thus far, we have considered a linear regression model, one that is linear in the relationship between the predictor variables and the outcome variable. We have also assumed that the error term follows a normal distribution. As discussed in Chapter 1, in order to check these assumptions, we may estimate bivariate scatterplots of the variables and the residuals. We may also use a normal probability plot to check the distribution of the error terms. Given that a large random sample of data often provides normally distributed variables, especially when we measure these variables as continuous, the linear model as represented by OLS regression is a powerful tool in the hands of the statistical modeler.

Unfortunately, many studies, especially in the social and behavioral sciences, do not normally collect data so that variables are measured continuously. As discussed in the introduction, variables are often measured in a discrete or categorical manner. Because so many of the concepts used in the social and behavioral sciences are not precise enough to be measured in a continuous fashion, a large number of studies rely on ordinal or nominal categories to measure social phenomena. When confronted with nominal or ordinal data, it is unwise to simply pretend that variables are continuous and use an OLS regression model to measure their associations.

For example, suppose a researcher has a sample of married couples and wishes to predict which couples are most likely to divorce. Perhaps the data gathered from these couples measure relationship satisfaction, family background, and demographic characteristics. Even if most of these data are continuous, the outcome of interest, divorce, is still measured in a *yes–no* format. To be precise, the variable *divorce* is a binary or dichotomous dependent variable. The researcher should not use OLS regression to predict divorce because it is not an appropriate statistical model when confronted with a dichotomous dependent variable. The implications of using OLS in this situation are discussed in Chapter 3.

Similarly, social scientists are often interested in public opinions about various political and social topics. A quick review of the General Social Survey (GSS) or the National Election Survey (NES), two widely used surveys designed to gauge public opinion in the United States, shows that most public opinion survey questions have a limited number of response categories. Survey respondents are often forced into categories such as agree or disagree. These response categories are sometimes broadened to include more choices. For instance, researchers may be interested in respondents' attitudes about some government policy such as: "The United States should provide humanitarian aid to Cuba." Respondents are then expected to reply in one of the following ways: Strongly Agree, Agree, Disagree, or Strongly Disagree. Imagine if you were asked to predict who tends to agree with this policy. How would you proceed? Many researchers would simply use this variable as the outcome in an OLS regression model with whatever independent variables their conceptual scheme justified. However, this is an unwise approach. Clearly this dependent variable is ordinal. Fortunately, advances in statistical theory and software provide a solution to the dilemma produced by discrete dependent variables.

The most significant advance in regression analysis in the last twenty years or so is the development of *generalized linear models*. This term refers to a class of regression models that allows us to generalize the linear regression approach to accommodate many types of dependent variables. We no longer have to assume that the outcome in our regression model is a continuous and normally distributed variable. Rather, particular generalized linear models may be used to estimate either continuous or discrete dependent variables, including those described in the preceding examples.

The Role of the Link Function

How does a generalized linear model accomplish this daunting task and why is it called "generalized"? Let's begin to answer these questions by thinking about the linear (OLS) regression model. This model may be specified using Equation 2.1 (the middle term that looks like a *u* with a long left tail is the Greek letter *mu*).

$$E(Y) = \mu = \sum_{k=1}^{K} \beta_K X_K \tag{2.1}$$

Recall from Chapter 1 that $E(Y)$ is the expected value of the dependent variable, Y. The symbol μ is thus also the expected value, or what is sometimes called the conditional mean, of Y. This is similar to the predicted values from an OLS regression equation. Notice how the usual regression equation has been condensed in Equation 2.1 using the summation sign, so that the β_K's represent the intercept and the regression coefficients, and the X_K's represent multiple independent variables. We may make Equation 2.1 more general by using the variable *eta* (the *n* with the long right tail), which is known as the linear predictor. So η is substituted for μ in Equation 2.2.

$$\eta = \sum_{k=1}^{K} \beta_K X_K \tag{2.2}$$

Whichever generalized linear model we use, the key is that the set of X's always linearly produces the η, which is a predictor of Y (remember the predicted values from the

OLS equation?). You are now probably scratching your head and wondering why we need this sleight-of-hand. Why not just stick with the old tried-and-true OLS regression model and eliminate the need for more Greek letters? Recall that OLS regression is not appropriate for discrete and even some continuous dependent variables. So we need some statistical sleight-of-hand to develop more appropriate regression models. Although understanding the precise way this is done requires substantial knowledge of statistical theory and its underlying mathematics (McCullagh and Nelder 1989), the logic behind these models is relatively simple.

The trick of the generalized linear model is to somehow "link" η and μ. We must find a function that does this: $g(\mu)$, so that $\eta = g(\mu)$. There are numerous ways to specify this link function. The *identity function*, for example, specifies that $\eta = \mu$, so we may use our standard linear regression model shown previously. And, assuming that the errors are distributed normally, we may use OLS to estimate such a regression model.

However, the identity function does not work for outcome variables that are not distributed normally. We must find some other link functions so that the X's linearly produce η. Fortunately, there are several link functions that accommodate a variety of statistical distributions.

The most common of these link functions, besides the identity function, is the *logit link*. It is specified using Equation 2.3.

$$\eta = \log_e \left[\frac{\mu}{1 - \mu} \right] \tag{2.3}$$

The term *log* refers to the natural or Napierian logarithm. It is given the subscript e to denote the type of logarithm (there are several) and to show its connection to the exponential function. The link implies that the expected value of the dependent variable is transformed by the function. When would this odd-looking function be useful? It turns out that it is useful when the variable is distributed as a binomial random variable. In practical terms, this means that the dependent variable is measured as a dichotomous or binary variable, usually coded [0,1]. The type of generalized linear model that normally uses this link function is called a logistic regression model and is described in Chapter 3.

Another type of link function that is appropriate for dichotomous dependent variables is the inverse normal. Recall from introductory statistics that variables are often transformed into z-scores using the formula $[x - \text{mean}(x) / \text{sd}(x)]$. Then, by looking at tables found in the appendices of most statistics textbooks, z-scores are found that correspond to areas under the standard normal curve. Imagine for a moment that underlying a dichotomous variable is a continuous scale that corresponds to probabilities. For instance, survey researchers may ask respondents whether or not they support the death penalty, but underlying their responses is a (hypothetical) continuous scale from supporting it under no circumstances to being a strong advocate for it. If we think about these continuous attitudes as probabilities that range from 0 (indicating support under no circumstances) to 1 (indicating extremely strong advocacy), with lots of possibilities in between, then we may begin to think about a threshold at which respondents shift from answering no to answering yes when asked about the death penalty. Statisticians and econometricians have spent quite a bit of time thinking about what this situation, generally speaking, means for a regression analysis. They have concluded that we may estimate a regression model that uses the standard normal distribution in a peculiar way: In order to transform the expected values of the dependent variable so they may be estimated with a regression model, the link function is the *inverse normal*, which is specified as

$$\eta = \Phi^{-1}(\mu) \tag{2.4}$$

The Greek capital letter *phi* (Φ) is used to indicate the standard normal distribution. Note, however, that it is accompanied by a superscript -1, which is used to indicate the inverse of a function. Hence the term *inverse normal*. The inverse normal link function leads to a probit regression model. Like logistic regression, this is also used for dichotomous dependent variables, usually coded [0,1]. It is also clear from Equation 2.4 how one transforms back from a probit model coefficient to the expected value (in this instance, a probability). One simply uses a table of z-scores to find the probability. In practical terms, the probit model coefficients may be transformed into conditional probabilities by using a table of z-scores, or by asking the software to do the transformation for you. Examples of how to do this transformation are provided in Chapter 3.

Another situation that concerns us is what to do when confronted with a count variable, that is, a variable that counts a number of possible outcomes. While it may seem reasonable to use an OLS regression model in this situation, keep in mind that counts cannot be negative numbers and many "counts" of interest to the research community (e.g., number of children, number of marriages, annual number of earthquakes in Guatemala) are rarely greater than two or three. Therefore, it is unlikely that a count variable will be distributed normally. The generalized linear models designed for count variables use the *natural logarithm link*.

$$\eta = \log_e \mu \tag{2.5}$$

Two of the most common regression models that use this link function are the Poisson and negative binomial models (discussed in Chapter 6). Note how this link function differs from the logit link function: There is no transformation of μ prior to taking the natural logarithm.

An explanatory caveat is in order at this point: It may appear that the log link implies a simple log-linear regression analysis, or that any of these link functions are asking us to transform that dependent variable directly. Recall from the OLS regression model that one approach when faced with a skewed dependent variable is to transform its values in some way. A very common transformation in this situation is to take the natural logarithm of the values of the dependent variable. This is useful when the distribution of the dependent variable has a long right "tail." After transformation, the researcher simply uses OLS to estimate the regression model. However, when one has discrete data and wishes to use a generalized linear model such as Poisson or negative binomial regression, the situation is more complicated than this. The values of the dependent variable are not transformed directly; rather, we transform μ, the expected value of the dependent variable, Y. An assumption is that the Y's (actually their residuals in a regression context) have a particular distribution, such as a Poisson or negative binomial distribution. These distributions are sometimes called *families*. (Technical note: The negative binomial regression model is not actually a generalized linear model because its distribution does not result from the exponential family of distributions, but we'll ignore this nuance and throw caution to the wind. See Lindsey (1997) for a discussion of this issue.)

Although there are several other link functions used in generalized linear models, the only other one that is of consequence for this presentation is a generalization of the logit link function

$$\eta_j = \log_e\left(\frac{\mu_j}{\mu_J}\right) \tag{2.6}$$

In the model that uses this link function there are *J* categories (usually more than 2). The issue addressed in the model—which is known as a multinomial logistic model—that uses the generalized logit link function is to compare explicit categories of a dependent variable. The multinomial logistic model is often used when the dependent variable is a set of unordered responses (e.g., Protestant, Catholic, and Jew; prefer federal government money spent on education, defense, or welfare assistance). This model is discussed in Chapter 5.

Note that these link functions share one characteristic: They all include taking the logarithm of some function. Recall that the natural logarithm is the inverse of the exponential function (e^x). Given this fact, statisticians often describe generalized linear models, which, of course, are based on these link functions, as developed primarily for variables that come from the exponential family of distributions (Gill 2000; Dobson 1990). In fact, even the normal distribution on which OLS regression is based is a special case of the exponential family of distributions. Hence linear regression is, technically speaking, a type of generalized linear model that uses the identity link function, $\mu = \eta$.

Before moving on, it is important to realize that the link function is determined by the random component of the dependent variable. A fundamental aspect of any regression analysis is that the researcher assumes that the model pulls out the systematic part of the Y's (the part related to the X's). What is left over (what were termed the errors or residuals in Chapter 1) is assumed to have a particular probability distribution, and it is this distribution that determines the link function. In fact, most of the books on generalized linear models begin with a discussion of the distinction between the random and systematic components of a model (Lindsey 1997; McCullagh and Nelder 1989).

Although much of this book addresses regression models that are based on these link functions, we should first understand a little more about the probability distributions (the *families*) on which they are based. Paralleling the remainder of the book, we'll discuss the binomial distribution, the multinomial distribution, the Poisson distribution, and the negative binomial distribution.

The Binomial Distribution

The binomial distribution concerns replications of a Bernoulli sequence of "trials." Bernoulli trials have only two outcomes, 0 if "unsuccessful" and 1 if "successful." So the binomial distribution is concerned with how many "successes" (labeled i) one finds in n trials. For example, one may be interested in how many heads come up in 10 flips of a coin, how many people out of 100 report marijuana use, how many respondents out of 2,000 support the death penalty, and so forth.

The *probability mass function*—the function that determines how the distribution *appears* and that assigns a probability to each value of the discrete variable—of the binomial distribution is given by the following:

$$P(i) = \binom{n}{i} p^i (1-p)^{n-i} \ where \ i \ = \ number \ of \ successes, \ 0 ... n \qquad (2.7)$$

In Equation 2.7 the symbol n over i in brackets denotes a *combinatorial*. Most scientific calculators compute a combinatorial using the key nCr, which is read as "n choose r." A combinatorial asks and answers the following question: Given n objects, in how many ways may we order r of them without repetition? So, for instance, I am interested in taking five books and placing three of them in order on my bookshelf. In how many ways can I do this? The answer is

$$\binom{5}{3} = 10$$

Suppose we flip a fair coin five times. Because it is labeled a fair coin, the probability of heads or tails is identical, 0.50. Using Equation 2.7, the probability mass function of this sequence of coin flips is then the following:

TABLE 2.1 *Probability of i Heads in Five Coin Flips*

i (number of heads)	0	1	2	3	4	5
P(i)		0.0313	0.1563	0.3125	0.3125	0.1563	0.0313

In other words, the probability that the sequence of five flips will result in no heads is 0.0313, the probability of exactly one head is 0.1563, and so forth. Another way of saying this is: If we were to consider five flips of a coin a "trial" and we were to conduct thousands of trials, we would expect about 3 percent of these trials to have zero heads, 15.6 percent to have one head, 31 percent to have two or three heads, and so forth. The most likely outcome, as shown by the highest probability, is either two or three heads out of five coin flips. As required by a probability mass function, the probabilities sum to 1.0. Note that the distribution is symmetric when the probability is 0.5.

Other interesting examples of a binomial distribution are the number of hits a baseball player gets given times at-bat (so hits are "successes" and at-bats are "trials"), the number of college graduates in a sample of workers (graduates are "successes" (literally?) and workers are "trials"), and the number of companies that offer daycare facilities among a sample of companies.

The *expected value* (which is more commonly labeled the *mean*) of successes in n trials is $n*p$ and the variance is $n * p * (1 - p)$. If the probability of cigarette use among adults is 0.25 and we have a sample of 1,000 adults, the expected value—in other words, the expected number of smokers—is $(0.25 * 1,000) = 250$ and the variance of this expected value is 187.5.

A practical use of the binomial distribution is when one wishes to predict statistically a variable that takes on only two values (e.g., yes vs. no; 0 vs. 1 or more). The binomial distribution is used in *logistic regression:* This regression technique assumes that the outcome variable is distributed as a binomial random variable. It is discussed in Chapter 3.

The Multinomial Distribution

Suppose, however, that there are multiple trials and, instead of only 2 outcomes, there are several outcomes. For example, a researcher might be interested in determining the probability of observing blue-eyed, brown-eyed, and green-eyed babies in a sample of newborns. Here there are three possible outcomes rather than only two. However, as we saw with the binomial distribution, the probabilities must still add up to one. For example, the probability of having a child with blue eyes might be 0.3, brown eyes 0.5, and green eyes 0.2.

The probability mass function for this *multinomial distribution* is

$$P\{X_1 = n_1, X_2 = n_2, \dots, X_r = n_r\} = \frac{n!}{n_1! n_2! \dots n_r!} p_1^{n_1} p_2^{n_2} \dots p_r^{n_r} \qquad (2.8)$$

In this function, r is the number of outcomes (e.g., blue, brown, or green) possible, the p's are the probability of each outcome, and the n's are the frequency with which we observe the particular outcome. The term $n!$ denotes $\{n * (n - 1) * (n - 2) * \dots * 2 * 1\}$ or the *factorial* of the number. The n in the numerator is the total number of trials.

For example, imagine that we observe five newborn babies, so we consider each observation a "trial" (an appropriate term according to many mothers experiencing labor). We know from past experience with these matters that the probability of the respective eye colors in the population of babies from which our sample is drawn is as stated previously $\{p(\text{blue}) = 0.3; p(\text{brown}) = 0.5; p(\text{green}) = 0.2\}$. In the sample drawn, we observe the following result: three brown-eyed babies, two blued-eyed babies, and zero green-eyed babies. Because we already have predetermined probabilities for each outcome, we may determine the probability that we observe the particular sequence of $\{3, 2, 0\}$ by using Equation 2.8.

$$P\{3, 2, 0\} = \frac{5!}{3! 2! 0!} (0.5)^3 (0.3)^2 (0.2)^0 = 0.1125 \qquad (2.9)$$

Note that $5! = \{5 * 4 * 3 * 2 * 1\} = 120$, $3! = 6$, $2! = 2$, and $0! = 1$. In words, the probability of observing a sequence $\{3, 2, 0\}$ is 0.1125, or if we were to take 1,000 samples, we would expect to find this sequence, on average, about 112 times. Now think about computing the probabilities for each possible combination of the three eye colors that could be observed among five babies. Although a challenging task, we know with certainty that these numbers would sum to 1.0.

A complicated aspect of the multinomial distribution is that, rather than one expected value, there are now as many expected values as there are groups. For instance, given the three probabilities listed previously, the expected number of brown-eyed babies out of, say, 10 is ($p_1 * n$ or 0.5 * 10) = 5, the expected number of blue-eyed babies is (0.3 * 10) = 3, and the expected number of green-eyed babies is (0.2 * 10) = 2. There are also variances to go with each expected value. The variances are computed using the formula $n * p_1(1 - p_1)$, so, for instance, the variance of the expected value for green-eyed babies is (10 * 0.2 * 0.8) or 1.6.

A practical use of the multinomial distribution is when there are more than two categorical outcomes. For example, perhaps the responses to a survey question about preferences for government funding are education, workfare, and drug abuse prevention. To model such a variable, which has a multinomial distribution, one could use multinomial logistic regression (see Chapter 5). An alternative that we will not spend time on, yet has a similar goal, is to use log-linear analysis (see Knoke and Burke 1980, and Christensen 1990 for thorough overviews of log-linear modeling techniques).

The Poisson Distribution

The social and behavioral sciences, and many other disciplines, are replete with variables that are designed to count some phenomenon (e.g., number of children, number of marriages, number of arrests, number of traffic accidents on California highways in 1999). There are three interesting characteristics of these count variables. First, they cannot be negative; the lower bound is zero. Second, these nonnegative numbers are integers, so that count variables are, strictly speaking, discrete rather than continuous variables. (It is unlikely that a family has 2.7 children; or that a person has been married 1.8 times, irrespective of what some spouses might claim.) Third, if we compute a histogram using a count variable, it has what is often termed a rapidly descending tail. Practically speaking, many count variables enumerate rare phenomena. So the distribution of these variables often peak at, say, one or two, and then become much rarer at higher values.

For example, if we took a sample of one hundred married adults in the United States and asked them how many children they have, we would find that most have one, two, or three with the peak probably at about two children per couple. Families with more children are relatively rare, so that, if plotted, the higher values would tend to "tail-off" rapidly. Based on the General Social Survey's 1996 (*GSS96*) data, Figure 2.1 shows what the distribution of children among married couples looks like.

It is evident that a plurality of married couples have two children, with a substantial proportion reporting zero, one, or three children. But notice what happens to the distribution as it moves past four children: The "tail" of the distribution diminishes rapidly. Because the GSS96 has a maximum value of "eight or more" children, we do not see how far to the right the tail actually goes, but it is extremely likely that very small proportions of married people have nine or more children.

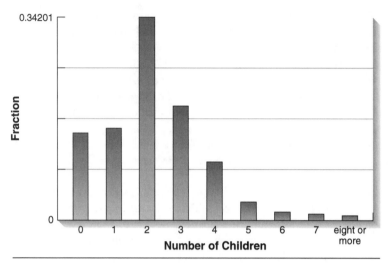

FIGURE 2.1

Count variables, especially when they gauge rare phenomena, often follow what is called a *Poisson distribution* (after Monsieur Simeon Poisson, a French mathematician). The probability mass function for a Poisson random variable is

$$P(i) = e^{-\lambda} \frac{\lambda^i}{i!} \tag{2.10}$$

Equation 2.10 indicates that the probability of observing some value (i) equals the exponentiated value of $-1 * \lambda$ multiplied by λ to the ith power divided by i factorial. The symbol that looks like an upside down y is the Greek letter *lambda*, also known as the *rate* in the context of a Poisson distribution. Note that it must be a positive number.

To see how this probability mass function operates, suppose that the rate of earthquakes per year in San Diego County, California, is some small number such as two. The values of the Poisson distribution when $\lambda = 2$ are shown in Table 2.2.

TABLE 2.2   *Probability of Number of Events in a Poisson Distribution*

i (number of events)	0	1	2	3	4	5
P(i)	0.1353	0.2707	0.2707	0.1804	0.0902	0.0361

If the average number of earthquakes per year in this California county, based on past data collection, equals two, then we expect the probability of only one earthquake in the next year to be 0.27, the probability of three earthquakes to be 0.18, and so forth. Notice that the probability of one or two earthquakes appears to be identical (0.2707). This is simply because we have rounded to only four decimal points. If we were to round further, then we would see that the probability is highest at two earthquakes. As with the other probabilities we have computed based on mass functions, these probabilities must add to one. A complication of the Poisson distribution is that we can conceivably compute probabilities for every positive integer, even though the probability of, say, 100 earthquakes is so small that we might as well claim that it is zero.

An interesting fact about the Poisson distribution is apparent from this table and was insinuated in the previous paragraph: The probability tends to peak when $i = \lambda$. Actually, the expected value or mean of a Poisson random variable equals the rate, λ. Symbolically, this implies that $\mu = \lambda$. Even more interesting, however, is that the variance also equals λ. In other words, when we assume that a variable follows a Poisson distribution, we also assume that the mean equals the variance. This is sometimes a restrictive assumption to make.

Figure 2.2 shows a simulated data set that uses the same mean (expected) number of children as those found among married people in the *GSS96*. The two histograms (compare Figures 2.1 and 2.2) are very similar, except the actual data have fewer one-child married couples than expected from a Poisson distribution.

A practical use of the Poisson distribution is its direct link to *Poisson regression* (see Chapter 6). When a dependent variable is measured as a count, especially when it involves some rare event, then Poisson regression is one of the preferred approaches. Count variables are very common in the social sciences. Some examples include the following: The number of stressful life events in a year; annual number of delinquent acts one commits; number of extracurricular activities among high school students; number of appointments to the Supreme Court by a president during his or her term; and many others.

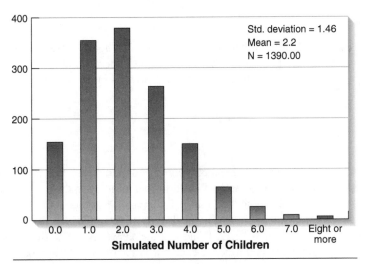

FIGURE 2.2

The Negative Binomial Distribution

Although it is common to assume that count variables follow a Poisson distribution, and, therefore, many researchers turn to Poisson regression to model dependent variables that count phenomena, the assumption that the mean equals the variance is often too stringent. Many count variables are *overdispersed*; that is, the variance is much larger than the mean. Annual "counts" of drug use and delinquency are common examples of overdispersed random variables that researchers have sought to predict (Hoffmann and Cerbone 1999; Land 1992). A rare situation, but one that does occur occasionally, is an *underdispersed* distribution in which the mean exceeds the variance. Overdispersion and underdispersion are known collectively as *extradispersion*.

When a dependent variable is overdispersed, many statistical modelers prefer to use an alternative approach known as a *negative binomial regression* model. This model is based on the negative binomial (NB) distribution. Similar to the binomial distribution, the NB distribution is concerned with "trials" (e.g., at bats) and "successes" (e.g., hits). However, there is a key difference between the binomial and negative binomial distributions. In the binomial distribution there are a fixed number of trials and the primary concern is analyzing the number of successes. In the negative binomial distribution the number of "successes" is fixed and the number of trials varies. An example of a NB distribution is the following. I have been hired by a hopeful politician. I need to gather r signatures (e.g., 100) in order to get my candidate on the ballot. I know, based on previous experience, that the probability of an individual signature is p. So if I approach a person on the street or I knock on a door in the neighborhood I have a 1 in $1/p$ chance of getting a signature. If we let n equal the number of people I must approach ("trials") to get r signatures ("successes"), then the probability mass function is

$$P(n) = \binom{n-1}{r-1} p^r (1-p)^{n-r} \tag{2.11}$$

Now suppose that the probability (p) is 0.60 and I need 10 signatures (I live in a small town). What is the probability that I will need to approach 20 people (n) to obtain these 10 signatures? I may simply plug the p's, r's, and n's into Equation 2.11 to obtain

$$P(20) = \binom{20-1}{10-1} (0.60)^{10} \, 0.40^{(20-10)} \tag{2.12}$$

Recall that the stacked numbers in brackets denote a combinatorial, or n items ordered in r ways. So, in this example, we compute 19 items ordered in 9 ways. Not surprisingly, this is a large number (92,378), indicating that if I attempted to order 9 of 19 books on my bookshelf in each possible way, I would probably waste several days.

Working through Equation 2.12, I find that the answer is 0.059. In words, if I were to undertake this exercise 1,000 times, I expect that I will have to approach exactly 20 people about 59 times; in other cases, I expect to approach more or fewer people. To see how the negative binomial distribution acts, Table 2.3 makes the same assumptions (p = 0.60 and r = 10) and shows probabilities using various values of n.

TABLE 2.3 ***Probability of Approaching n People to Get 10 Signatures***

***n* (number of people approached)**	10	15	20	25	30
P(*n*)	0.006	0.124	0.059	0.009	0.0007

Similar to the Poisson distribution, the values peak around the mean, but they tail off rapidly. The mean of the negative binomial distribution is r / p and the variance is $r(1 - p) / p^2$. So for the preceding distribution the mean is 10/0.60 = 16.67 and the variance is $10(0.40) / 0.60^2 = 11.11$. On average, I will need to approach about 17 people to get 10 signatures.

The connection between the NB distribution and the typical count variables encountered in the social sciences is not as clear as it is for the other distributions we have seen thus far. One way to think about this connection, however, is to imagine that we are "counting" the number of people we need to sample to find x number of positive observations. For example, how many people do you need to observe to find 100 marijuana users if the probability of marijuana use is 0.15? Another way of thinking about it is how many times does an average person use marijuana in a year.

As already mentioned, many statisticians prefer to use the NB distribution rather than the Poisson distribution when investigating count variables because their variances often exceed their means (hence we have *overdispersion*). For instance, when $r = 5$ and $p = 0.10$, the mean of the negative binomial is 50 and the variance is 450. Even when this is not the case and the Poisson assumption holds, the results of negative binomial regression and Poisson regression are often very similar. We shall explore this issue in more detail in Chapter 6.

There are many other distributions that may apply in a regression context, such as the gamma, exponential, and Weibull. We will focus primarily on those already described, although we return to some of these other distributions in Chapter 7 when event history models are discussed. The interested (and brave) reader should consult Lindsey (1997) or a book on probability theory (e.g., Ross 1994) for a full description of other applicable probability distributions.

How Do We Estimate Regression Models Based on These Distributions?

Now that we have some background on discrete variables, link functions, and probability distributions, the question is, what is needed to estimate regression models based on these functions and distributions? In the linear regression model detailed in Chapter 1, ordinary least squares (OLS) was the preferred approach to estimation. In other words, given a set of variables, some are specified as the independent variables and one as the dependent variable. The researcher (well, actually the computer) then computes a set of linear combinations that minimize the sum of squared errors to produce the regression equation. Considering the extra complications presented by the preceding distributions, OLS does not work well when investigating discrete dependent variables. Thus, an alternative is needed. The most common approach for estimating regression models based on the various distributions is by a technique known as *maximum likelihood estimation (MLE)*. A good description of MLE is found in Eliason (1992). Because the mathematics of MLE techniques are challenging, we will cover only the most elementary aspects. Once these are presented, we will learn about some measures of model fit based on MLE.

A common probability theory exercise is to find the probability of obtaining three heads after flipping a coin five times. If the coin is fair, the probability of obtaining heads any one time is 0.50. So the probability of getting three heads is simple to compute with the binomial formula. Similarly, if past experience indicates that the mean number of earthquakes in a particular county in California in any one year is two and a researcher wishes to determine the probability that this county will experience four or more earthquakes this year, then it is simple to use the Poisson distribution to calculate this probability. Exercises such as these form much of the core of probability theory courses.

But a more realistic situation in statistics is that the researcher observes a number of "trials" (e.g., flips of a coin; data gathered from respondents in a survey) and the number of "successes" (e.g., number of heads; number of married respondents), and then needs to estimate a probability or the rate of some occurrence (e.g., a rate (λ) in the Poisson distribution). For example, if we observe three heads in five flips, what is the likelihood that the probability of heads for this coin is 0.50? In other words, it is obvious that the number of heads in n coin flips follows a binomial distribution and that, normally, we know that $p = 0.50$. Typically we do not know the probability of obtaining, say, six heads out of ten flips; but we can easily determine this particular probability using the binomial distribution. But suppose we do not trust the coin manufacturer and we wish to determine if the initial p actually does equal 0.50. Determining the most likely p or some other parameter (e.g., λ, β, etc.) given a set of data is the goal of maximum likelihood estimation. In other words, MLE *finds the value* of the parameter that makes the *observed data most likely*.

In probability theory when *probability functions* are explored, we typically allow the i's to vary and then check the probabilities (see the preceding tables). When using *likelihood functions* we hold the i's and N's constant, and allow the parameters (e.g., p, λ, β, etc.) to vary. For instance, for the binomial model the value of p is allowed to vary in the likelihood function. If we observe three heads in five flips of a coin then the binomial distribution becomes the following likelihood function:

$$L(p \mid i = 3, n = 5) = \binom{5}{3} p^3 (1-p)^2 \qquad (2.13)$$

The maximum likelihood estimate is that estimated value of p that *maximizes the likelihood* of observing the sample data that were obtained. The $i = 3$, $n = 5$ in the function indicate these sample data. This maximum value is typically derived with calculus (e.g., setting the partial derivative of the likelihood function with respect to p to zero and solving), but computers often use an interative approximation approach to arrive at the ML estimators. It is often easier computationally to use the natural log of the likelihood function, so typically the values of the log-likelihood are reported.

Using Equation 2.13 we can try out some values and make educated guesses. Because we observed three heads in five flips, the most applicable column in Table 2.4 is $i = 3$.

TABLE 2.4   *Likelihood of Obtaining i Heads in Five Coin Flips*

	$i = 1$	$i = 2$	$i = 3$	$i = 4$
$p = 0.4$	0.259	0.346	0.230	0.077
$p = 0.5$	0.156	0.313	0.313	0.156
$p = 0.6$	0.077	0.230	0.346	0.259
$p = 0.7$	0.028	0.132	0.309	0.360

The p's in this table could also be β's, *SE*'s, λ's. etc.

Assuming the coin tosses follow a binomial distribution (a logical assumption to make) and that the tosses result in three heads, the maximum likelihood approach to estimating the value of p (which we might assume initially is 0.5—a fair coin) indicates the most likely value of p is 0.6. The maximum value of 0.346 corresponds to $p = 0.6$. Of course, we would probably want to have far more than five trials (e.g., coin flips) to come up with a good estimate (especially if you were ready to complain to that coin manufacturer about the fairness of its coins!).

In fact, this is a common criticism of ML estimators: They require large sample sizes to be unbiased. However, as demonstrated from an abundance of statistical work, ML estimators also have the following desirable statistical properties ("asymptotically" may be interpreted as meaning "large sample"):

1. *Consistency:* As the sample size grows larger, the bias grows smaller.
2. *Asymptotically efficient:* The smallest variance among consistent estimators.
3. *Asymptotically normally distributed:* Allows powerful hypothesis testing.

Given these qualities, MLE has become the preferred choice of analysts who use generalized linear models. ML techniques are general enough to accommodate any of the probability distributions already described. Although showing this is beyond the scope of this presentation, many books on generalized linear models work through the mathematics of MLE with these various distributions (see, e.g., Dobson 1990). Hardin and Hilbe (2001) describe various algorithms that are used in software such as Stata to calculate maximum likelihood estimates.

How to Check the Significance of Coefficients and the "Fit" of the Model

In linear regression one of the goals is to determine the overall fit of the model and to compare models with different subsets of independent variables. We may use, for example, the adjusted R^2, nested F-tests, and the root mean square error (RMSE) to check for goodness-of-fit. There is also interest in determining whether individual coefficients (β's) are significantly different from zero. The most common approach is to use t-tests and associated p-values to do hypothesis testing for single coefficients. Sufficiently large t-values and accompanying small p-values (e.g., $p < 0.05$) answer the question of whether there is a statistically significant relationship between an independent and the dependent variable. The question remains, however: What does the researcher do when confronted with a generalized linear model?

For single coefficients (such as β's), the fact that ML estimators are asymptotically normally distributed suggests that, given a large enough sample, we may simply use a z-test to check for statistical significance. The z-value may be used in the same way that the t-value is used in OLS regression: Look for z-values with absolute values greater than 1.96 if the rule of thumb used is a p-value of less than 0.05 (2-tailed test). Many statistical programs such as Stata provide a z-test associated with each coefficient in a generalized linear model.

Another commonly used approach is the *Wald test*. It looks very similar to the t-test, as follows:

$$W = \left[\frac{\hat{\beta}_1 - \beta^*}{\hat{\sigma}_{\hat{\beta}_1}}\right]^2 \tag{2.14}$$

A difference between the Wald test and the t-test is that the term in brackets is squared. Note that β^* is equal to zero in many analyses because we wish to determine whether the coefficient is significantly different from zero. So in many situations we may simply use the coefficient divided by its standard error. SAS and SPSS provide a Wald test in their logistic regression routines. The Wald test is distributed *chi-square* (χ^2; recall that a chi-square value in OLS regression may be obtained by squaring a t-value). An advantage of the Wald test is that the researcher may test whether more than one coefficient is significantly different from zero, and may also test whether two coefficients equal one another using the following formula:

$$W = \frac{\left(\hat{\beta}_2 - \hat{\beta}_1\right)^2}{\hat{\sigma}^2_{\hat{\beta}_2} + \hat{\sigma}^2_{\hat{\beta}_1} - 2\hat{Cov}\left(\hat{\beta}_2, \hat{\beta}_1\right)} \tag{2.15}$$

As long as the statistical software allows estimation of the covariance between two coefficients, analysts may use the preceding formula to compare coefficients in generalized linear models. For those who prefer confidence intervals (CIs), Liao (2000) has recently developed some simple tools for obtaining them.

In OLS regression, most researchers use the adjusted R^2 to determine the overall fit of the model. The adjusted R^2 indicates the proportion of variability in the dependent variable that is "explained" by the independent variables. It is "adjusted" to take into account the number of independent variables in the model (see Chapter 1). Some analysts also use the root mean squared error (RMSE) because it measures the variability left over in the dependent variable once its systematic component that is related to the independent variables has been removed. Smaller RMSE's indicate better fitting models.

To test the overall fit of the generalized linear model, there is no direct parallel to the adjusted R^2 or the RMSE. There are, however, several alternative approaches to testing the fit of the model. The most common are based on the *Likelihood Ratio (LR) Test*. The LR test, in general, compares the likelihood function of the *constrained model* (M_C) and the likelihood function of the *unconstrained model* (M_U). The constrained model may take one of two forms. In the first form, some of the coefficients are assumed to equal zero. In practical terms, this means that some of the independent variables of interest are left out of the model. In the second form, all of the coefficients are assumed to equal zero. In this situation, the constrained model is known as the *null model* or *intercept-only* model (e.g., $Y = \alpha$). The unconstrained model is typically the hypothesized model, or the model with all of the relevant independent variables included.

As already mentioned, the most common approach to computing likelihood functions is to take their natural logs ($\log_e$). Not only does this simplify the computations, but it also results in log-likelihood functions from different models that may be subtracted to yield LR tests. Moreover, with just a little further mathematical manipulation, this subtraction results in a quantity that is distributed χ^2, so that we may use a regular χ^2 test to assess significance. LR tests look like the following:

$$\text{LR test} = \{2 * \ln L(M_U)\} - \{2 * \ln L(M_C)\} \tag{2.16}$$

This test explicitly compares the log-likelihood from the unconstrained model (M_U) to the log-likelihood from the constrained model (M_C). (Note: Most presentations of log-likelihoods use *ln* to indicate the natural logarithm, or what we have earlier labeled $\log_e$. We will follow the convention of using *ln* when presenting log-likelihoods and measures based on them.) Most analysis software supplies these log-likelihoods or similar numbers that may be transformed into log-likelihoods.

The most common approach is to define the unconstrained model as the hypothesized model and the constrained model as the null model. This is similar to the R^2 test in OLS regression that compares, implicitly, the hypothesized model to the intercept-only model. However, the LR test may also be used to compare two models that are nested; that is, that have a set and a subset of independent variables. This is similar to using nested F-tests in OLS regression to compare nested models. In general, the just-described LR test is known as the *likelihood ratio chi-square test*. Many statistical programs provide it, often labeling it G^2. The degrees of freedom (*df*) used for determining whether the χ^2 value is significant is the difference in the number of independent variables between the constrained and unconstrained models. If the constrained model is the null model, then the *df* are simply the number of independent variables in the model. An example of the LR test is given in Table 2.5, but first we will examine several other model fit statistics.

Another common approach based on the same principle uses what is termed the *De-viance*. This approach also uses the unconstrained (hypothesized) model, but compares it to the *full* or *saturated* model (M_F). The full model has one parameter for each observation. In other words, the full model assumes that we have perfect knowledge of the patterns in the data. A *Deviance* asks whether the full model improves the fit over the hypothesized model (you obviously do not want this because it indicates that you may get a better model with more parameters). When the full model is fit, the log-likelihood is zero, so the Deviance is computed as

$$\text{Deviance} = \{2 * \ln L(M_F)\} - \{2 * \ln L(M_U)\} = -2 * \ln L(M_U) \qquad (2.17)$$

The Deviance is distributed χ^2, but there has been some statistical research that indicates that it is not useful when the model is based on a small sample. Smaller Deviance values generally indicate better fitting models.

Measures of overall fit similar to the OLS R^2 statistic have also been proposed. Most of these manipulate the log-likelihoods to compare regression models. One such measure is the McFadden (pseudo) adjusted R^2.

$$\bar{R}^2{}_{McF} = 1 - \frac{\ln L(M_U) - (k+1)}{\ln L(M_C)} \qquad (2.18)$$

This measure is similar to an adjusted R^2 with k equal to the number of independent variables estimated in the model. It ranges from 0 to 1, much like an adjusted R^2. A difference is that, unlike the many rules of thumb that have emerged among those who study the R^2, no one has concluded how large is "large" for the McFadden adjusted R^2 (Greene 2000; Long 1997). Note that the log-likelihoods are not multiplied by 2 in Equation 2.18.

Another similar measure is known simply as the pseudo-R^2 measure.

$$\text{Pseudo-}R^2 = \frac{\left[\text{Deviance}(M_C) - \text{Deviance}(M_U)\right]}{\text{Deviance}(M_C)} \qquad (2.19)$$

Values of the pseudo-R^2 measure tend to be very similar to the McFadden adjusted R^2 measure. Like the McFadden adjusted R^2, how large is "large" is also a problem for this measure of fit. Note that the constrained model used in computing these two pseudo R^2 measures is the null model.

Finally, a growing consensus has emerged that comparing models should be accomplished with what are known generally as *Information Measures*. We'll discuss the two most common.

Akaike's Information Criterion (AIC) is computed by the following formula:

$$AIC = \frac{\text{Deviance}(M_U) + 2C}{N} \qquad (2.20)$$

Equation 2.20 involves the deviance of the unconstrained (hypothesized) model plus 2 multiplied by the number of coefficients (independent variables + intercept), divided by the sample size. To compare models, the rule of thumb is that the smaller the AIC, the better the model fits the data.

Another information measure is known as the *Bayesian Information Criterion (BIC)*. Similar to the AIC, the smaller the value of the BIC, the better the model fits the data. But this can be tricky to interpret because the BIC is often a negative number. The BIC is computed by the following formula:

$$BIC = \text{Deviance}(M_U) - (df_k \times \ln N) \qquad (2.21)$$

One simply computes the deviance statistic for the hypothesized model and subtracts its degrees of freedom (this is the sample size *minus* the number of coefficients) multiplied by the natural logarithm of its sample size. If the BIC is larger than 0, then the full (saturated) model provides a better fit. When it is less than 0, you should compare models and see which BIC is smaller. The rationale behind these information measures is provided in detail in Raftery (1995) or Zucchini (2000).

To pull this all together, Example 2.1 uses the statistical software Stata to estimate a couple of linear regression models. Unlike the models shown in Chapter 1, we will use the MLE approach to produce these regression models. The goal is not to show that the MLE and the OLS approaches yield similar results, although they do when the assumptions of OLS are met (especially normally distributed errors). Rather the goal is to show the ease with which these various fit statistics may be computed.

The example uses Stata and the data file *GSS96.dta* to analyze religious service attendance. Note that this variable, labeled *attend*, is not a continuous variable, but we are treating it as such for exposition purposes. After opening Stata and the data file, the following commands are entered:

EXAMPLE 2.1   *A Linear Regression Model of Religious Service Attendance Estimated with Maximum Likelihood*

---

*First we compute the *null* model using MLE.*

---

glm attend , family(gaussian) link(identity)   *Note that GLM specifies the   *
                                                       *generalized linear model, family *
                                                       *is normal(gaussian), and the   *
                                                       *link function is identity   *

Iteration 1 : deviance = 15508.8447

Residual df	=	2613	No. of obs	=	2614
Pearson X2	=	15508.84	Deviance	=	15508.84
Dispersion	=	5.935264	Dispersion	=	5.935264

Gaussian (normal) distribution, identity link

attend	Coef.	Std. Err.	t	P > |t|	[95% Conf. Interval]	
_cons	3.35807	.047651	70.473	0.000	3.264635	3.451508

(Model is ordinary regression, use regress instead)

Because Stata does not provide the value of the likelihood functions, we'll have to compute them based on the deviance statistics.

Next we compute an initial hypothesized model.

glm attend gender race educate, family(gaussian) link(identity)

Residual df	=	2602	No. of obs	=	2606
Pearson X2	=	15088.38	Deviance	=	15088.38
Dispersion	=	5.798762	Dispersion	=	5.798762

Gaussian (normal) distribution, identity link

attend	Coef.	Std. Err.	t	P > ItI	[95% Conf. Interval]	
gender	.609373	.094997	6.415	0.000	.423096	.795651
race	.455039	.122122	3.726	0.000	.694504	.215573
educate	.051745	.016337	3.167	0.002	.019710	.083781
_cons	2.709408	.246479	10.992	0.000	2.226110	3.192722

(Model is ordinary regression, use regress instead)

*Finally, we estimate a third model that includes the variable *prayer*.*

glm attend gender race educate prayer, family(gaussian) link(identity)

Iteration 1 : deviance = 8837.8135

Residual df	=	2601	No. of obs	=	2606
Pearson X2	=	8837.814	Deviance	=	8837.814
Dispersion	=	3.397852	Dispersion	=	3.397852

Gaussian (normal) distribution, identity link

attend	Coef.	Std. Err.	t	P > ItI	[95% Conf. Interval]	
gender	.151166	.073499	2.057	0.040	.007043	.295289
race	−.231968	.094844	−2.446	0.015	−.045990	−.417946
educate	.080035	.012523	6.391	0.000	.055478	.104592
prayer	1.495438	.034867	42.890	0.000	1.427068	1.563811
_cons	−4.225179	.248474	−17.005	0.000	−4.712406	−3.737952

(Model is ordinary regression, use regress instead)

We may now use the results of these three models to compute the fit statistics outlined previously. But before doing this, we should discuss some characteristics of the Stata printout. First, note that, at the bottom of each printout, Stata indicates that the model involves what it terms an *ordinary regression* and advises the analyst to use *regress* instead.

In other words, we have conducted a linear regression—which is normally estimated with OLS—using MLE. Second, notice that Stata's GLM routine does not provide the log-likelihoods for the models. However, recall that the deviance, which is supplied, is simply −2*log-likelihood so we may divide the deviance by −2 to compute the log-likelihood for each model. For example, the log-likelihood for the final model is 8,837.814 / −2 = − 4418.907. Finally, the coefficients, standard errors, *t*-values, and *p*-values may all be used the same way in this model as in an OLS regression model. Of course, once we shift focus to discrete dependent variables, this will change.

Table 2.5 shows many of the statistics discussed previously. Note first that the deviance decreases as we move from the null model (also known as the intercept-only model) to Model 2. This provides a rough indicator that the model fit improves as we add the independent variables. The most dramatic change occurs when we move from Model 1 to Model 2. This is because the variable *prayer* has such a strong statistical association with religious service attendance. The log-likelihood for the unconstrained model (M_U) also changes as we move across models—it gets closer to zero, which also indicates, roughly speaking, that the model fit improves.

The number provided by the likelihood ratio χ^2 test is distributed χ^2 with $df = 3$ in Model 1 and $df = 4$ in Model 2. The large values associated with both models indicate that we improve the model fit significantly as we add independent variables. Finally, the

TABLE 2.5   *Fit Statistics from MLE Linear Regression Models of Religious Service Attendance*

	Null Model	*Model 1*	*Model 2*
Deviance	15,508.84	15,088.38	8,837.81
ln L(M_U)	–	−7,544.19	−4,418.91
ln L(M_C)	−7,754.42	−7,754.42	−7,754.42
LR χ^2 test (G^2)		420.46	6,671.03
df_{LR}		3	4
R^2_{McF}		0.03	0.43
Pseudo-R^2		0.03	0.43
AIC	5.93	5.79	3.40
BIC	−5,051.91	−5,377.84	−11,620.54
df_{BIC}	2,613	2,602	2,601
Sample Size	2,614	2,606	2,606

pseudo-R^2 values and the information measures confirm that Model 2 fits the data much better than Model 1. Not only do the pseudo-R^2 measures increase dramatically, but the AIC and BIC decrease substantially. It would be easy to conclude, therefore, that Model 2 provides a good fit to the data. Of course, this is primarily because we have included a variable, *prayer,* that is strongly related to the dependent variable.

Conclusion

This chapter has covered a substantial amount of information about generalized linear models, including descriptions of the link functions and the distributions that they support. A thorough understanding of the information provided in this chapter should furnish a solid foundation for the remaining material in this book. To summarize: OLS regression is not appropriate when the dependent variable is measured as a discrete variable, whether binomial, ordinal, multinomial, or as a count. Fortunately, by generalizing the linear model through the use of link functions that equate the expected value of the dependent variable with a particular distribution, we may derive regression models that are appropriate for a number of types of dependent variables. By understanding how the dependent variable is distributed, it is a simple matter to find the appropriate link function and use available statistical software to estimate regression models. We may then use the various model fit statistics to compare models and determine whether we have done a good job of "explaining" the dependent variable with our independent variables. In order to understand more fully the specific models that we should use, the following chapters describe several in detail. The reader who would like a more advanced treatment of the statistical theory underlying generalized linear models may consult McCullagh and Nelder (1989), Dobson (1990), Hilbe (1994), Lindsey (1997) or Hardin and Hilbe (2001).

Exercises

1. Specify the probability distributions that best describe the following variables:

   a. A measure of the number of avalanches that occur per year in the Wasatch mountain range of Utah.

   b. A measure of whether or not members of a large, nationally representative sample of adults smoke cigarettes.

   c. A measure of the temperature (in Kelvin) inside a sample of volcanoes in Japan.

   d. A measure of whether members of a sample have done one of the following mutually exclusive events in the past year: Remained with their religious denomination, joined a different religious denomination, or left their religious denomination without joining another.

   e. A measure of whether or not firms in a national registry have adopted a public venture capital program.

   f. A measure of whether members of a sample of workers have either quit a job, been laid-off from a job, been fired from a job, or remained in their jobs in the past year.

g. In a sample of adult probationers in Oregon, a measure of the number of times arrested in the previous ten years.

2. Suppose you wished to analyze each of these variables using regression techniques. Select the most likely link function for each distribution.

3. Compute the expected values (means) and variances for each of the following variables:

   a. A sample of 1,500 adults in which the probability of alcohol use in 0.65.

   b. A sample of 200 adults with the following probabilities of involvement in the workforce: 0.55 of being employed full-time, 0.15 of being employed part-time, 0.10 of being unemployed, and 0.20 of not participating in the workforce (e.g., homemakers, students).

   c. A sample of 850 adolescents with the following probabilities of low and high self-esteem: 0.45, low self-esteem; and 0.55, high self-esteem.

   d. A sample of traffic accidents per day along a 10-mile stretch of I-95 in Virginia that yielded the following results:

Number of Accidents	Frequency
0	121
1	199
2	21
3	12
4	5
5	4
6	2
7	1

4. We have been asked to collect 12 signatures for a petition that asks the state government for more money to clean up garbage on public land. The probability of getting a signature from a person approached is 0.40. After finding the mean and variance, answer the following: What is the probability we will have to approach exactly 30 people to get the 12 signatures?

5. Suppose that we survey six people and find that two of them say they read a newspaper every day and the other four say they do not. We wish to determine the maximum likelihood estimate of p, or the probability of daily newspaper reading among this sample. Use the likelihood function for the binomial distribution to fill in the cells of the following table:

	$i = 2$
$p = 0.1$	
$p = 0.2$	
$p = 0.3$	
$p = 0.4$	

From this table, what is the most likely value of p?

6. The data file *USData* (available in Stata, SAS, and SPSS formats) contains a number of variables from the 50 states in the United States. In this exercise we are interested in using linear regression to predict *violrate*, the rate of violent crimes such as murder, robbery, and assault per 100,000 population in 1995. We shall use the following independent variables: *unemprat* (average monthly unemployment rate in 1995), *density* (population density in 1995), and *gsprod* (gross state product in 1995—a measure of the state's economic productivity). Using either Stata or SAS, estimate two linear regression models using MLE (hence, use either Stata's *glm* command or SAS's *Proc Genmod*; SPSS will not estimate a linear regression model using MLE). The first model is the null model, while the second includes the three independent variables. Use the output from these models to compute the following fit statistics from the second model: McFadden adjusted R^2 and the pseudo-R^2. Then compute the AIC and BIC from both models.

3

Logistic and Probit Regression Models

This chapter begins the discussion of how to apply generalized linear models to specific types of categorical or discrete dependent variables. The first type of discrete variable addressed is probably the most common: a binary or dichotomous dependent variable. As we shall see shortly, it is unwise to use OLS regression when confronted with a binary dependent variable. But there are two alternative regression models that are easily implemented in this situation.

Suppose we are interested in explaining the distribution of some dependent variable, yet it has only two possible outcomes. For example, this dependent variable might measure whether or not respondents in a sample support the death penalty, whether or not respondents graduated from college, whether companies in a sample of Fortune 500s have adopted a particular employee assistance program, or whether people vote. In each of these examples, the variable is often coded as [0,1], with 0 indicating "no" and 1 indicating "yes." Most binary variables may be coded in this way. When used as independent variables, we often use the label "dummy variables." For instance, we may have a dummy variable that measures gender and is coded 0 = male and 1 = female. This type of binary measure presents no particular problems for an OLS regression analysis when used as an independent variable. Example 1.1 of Chapter 1 provides a model that uses the dummy variable *gender* and shows how to interpret its coefficient.

The main difficulty for a regression model occurs when the researcher wishes to use a binary variable as the dependent variable. Given what we have learned in Chapter 2, it should be clear that this variable does not—and will not—follow a normal or Gaussian distribution. Rather, it is distributed as a binomial random variable. But the researcher may still want to predict this variable within a regression-like context. What should one do?

Let us begin by seeing what happens when we assume that a binary dependent variable is distributed normally and use OLS regression to explain its variability. The following example uses the SPSS data set *Depress.sav* (also available in Stata and SAS formats). The dependent variable of interest is a measure of life satisfaction, labeled *satlife*. This variable is coded so that *0 = low life satisfaction* and *1 = high life satisfaction*. (You may

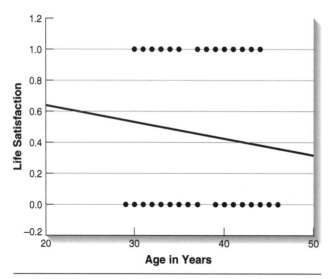

FIGURE 3.1

wish to run a frequency table to see how many respondents fall within each category of life satisfaction.) Suppose we wish to see how life satisfaction varies with age; our hypothesis is that life satisfaction decreases as one gets older. Rather than starting with a regression model, it is useful to compute a scatterplot of the two variables. Figure 3.1 is generated in SPSS for Windows using the *graphs-scatter* option. By double-clicking on the SPSS scatterplot in the output window and clicking *chart-options-fit line* we may include an estimated linear regression line like the one shown.

This figure shows a clear problem with a proposed OLS regression model. Note that all the values of *satlife* line up to correspond to either zero or one. If we connect the regression line to the data points, we will see there is clearly a *heteroscedasticity problem* in the linear relationship between life satisfaction and age. Moreover, if we estimate an OLS regression model and check the distribution of the residuals, we will find that they are not distributed normally (try this). Therefore, when using OLS regression with a binary dependent variable, we violate at least two of the assumptions that underlie this model. Another problem with using OLS regression to estimate this relationship is that, although the dependent variable is bounded by [0,1], it is possible to obtain predicted values that fall outside of this boundary. In other words, we might predict that someone's life satisfaction is a meaningless 1.5.

What Are the Alternatives to the Linear Regression Model?

There are two alternative regression models that are used most often when dealing with a binary dependent variable: logistic regression and probit regression. As noted in Chapter 2, these two models use different link functions, but usually yield similar results. We shall begin by discussing logistic regression.

The Logistic Regression Model

This regression model is perhaps the most widely used among researchers whose goal is to model binary dependent variables. In fact, entire books have been written about this one type of model (see, e.g., Hosmer and Lemeshow 1989; Kleinbaum 1994). The key to the model is that, rather than modeling the dependent variable directly (i.e., estimating the expected value of the dependent variable, Y, for some combination of independent variables, X_k), we estimate the *probability that Y = 1*. Just like in linear regression we assume that some set of X variables is useful for predicting the Y values, but we are claiming that this set predicts the probability that $Y = 1$ (assuming we have coded the dependent variable as [0, 1]). This transformation from directly modeling the dependent variable to modeling some variation of it should jog in your memory the concept of link functions. Before "linking" the particular link function to logistic regression, it is important to understand a few other things about this model.

The basic formula for estimating $Y = 1$ consists of transforming the regression equation to look like Equation 3.1.

$$P(Y = 1) = \frac{1}{1 + \exp\left[-(\alpha + \beta_1 X_1 + \beta_2 X_2 + \ldots + \beta_k X_k)\right]} \tag{3.1}$$

The part of the denominator in parentheses should remind us of the standard linear regression model. But note that in this function it is transformed in what seems to be an unusual way. This part is multiplied by −1, exponentiated, added to 1 and then inverted. Fortunately, most of us will never have to compute this function by hand, or even with a hand calculator; we simply let the computer do the dirty work. The whole function is called the *logistic function* and it is estimated by maximum likelihood (ML) techniques. An advantage of this function is that it guarantees that the probability ranges from 0 to 1 as the regression equation predicts values from negative infinity to positive infinity. (Try plugging various α's and β's into the logistic function and see what happens.). Thus, it does not suffer from the above-mentioned disadvantage of OLS regression when dealing with a binary dependent variable.

The other advantage is that if we plot the logistic function we come up with a shape that looks like Figure 3.2. Keeping in mind that we are concerned with probabilities (e.g., what is the probability that person z supports the death penalty?), this is often an accurate portrayal of probabilities in social and behavioral research. At the low end of a probability scale it is difficult to get much action, in the middle things move more quickly, and at the high end the probability moves more slowly. So, for example, only small groups are adamantly opposed to or very strong advocates of the death penalty, while many people are in the middle with some opposition and some support for this extreme form of punishment.

Most of us probably understand a probability. We know that the probability of obtaining a head when flipping a fair coin is 0.50. In practical terms, we expect that about half of our coin flips will yield heads and half will yield tails. While probabilities help us, in part, to understand logistic regression, there is another essential aspect of logistic regression that we also must understand. This is something known as an *Odds Ratio (OR)*.

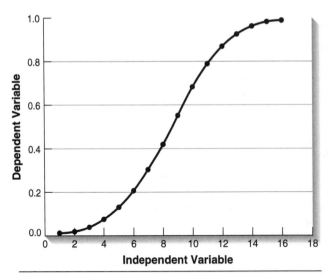

FIGURE 3.2

But what is an odds ratio? More fundamentally, what is an odds? It is probably easiest to explain odds and odds ratios using an example.

Suppose we know, based on extensive research, that the probability of illegal drug use among some population of adolescents is 0.25. Hence we expect that 25 percent of this population of adolescents has used illegal drugs at some point. We may use this information to compute the *odds* of illegal drug use among these adolescents using the general formula $p / (1 - p)$. The odds of illegal drug use are therefore

$$p(\text{drug use}) / (1 - p(\text{drug use})) = 0.25 / (1 - 0.25) = 1/3 \qquad (3.2)$$

This is equivalent to saying that the odds are "3 to 1" that an adolescent from this population will *not use* illegal drugs. Another interpretation is that three times as many adolescents are expected to not use illegal drugs as to use illegal drugs.

An odds ratio is just what it sounds like: the ratio of two odds. The usefulness of this concept is apparent as we continue our adolescent drug use example. Suppose we wish to compare the odds of illegal drug use among male and female adolescents. Then, symbolically speaking, we would be interested in the following:

$$\text{OR}_{\text{males vs. females}} = \frac{\text{odds}(\text{D males})}{\text{odds}(\text{D females})} = \frac{p(\text{D males})}{1 - p(\text{D males})} \bigg/ \frac{p(\text{D females})}{1 - p(\text{D females})} \qquad (3.3)$$

where D is illegal drug use among the group indicated. Our research indicates that 25 percent of males but only 10 percent of females used illegal drugs. As previously, by treating these percentages as probabilities, we may compute the following odds ratio:

$$\text{OR}_{\text{males vs. females}} = [0.25 / 0.75] / [0.10 / 0.90] = (1 / 3) / (1 / 9) = 3 \qquad (3.4)$$

In words, the odds of using illegal drugs among males is three times the odds of using illegal drugs among females. Some researchers use the shorthand phrase that males are three times as likely as females to use illegal drugs. However, this latter phrase is imprecise because saying something is more or less "likely" may refer to odds or probabilities. It should be clear that odds and probabilities are not the same thing.

Essentially an odds ratio is just two odds that are compared to determine whether one group has a higher or lower odds of some binary outcome. A number greater than one indicates a positive association between an independent variable and the dependent variable (of course, this is driven by the coding of the independent variable), while a number between zero and one indicates a negative association. Note that in the preceding example, we are assuming the variable measuring gender is coded male = 1 and female = 0. What if there are no differences between two or more groups? Then we expect to find an odds ratio of 1.00, which means that the odds are the same for the groups. In our example, if the percentage of illegal drug use is the same for males and females, let's say 0.25, then the odds are identical for both groups (0.25 / 0.75 = 0.33) and the odds ratio (0.33 / 0.33) equals 1. We would thus conclude that there are no gender differences in the likelihood of illicit drug use among females and males.

Returning to the logistic function, a nice property is that we may write it as

$$\text{logit}\,[p\,(Y = 1)] = \alpha + \beta_1 X_1 + \beta_2 X_2 + ... + \beta_k X_k$$

$$(3.5)$$

$$\text{where the } logit\,[p\,(Y = 1)] = \log_e\left[\frac{p\,(Y = 1)}{1 - p\,(Y = 1)}\right] \text{ i.e., log–odds}$$

Before moving on, look back at the *link function* for the *logit link* shown in Chapter 2. It is simply the formula in Equation 3.5. The logit link function, however, uses μ to represent $p(Y = 1)$. Another name for the logit is the log-odds.

Going back to the example from the SPSS data set *Depress.sav*, we still wish to predict life satisfaction, but, as noted earlier in the chapter, it is coded as a binary variable. Fortunately, we now have some additional statistical tools that come in handy as we ponder this dependent variable. Let's extend the example by looking at gender differences in life satisfaction. A simple way is to use our statistical software to look at a cross-tabulation of *satlife* and *gender* (coded as 0 = female, 1 = male). In SPSS for Windows this is accomplished using the option *analyze-descriptive statistics-crosstab*, in Stata use the command *table* or *tabulate*, and in SAS use the command *Proc Freq*. Here is the SPSS *crosstab* result.

EXAMPLE 3.1   *Cross-Tabulation of Gender and Life Satisfaction*

SATLIFE * GENDER Crosstabulation

Count

		Female (0)	Male (1)	Total
SATLIFE	Low (0)	58	7	65
	High (1)	38	14	52
Total		96	21	117

The probability that males are *high* on life satisfaction is 14 / 21 = 0.67; the probability that females are *high* on life satisfaction is 38 / 96 = 0.40. (What is the probability of *low* life satisfaction for each group?) What are the odds that males are high on life satisfaction relative to females? As we learned previously, this is the *odds ratio*.

$$\text{OR}_{\text{males vs. females}}: [0.67 / 0.33] / [0.40 / 0.60] = 3.05 \tag{3.6}$$

A quick method for computing this odds ratio when faced with a 2×2 cross-tabulation is with the formula *ad / bc*, where the cells of the table are labeled from left to right, top to bottom as *a, b, c,* and *d.*

a	b
c	d

Thus, in the frequency table, the odds ratio is (58)(14) / (38)(7) = 3.05. In words, the odds of high life satisfaction among males is three times the odds of high life satisfaction among females. This is simple to compute when we are faced with two binary variables, such as *gender* and *satlife*. But what happens when we are confronted with a continuous independent variable or multiple independent variables? It is obvious that the model quickly becomes much more complicated.

In these situations, we may take advantage of the logistic regression model to determine associations in the data. Before moving directly to a more complicated model, let's first see what SPSS's logistic regression routine produces. An important question to ask is whether we can reproduce the simple analysis we just looked at. Using the SPSS for Windows option *analyze-regression-binary logistic* and then choosing *satlife* as the dependent variable and *gender* as the covariate, we discover the following results:

EXAMPLE 3.2   *A Logistic Regression Model of Gender and Life Satisfaction*

Variable	B	S.E.	Wald	df	Sig	R	Exp(B)
GENDER	1.1159	.5078	4.8295	1	.0280	.1327	3.0523
Constant	−.4229	.2087	4.1051	1	.0428		

Variables in the Equation

Note that the printout looks similar to an OLS regression printout, with B's, S.E.'s and Sig's (*p*-values). However, as explained in Chapter 2, we now determine statistical signifi-cance with a Wald value, although, for most purposes, we may use this value much the way we used *t*-values in OLS regression. To obtain the odds ratio, simply take the B value and exponentiate it. This is provided in the SPSS output under Exp(B) and is interpreted in the same way as the odds ratio previously computed. As should be the case, the logistic regression model indicates that the odds of high life satisfaction among males is three times the odds of high life satisfaction among females. An added advantage of the logistic regression model is that we may now conclude that the gender difference is statistically significant at the *p* = .028 level. (What does this mean?)

Many researchers who feel compelled to use logistic regression, especially novice users, are not comfortable interpreting odds ratios. Fortunately, it is rather simple, espe-cially with contemporary statistical software, to convert these results into probabilities. In this simple model (and even in more sophisticated models), we may use Equation 3.7—which is clearly based directly on the logistic function—to compute probabilities.

$$P\left(y_i = 1 \mid \mathbf{x}_i\right) = \frac{1}{1 + e^{(-\mathbf{x}_i \mathbf{b})}} \tag{3.7}$$

Notice that the *x* and *b* in Equation 3.7 are bolded. This suggests they include values of the independent variables, coefficients, *and* the intercept (see the logistic function). A key characteristic of Equation 3.7 is that we must choose particular values of the indepen-dent variables when computing probabilities. When faced with a single dummy variable, such as gender, this is a simple task because there are only two possible values. For ex-ample, among females in the *Depress* data set, the probability of high life satisfaction is $[1 + \exp-\{-.423 + (0)(1.12)\}]^{-1} = 0.40$. The probability of high life satisfaction among males is $[1 + \exp-\{-.423 + (1)(1.12)\}]^{-1} = 0.67$. These probabilities are identical to those that we computed using the cross-tabulation of *satlife* and *gender*. All of the software packages discussed in this presentation—SPSS, Stata, and SAS (as well as others such as S-Plus, LIMDEP, Systat, and Minitab)—also allow the user to save the predicted prob-abilities from the logistic regression model.

When a model includes multiple independent variables, a common approach when computing probabilities is to choose the means of the independent variables. Of course, this does not work well when using dummy variables, so the researcher typically chooses a relevant category. A model might be used, for instance, to predict the probability of high life satisfaction among female, 30-year-olds with one child. Examples of this procedure are provided in the next section.

What about a More Sophisticated Model?

The following multivariable logistic regression model is designed to determine the statistical association of life satisfaction and the following independent variables: *Gender* (0 = female, 1 = male), *IQ*, *age* (in years), and *weight* (in *z*-scores). We are particularly interested in whether there are still significant gender differences in life satisfaction after controlling for the effects of these other variables. SPSS's *binary logistic* routine is used to estimate the model.

EXAMPLE 3.3   *A Logistic Regression Model of Life Satisfaction with Multiple Independent Variables*

			Variables in the Equation				
Variable	B	S.E.	Wald	df	Sig	R	Exp(B)
GENDER	1.2792	.5597	5.2236	1	.0223	.1545	3.5939
IQ	−.0728	.0536	1.8439	1	.1745	.0000	.9298
AGE	−.0411	.0525	.6137	1	.4334	.0000	.9597
WEIGHT	−.0377	.0889	.1799	1	.6715	.0000	.9630
Constant	7.7413	5.9431	1.6967	1	.1927		

In this model we have computed *Adjusted Odds Ratios*; that is, odds ratios that are adjusted for the effects of the other variables in the model. For example, after controlling for the effects of *IQ*, *age*, and *weight*, the odds of high life satisfaction among males is about 3.6 times the odds of high life satisfaction among females. So the relationship between life satisfaction and gender seems to increase once we control for the effects of these other variables. (But it may not increase *significantly*.) We may also work out predicted odds for particular groups using the same algebraic approach as in OLS regression. For instance, if we wish to know the odds of high life satisfaction among females and males at the mean of *age* (mean = 37), *IQ* (mean = 92), and *weight* (mean = 0), we find

$$\text{Odds}_{females}: \exp[7.74 + (92)(-.07) + (37)(-.04)] = 0.84$$

$$(3.8)$$

$$\text{Odds}_{males}: \exp[7.74 + (1)(1.28) + (92)(-.07) + (37)(-.04)] = 3.00$$

(Note that the weight coefficient does not appear in Equation 3.8 because it has a mean of zero.) The odds ratio associated with these two odds should correspond with the odds ratio in the logistic regression table (within rounding error). Keeping our respective fingers crossed, we find 3.00 / 0.84 = 3.57. Compare this to the table's *gender* odds ratio of 3.59.

Finally, we may compute predicted probabilities using Equation 3.7. This is done at particular values of the independent variables, usually at their respective means. Using the formula for converting logistic regression coefficients into probabilities, we may use the model coefficients to come up with the following fascinating results:

> The probability of high life satisfaction among females who are at the average on *IQ* (92), *age* (37), and *weight* (mean = 0): 0.387.

> The probability of high life satisfaction among males who are at the mean on *IQ, age,* and *weight:* 0.695.

Let's develop another example, but this time, instead of using SPSS, we shall use Stata to estimate the logistic regression model. The Stata data file *GSS96.dta* includes a variable labeled *volrelig*, which indicates whether or not a respondent volunteered for a religious organization in the previous year (coded 0 = no, 1 = yes). A hypothesis we wish to explore is that females are more likely than males to volunteer for religious organizations. Hence, in this data set, we code *gender* as 0 = male and 1 = female. In order to preclude the possibility that age and education explain the proposed association between *gender* and *volrelig*, we include these variables in the model after transforming them into z-scores. An advantage of this transformation is that it becomes a simple exercise to compute odds or probabilities for males and females at the mean of age and education, because these variables have now been transformed to have a mean of zero.

After opening *GSS96.dta* in Stata, we specify the following logistic regression model using Stata's *logit* command (it may also be estimated using Stata's *glm* command with *link(logit)* and *family(binomial)*):

EXAMPLE 3.4   *A Logistic Regression Model of Volunteer Work Using Stata*

logit volrelig zeduc zage gender   *This appears on the command line*

Logit estimates					Number of obs	=	2890
					LR chi2(3)	=	29.23
					Prob > chi2	=	0.0000
Log likelihood = −727.93848					Pseudo R2	=	0.0197

volrelig	Coef.	Std. Err.	z	P > |z|	[95% Conf. Interval]	
zeduc	.354176	.073655	4.809	0.000	.209815	.498537
zage	.140682	.073947	1.902	0.057	−.004252	.285615
gender	.355627	.150303	2.366	0.018	.061038	.650216
_cons	−2.830669	.121425	−23.312	0.000	−3.068655	−2.592680

Note first that, unlike the SPSS output, the Stata logit output includes z-values rather than Wald values. The associated *p*-values are approximately the same using either approach. Stata also does not automatically provide odds ratios, although these are easy to obtain. In fact, if we specify Stata's *logistic* command rather than *logit*, the output provides odds ratios rather than coefficients. The initial part of the output also provides the log-likelihood value and the LR test that compares the null model to the model that we specified. The LR test provides a χ^2 value of 29.23 with 3 degrees of freedom. This is significant at the $p < .0001$ level. However, the pseudo-R^2 measure shows a very unimpressive model fit.

The interpretation of the coefficients is much the same as those we have seen so far. For example, after controlling for the effects of education and age (because they are standardized we are estimating the association of *volrelig* and *gender* at the mean of age and education), the odds of female volunteer work is $\exp(0.356) = 1.43$ times higher than the odds of male volunteer work. But what about the "continuous" variables such as education and age? We may interpret their coefficients much like we interpret coefficients in OLS regression, except we should keep in mind that we are now dealing with log-odds ratios, or, after exponentiation, odds ratios. For example, with each one standard deviation unit increase in education, we expect the odds of volunteer work to increase by a factor of about $\exp(0.354) = 1.42$, holding gender and age constant.

A useful method for interpreting coefficients from generalized linear models that use the log or logit link function is provided by the following formula: $([\exp(\beta) - 1] * 100)$. In the case of logistic regression, the result of this formula is interpreted as the percent change in the odds of the dependent variable that is associated with unit change in the independent variable (Long 1997). Hence, another way of interpreting the association in our example is to say that with each standard deviation unit increase in education, we expect the odds of volunteer work to increase by about $([\exp(0.354) - 1] * 100) = 42$ percent. Similarly, we may say that, after controlling for the effects of education and age, the odds that females volunteer are about 43 percent higher than the odds that males volunteer for a religious organization.

Finally, we may also compute odds and probabilities for particular groups directly from the coefficients.

> Controlling for age and education, the odds of volunteering among males is $\exp(-2.83) = .059$, and the odds of volunteering among females is $\exp(-2.83 + 0.354) = .084$. (What, then, is the odds ratio?)

> Controlling for age and education, the probability of volunteering among males is .056 and the probability of volunteering among females is .078. (Use these probabilities to compute the odds ratio for gender.)

Note that these odds and probabilities are similar. This often occurs when we are dealing with probabilities that are relatively close to zero; in other words, it is a common occurrence for *rare* events. To see this, simply compute a cross-tabulation of *volrelig* and *gender* and compare the odds and probabilities. Then try it out for any rare event you may wish to simulate.

The Probit Regression Model

Although the logistic regression approach offers a relatively simple and widely used technique for modeling binary variables, there are other approaches that may be used as well.

Perhaps the most common alternative is probit regression. This model is used widely by econometricians and is described in detail in any introductory econometrics textbook (e.g., Kennedy 1992). It is not clear why some disciplines prefer the logistic regression model while others prefer the probit regression model, but it may have its roots in what appears to be the complicated functional form of the probit model. Unlike the logistic function, the functional form of the probit model has one of those frightening calculus symbols, the dreaded integral ($\int$). Nonetheless, given the statistical tools available in most software, it is unlikely that the researcher ever has to figure out the calculus underlying the probit function. Moreover, the shapes of the distributions implied by the logistic function and the probit function are very similar. Equation 3.9 demonstrates the functional form of the probit model.

$$P\left(Y_i\right) = F\left(Z_i\right) = \frac{1}{\sqrt{2\pi}} \int_{-\infty}^{Z_i} e^{-s^2/2} ds \qquad (3.9)$$

Readers who have had exposure to probability theory will quickly recognize this function as the cumulative distribution function of a standard normal variable. The lower-case s represents a normally distributed variable with mean of zero and standard deviation of one. Equation 3.9 indicates that the probability of Y falls between 0 and 1. Recall from Chapter 2 that the probit model assumes that the binary variable measured denotes an underlying, yet unobserved, continuous scale. This is represented in the function by the Z. In other words, Z signifies an unobserved continuous scale underlying Y. Because we don't observe Z directly, we take the binary indicator Y as its proxy.

One advantage of the probit model over the logistic model is that the coefficients may be transformed directly into probabilities at particular levels of the independent variables simply by using values from a standard normal distribution table (i.e., a table of z-values). To show this advantage directly, let's return to the example of gender and life satisfaction using Stata and the file *Depress.dta*. We begin with the same simple model that was previously estimated.

EXAMPLE 3.5   *A Probit Regression Model of Life Satisfaction*

probit satlife gender   *This appears on the command line*

Probit estimates				Number of obs	=	117
				LR chi2(1)	=	5.13
				Prob > chi2	=	0.0235
Log likelihood = −77.810255				Pseudo R2	=	0.0319

satlife	Coef.	Std. Err.	z	P > |z|	[95% Conf. Interval]	
gender	.694874	.311168	2.23	0.026	.084997	1.304752
_cons	−.264147	.129551	−2.04	0.041	−.518062	−.010232

Using these probit regression results, we may use a table of z-scores (found in most elementary statistics textbooks) to determine the probabilities of high life satisfaction. Because there are only two gender categories, we are interested in two probabilities, as follows:

Probability that females are high on life satisfaction: $z(-0.26) = 0.40$

Probability that males are high on life satisfaction: $z(-0.26 + 0.69) = z(0.43) = 0.67$

Of course, these probabilities are identical to those we estimated from the initial cross-tabulation of *gender* and *satlife* (see Example 3.1).

Fortunately, if we have access to Stata or other statistical software, there is no need to carry around a table of z-values to transform probit coefficients to probabilities. A simple way to transform these coefficients is with Stata's *display* command. This command allows us to use Stata as a glorified calculator. To convert z-scores to probabilities type *display normprob(z-score),* where you place the probit coefficient in place of *z-score.* For example, to get the probabilities above, type *display normprob(–0.26)* on Stata's command line. Stata displays 0.397. Type *display normprob(–0.26 + 0.69)* and Stata displays 0.6664.

These results agree with what we found previously, and eliminate the need to consider odds and odds ratios. Although researchers often get comfortable using odds and odds ratios, some prefer to go straight to probabilities. We will discuss more about these probabilities, especially different ways of representing them, when we consider the following more sophisticated probit model.

Continuing our use of the probit model to predict life satisfaction, let's move to a model with more independent variables. In this model, we are still interested in gender differences, but we also wish to consider sleeping habits. We therefore include a binary independent variable, *sleep,* which is coded as 0 = poor sleeper and 1 = adequate or good sleeper. There are two additional variables in the model, *age* and *IQ.* Both are transformed into z-scores, so they have means of zero.

EXAMPLE 3.6 *A Probit Regression Model of Life Satisfaction with Multiple Independent Variables*

probit satlife gender sleep zage z_iq   *This appears on the command line*

Probit estimates					Number of obs	=	104
					LR chi2(4)	=	19.20
					Prob > chi2	=	0.0007
Log likelihood = –62.181176					Pseudo R2	=	0.1337

satlife	Coef.	Std. Err.	z	P > |z|	[95% Conf. Interval]	
gender	.652573	.359239	1.817	0.069	–.051523	1.356669
sleep	1.451607	.527266	2.753	0.006	.418185	2.485028
zage	–.036661	.030742	–1.193	0.233	–.096913	.023591
z_iq	–.026244	.031431	–0.835	0.404	–.087848	.035360
_cons	–.355077	.145204	–2.445	0.014	–.639671	–.070483

Before interpreting the probit coefficients, let's review the model fit information. The log-likelihood is -62.181, which implies a deviance value of $-2 * (-62.181) =$ 124.362. The LR test gives a χ^2 value of 19.20 with 4 degrees of freedom (corresponding to 4 independent variables). This is statistically significant at the $p = .0007$ level, or, what is typically reported is that it is statistically significant at the $p < .001$ level. The pseudo-R^2 value is 0.134, which is quite a bit higher than the pseudo-R^2 reported in the earlier models. We may also compute other fit statistics using the information provided in the table. For instance, what is the AIC for this model? Recalling its formula from Chapter 2, it is simply $[124.362 + (2 * 5)] / 104 = 1.29$. The BIC is $124.362 - [(104-5) * ln(104)] = -335.27$.

Moving to the coefficients, what does the gender effect mean? (Assume for now that it remains statistically significant at the $p < .05$ level.) Should we interpret it using predicted probabilities? Keeping in mind that we now have two continuous variables and two binary independent variables, we need to decide how to compute these predicted probabilities. One possibility is to compute predicted probabilities for males and females at the mean of the other variables. This is similar to what we did previously, where we plug the means of the other variables in an equation and then transform the resultant z-score using a table or Stata's *display* function. Because age and IQ are z-scores, with means of zero, this is simple to do. But what do we do about the sleep variable; it has only two values? Perhaps rather than predicting two probabilities, male and female, we should predict four probabilities identifying the four groups that result from cross-classifying *gender* and *sleep*. The resulting probabilities are

Female, poor sleeper:	$z(-.36) = 0.36$
Male, poor sleeper:	$z(-.36 + 0.65) = z(0.29) = 0.61$
Female, good sleeper:	$z(-.36 + 1.45) = z(1.09) = 0.86$
Male, good sleeper:	$z(-.36 + 0.65 + 1.45) = z(1.74) = 0.96$

In words, we expect about 36 percent of poor sleeping females and 61 percent of poor sleeping males to report high life satisfaction. Similarly, we expect 86 percent of good sleeping females and 96 percent of good sleeping males to report high life satisfaction. Getting a good night's sleep appears to be especially important for one's life satisfaction.

We may also use Stata to compute these probabilities without reference to a table of z-scores. The *display* command combined with the *normprob* function yields the following precise results:

```
display normprob(-.355077)
.361266
display normprob(-.355077 + .652573)
.6169561
display normprob(-.355077 + 1.451611)
.863577
display normprob(-.355077 +.652573 + 1.45161)
.9598634
```

Another way to interpret these results is by computing the *discrete change* in the outcome variable given a change in the independent variable. A simple way to do this with dummy variables is to to subtract one probability from another. So if we wish to determine the discrete change in life satisfaction as we move from poor sleep to good sleep among females, we subtract 0.36 from 0.86:

Change among females associated with good vs. poor sleep: $0.86 - 0.36 = 0.50$

For continuous variables, the discrete change is harder to compute, but the interpretation is similar. Equation 3.10 shows a formula that is useful for computing discrete changes in general (see Long 1997).

$$\frac{\Delta P(y = 1 \mid \bar{\mathbf{x}})}{\Delta x_k} = P(y = 1 \mid \bar{\mathbf{x}}, \bar{x}_k + 1) - P(y = 1 \mid \bar{\mathbf{x}}, \bar{x}_k) \tag{3.10}$$

The Greek letter delta (Δ) is often used in mathematics and statistics to signify change. Hence this formula says that the change in the probability of the dependent variable given some change in the independent variable (here denoted as an increase of one unit) is given by subtracting one estimated probability from another. This formula also implies that all the other independent variables are set at their mean value. But for dummy variables, we still must choose a category. For example, from the current model let's assume that the age coefficient is significant and not standardized and we want to see what effect a discrete change in age—five years—has on the probability of high life satisfaction among females who get little sleep. This is computed as

$$P(y = 1 \mid \bar{\mathbf{x}}, \bar{x}_k) = z(-0.36), \ P(y = 1 \mid \bar{\mathbf{x}}, \bar{x}_k + 5) = z(-0.36 - \{5 * 0.036\})$$
$$\tag{3.11}$$
$$z(-0.36 - 0.18) - z(-0.36) = z(-0.54) - z(-0.36) = 0.295 - 0.359 = -0.064$$

Hence, an increase of five years in age is expected to decrease the probability of high life satisfaction among females who get little sleep by about –0.06. Similarly, an increase of five years in age is expected to shift the probability of high life satisfaction among males who get little sleep by about $z(\{-0.36 + 0.65\} - 0.18) - z(-0.36 + 0.65) = 0.544 - 0.614 = -0.07$.

Note that, if we computed gender differences at a variety of ages, there would be little relative difference in the probabilities. This is because we have assumed that the effects of age and gender are independent, so we obviously will find similar gender differences anywhere along the age distribution. If we think that the gender differences in life satisfaction increase or decrease with age, then we should include a gender-by-age interaction term in the model.

Stata will automate the process of determining discrete changes for us somewhat. If we ask for *dprobit* rather than *probit*, we obtain the following results:

EXAMPLE 3.7   *Using Stata's DProbit Command to Compute Discrete Changes in Life Satisfaction*

dprobit satlife gender sleep z_iq zage   *This appears on the command line*

satlife	dF/dx	Std. Err.	z	P > |z|	x-bar	[95% C.I.]	
gender*	.253169	.130574	1.82	0.069	.182692	−.002751	.509089
sleep*	.482463	.111551	2.75	0.006	.125	.263827	.701099
z_iq	−.010450	.012514	−0.83	0.404	−.174615	−.034978	.014077
zage	−.014599	.012240	−1.19	0.233	.302015	−.038588	.009391
obs. P	.461539						
pred. P	.475721	(at x-bar)		/*Predicted at mean of all variables*/			

(*) dF/dx is for discrete change of dummy variable from 0 to 1
     z and P > \| z \| are the test of the underlying coefficient being 0

Rather than coefficients, Stata provides a column labeled dF/dx. This is simply calculus shorthand for a change in the probability of the dependent variable given a one-unit change in the independent variable. But notice that Stata recognizes that the model includes dummy variables (denoted with an asterisk) and tells the user that the dF/dx column specifies the discrete change from 0 to 1, the most common coding of dummy variables. These discrete changes are therefore computed for dummy variables as they shift from 0 to 1 and for continuous variables as they increase by one unit. So we anticipate a gender difference in probabilities, on average, of 0.25; and a sleep difference of 0.48. Each unit increase in age, or a one standard deviation unit increase, is expected to decrease the probability by about 0.015. If we multiply this number by 5, we find an expected decrease of 0.075, which, with all due respect to rounding error, is similar to what we found previously. But keep in mind that this result associated with age *does not* reflect a significant difference in the population (look at the z-value and its p-value). It appears that a good night's sleep is much more consequential for high life satisfaction than is one's gender, age, or IQ.

Diagnostic Tests for the Logistic Regression Model

This final substantive section discusses briefly some useful ways to diagnose problems in a logistic regression model. Although these same problems can occur for probit models, the techniques discussed in this section have been developed primarily for logistic regression models, and the relevant software has followed suit. The post-estimation commands allowed in Stata, SAS, and SPSS following probit models are limited primarily to predicted values and do not include the host of residuals that are useful for regression diagnostics.

Recall from Chapter 1 that predicted values, residuals, and various transformations of them are used to diagnose nasty problems such as heteroscedasticity and influential observations. In a similar manner, we may use predicted probabilities and residuals from a logistic regression model to diagnose potential problems with fit. Although there are numerous approaches for doing this, we will focus on only a couple. The interested reader should consult Hosmer and Lemeshow (1989), McCullagh and Nelder (1989), Hamilton (1992), or Myers, Montgomery, and Vining (2002) for a more thorough review of diagnostic approaches for logistic regression and other generalized linear models.

Before showing an example of some simple diagnostic plots for a logistic regression model, let's review predicted values and residuals. The most common predicted values from a logistic regression model are simply the predicted probabilities, which may range from zero to one. We have already seen how to ask Stata for predicted probabilities. Obtaining predicted probabilities from SPSS, SAS, or most other statistical software is also a simple matter. Now, recall from Chapter 1 how to compute residuals from an OLS regression model. They are simply $r_i = \{Y_i - \hat{Y}_i\}$. This type of residual may then be transformed in various ways (e.g., standardized, studentized) and used to diagnose potential problems with the OLS regression model.

It turns out that a residual computed in a similar manner is not appropriate for a logistic regression model, nor for most other types of generalized linear models, because the preceding formula assumes that the variance of the dependent variable is constant. Clearly, this is not the case in logistic regression. There are two generally used alternatives in this situation: the Pearson's residual (r_p) and the deviance residual (r_d). These are computed as

$$ r_p = \frac{Y_i - \hat{\mu}_i}{\sqrt{\text{var } Y_i}} $$

(3.12)

$$ r_d = \left[\text{sign}\left(Y_i - \hat{\mu}_i\right)\right] \times \sqrt{d_i} $$

An interesting property of the deviance residuals is that the sum of their squared values equals the model deviance, which was shown in Chapter 2 to be –2 times the log of the likelihood function of the model. More details on how to compute these quantities are in McCullagh and Nelder (1989). Fortunately, the software will compute these residuals for us. Because research indicates that deviance residuals are probably the best available technique for diagnosing problems in models with discrete dependent variables (Davison and Gigli 1989; Pierce and Schafer 1986), we will rely on them in this discussion.

What do we do with deviance residuals? Perhaps their most useful purpose is in finding areas where the model does not fit the data well. Hosmer and Lemeshow (1989) recommend that information from the deviance residual be combined with the leverage values (see Chapter 1) to come up with a measure they label ΔD_i. This is computed as follows:

$$ \Delta D_i = \frac{r_d^2}{\left(1 - h_i\right)} $$

(3.13)

The quantity h_i is the leverage value of the observation (see Hosmer and Lemeshow 1989, p. 151, for the formula to compute leverage values from a logistic regression model). They then recommend plotting the ΔD_i's by the predicted probabilities to determine areas where the model may not fit the data well. A recommended cut-off point for the ΔD_i's is 4, with values higher than this suggesting influential observations. At this point an example is valuable.

Earlier in the chapter we estimated a logistic regression model designed to predict volunteer work for a religious organization. Using the *GSS96* data and Stata the model is estimated as

EXAMPLE 3.8 *A Logistic Regression Model of Volunteer Work*

logit volrelig gender age educate   *This is placed on the command line*

Logit estimates						
				Number of obs	=	2890
				LR chi2(3)	=	29.23
				Prob > chi2	=	0.0000
Log likelihood = −727.93848				Pseudo R2	=	0.0197

volrelig	Coef.	Std. Err.	z	P > |z|	[95% Conf. Interval]	
gender	.355627	.150303	2.37	0.018	.061038	.650216
age	.008340	.004384	1.90	0.057	−.000252	.016933
educate	.120903	.025143	4.81	0.000	.071623	.170183
_cons	−4.819976	.452735	−10.65	0.000	−5.707311	−3.93262

A number of predicted values may then be computed in Stata, including probabilities, deviance residuals, and ΔD_i's, which Stata labels *ddeviance*. They are computed in Stata using the predict postcommand as follows:

```
predict pred, p              * computes predicted values *
predict dev, deviance        * computes deviance residuals *
predict delta, ddeviance     * computes ΔD_i *
```

We may then plot the predicted values against the ΔD_i's to check for influential observations. Figure 3.3 shows this plot.

It is clear that there are some observations that may be considered influential. Note, for instance, the two circles at the top of the graph. These actually correspond to twelve observations that have ΔD_i values in excess of eight. One way to view all observations with ΔD_i values in excess of four is to ask Stata to list *id* and *delta* restricted to those values in excess of four, as follows:

```
list id delta if delta > 4
```

It will be apparent that there are many observations in excess of this number. However, we should remember that four is an arbitrary cut-off point, so we must rely on our understand-

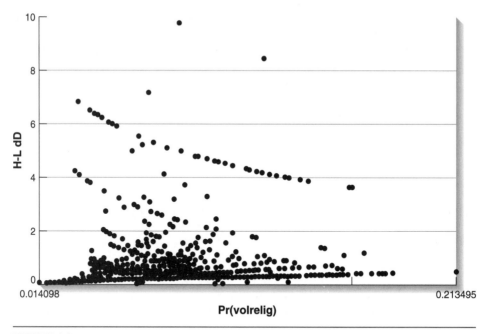

FIGURE 3.3

ing of the relationships to determine what step to take next. But suppose that we take the extreme step and decide to re-estimate the model and omit all ΔD_i values in excess of four. The following model does this:

EXAMPLE 3.8   (Continued)

logit volrelig gender age educate if delta < 4   *This appears on the command line*

Logit estimates

Log likelihood = −593.00643

		Number of obs	=	2819
		LR chi2(3)	=	25.87
		Prob > chi2	=	0.0000
		Pseudo R2	=	0.0214

volrelig	Coef.	Std. Err.	z	P > |z|	[95% Conf. Interval]	
gender	.328057	.169883	1.93	0.053	−.004908	.661023
age	.001848	.005128	0.36	0.719	−.008202	.011898
educate	.138051	.028894	4.78	0.000	.081420	.194681
_cons	−5.018370	.512610	−9.79	0.000	−6.023068	−4.013673

Note that, using a $p < .05$ to determine whether a coefficient is statistically signifi-cant, only *educate* remains significantly associated with *volrelig*. Of course, further diagnostic exploration is in order. For example, we may wish to review the observations that have ΔD_i values in excess of four to determine whether they represent an unusual subsample (e.g., are they older people? younger people? females?).

Other recommended diagnostic plots include ΔD_i values by the leverage values, although experience suggests that this provides little additional information beyond what we have already determined from the plot above. See McCullagh and Nelder (1989) and Hosmer and Lemeshow (1989) for additional suggestions about diagnostic plots. Finally, there are other diagnostic tools that may be used with logistic regression, such as condition indices to check for multicollinearity (Kleinbaum 1994), but these are not as yet widely available in statistical software.

Conclusion

This chapter has described some statistical tools for estimating regression models with binary dependent variables. The logistic and probit models are designed specifically to carry out this important and common task. Considering the many variables that are of interest to social and behavioral scientists, yet are measured using only two outcomes, these models are highly useful (see, e.g., Cunradi, Caetano, and Schafer 2002; Wayman 2002; Neeley and Richardson 2001; Powell 2000; Dispensa 1997; Carothers and Murray 1990; Danes and Winter 1990). Nevertheless, we have not exhausted the number of models that may be used to predict binary dependent variables. Although beyond the scope of this presentation, there are many situations, especially when all of the variables are measured discretely, when log-linear models are used (Powers and Xie 2000, Chapter 4; Tansey, White, and Long 1996; Christensen 1990). These are computationally similar to the logistic regression model, but are the preferred approach when many interaction terms are hypothesized. They are also useful when the distinction between dependent and independent variables is not well defined. Nonetheless, the logistic and probit regression models are appropriate for a large number of modeling tasks.

Exercises

1. For the following 2×2 table, determine the odds and the probabilities of marijuana use among males and females. Then compute the odds ratio of marijuana use that compares males to females.

	Gender	
Marijuana Use	**Male**	**Female**
Yes	10	6
No	30	34

2. The data file *Religion* (available in Stata, SPSS, and SAS formats) contains a variable labeled *relschol*, which indicates whether or not the survey respondent attends a secondary

school affiliated with a religious institution. The variable is coded as 0 = no and 1 = yes. Conduct the following analyses:

a. Compute the overall odds and probability of attending a religious school.

b. Cross-tabulate *relschol* with *race* (coded 0 = non-white, 1 = white). What are the probabilities that non-white students and white students attend religious schools? What are the odds that white students and non-white students attend religious schools? What is the odds ratio that compares white and non-white students?

3. Estimate two logistic regression models that are designed to predict *relschol*. In the first model include only the variable *race*. In the second model, include *race*, *attend* (religious service attendance), and *income* (family income), treating the latter two as continuous variables. Answer the following questions:

a. Based on the first model, what is the odds ratio that compares white and non-white students? Compare this to the odds ratio computed in Exercise 2.b.

b. What are the AICs and BICs for the two models? Based on these measures of fit, which model do you prefer?

c. For those who attend religious services five days per month (*attend* = 5) and have a family income of $20,000–29,999 (*income* = 4), what are the predicted odds of attending a religious school for white and non-white students?

d. What is the adjusted odds ratio for *race*? Interpret this odds ratio.

4. Re-estimate the two models outlined in Exercise 3, but use a probit model. Answer the following questions:

a. Based on the first model, what is the predicted probability that white and non-white students attend a religious school? Compare these results to those found in Exercise 2.b.

b. What are the AICs and BICs for the two models? Compare these to the AICs and BICs computed in Exercise 3.b.

c. For those who attend religious services five days per month (*attend* = 5) and have a family income of $20,000–29,999 (*income* = 4), what are the predicted probabilities that a white student and a non-white student attend a religious school?

d. Compute the discrete change in probability under the following scenario: A non-white student whose *attend* value equals 4 with a shift in family income (*income*) from a value of 4 ($20,000–29,999) to a value of 10 ($80,000–99,999).

5. In plain English, what do you conclude about the relationship between a student's race/ethnicity, religious service attendance, family income, and attending a religious school?

4

Ordered Logistic and Ordered Probit Regression Models

Given what we have now learned about modeling binary (two-category) discrete outcomes, we should find it relatively simple to generalize to multiple categories. This chapter and the next show how to generalize the case of multiple categories in two ways. In this chapter, we will assume that there is a natural ordering to the categories. In other words, our goal is to analyze ordinal variables as dependent variables. In Chapter 5 we will not assume that the categories of the dependent variable can be ordered; rather, the dependent variable is treated as being free from ordered responses. Hence, it is considered a nominal dependent variable.

Ordinal variables should be familiar from elementary statistics. They are used widely in survey research and to represent poorly measured constructs. One example of an ordinal variable might be educational outcomes such as the following three mutually exclusive categories: high school graduate, college graduate, or attended graduate/professional school. A common set of response categories from opinion surveys when asking about social issues illustrates another example—"Do you strongly disagree, disagree, agree, or strongly agree that we should have prayer in public schools?" The four choices are then coded as 1–4, or 0–3. In social stratification research, occupational prestige is often measured in a continuous manner, but sometimes is categorized into low, medium, and high categories. In survey data, the creators of the data set often force a continuous variable into ordinal categories: "How many times have you used marijuana in your lifetime? 0 times, 1–2 times, 3–4 times, 5–9 times, or 10 or more times." So we are left with an ordinal variable, but we may still wish to predict the particular outcome.

For all the reasons discussed in previous chapters, it is not wise to use a linear regression model to predict ordinal outcomes. There is a rule of thumb that seems to remain popular in the social and behavioral sciences that once a variable has seven or more categories (some claim it is five), an OLS regression model is acceptable. However, this assumption depends strongly on the distribution of the categories. If the ordinal variable does not approximate a normal distribution, then biased estimates are highly likely. Experience suggests that ordinal variables rarely give the appearance of a normal distribution.

In addition, an OLS regression model is forced into the strong assumption that the "distance" between categories is constant. In some situations, researchers may adopt various scoring schemes so that ordinal variables mimic continuous variables. A common strategy is to assign midpoints to categories or to transform the variable using normal scores (Powers and Xie 2000). Although this may obviate the problems associated with using OLS regression for ordinal dependent variables, the models described in this chapter provide a more efficient approach. In virtually any situation, it is preferable to use regression techniques that are designed explicitly for ordinal outcomes.

As an initial example of an ordinal dependent variable, let's look at the relationship between support for corporal punishment and education. We'll use the variable *spanking* from the *GSS96* data set. The pertinent question asks "Do you strongly agree, agree, disagree, or strongly disagree that it is sometimes necessary to discipline a child with a good, hard spanking?" The possible answers are coded as $1 =$ strongly agree, $2 =$ agree, $3 =$ disagree, and $4 =$ strongly disagree. A common hypothesis is that support for corporal punishment of children decreases at higher levels of education. A scatterplot with *educate* as the X variable and *spanking* as the Y variable is shown in Figure 4.1.

Now, let's take a look at the normal probability (Q-Q) plot of the residuals of an OLS regression model with *spanking* as the dependent variable and *educate* as the independent variable (see Figure 4.2).

Both the scatterplot and normal probability plot of the residuals immediately demonstrate problems indicative of violating some important assumptions about the OLS regression model. First, as with the binary variable situation discussed in Chapter 3, there is likely a serious problem with heteroscedastic errors. Second, the residuals are not normally distributed. In fact, you can easily see the effect of having a four-category variable

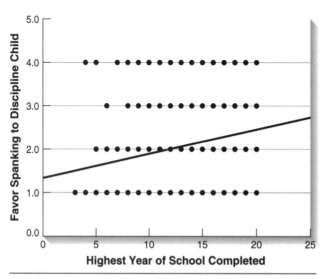

FIGURE 4.1

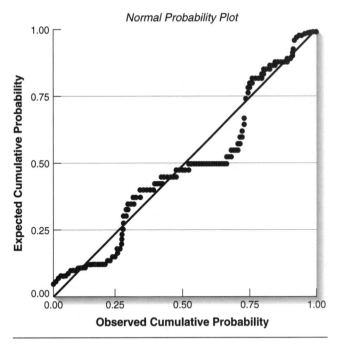

FIGURE 4.2

rather than a continuous variable in the normal probability plot (Figure 4.2). This type of snaking pattern is common when examining residuals from an OLS model with an ordinal dependent variable.

Alternative Models for Ordinal Dependent Variables

When faced with an ordinal dependent variable, we have two widely used alternatives: the ordered logistic regression model and the ordered probit regression model (sometimes known as ordinal logistic or ordinal probit). There are actually several types of logistic and probit regression models for ordinal outcomes. This chapter discusses the most widely used models, the cumulative logistic and probit models (sometimes labeled *proportional odds models* for reasons that will become apparent). Other models for ordinal variables, such as adjacent category and stereotype models, are mentioned in the conclusion.

As with binary logistic and probit regression, we must make an assumption about the error terms (the part that is left unexplained). For the ordered probit model we assume that the errors follow a normal distribution, and for the ordered logistic model we assume that the errors follow a logistic distribution.

An important issue that arises for both models involves what are frequently called the "cut-points" of the distribution. These cut-points are simply the points at which the categories are separated and may be thought of as separate intercepts. Note that there is only one cut-point for the binary variable because there are only two categories. However, the ordinal variable has more than one cut-point; it has $q - 1$ cut-points, where q is the number of categories.

An easy way to think about cut-points for ordinal variables is in terms of probabilities. For instance, what is the probability that someone falls in one group relative to their probability of falling into another group or in any other group? Using the preceding spanking example, let's look at the probability that males and females support the diverse attitudes about spanking. Using Stata and the *GSS96.dta* data set, I constructed the following table (note: *gender* is coded 0 = male, 1 = female):

EXAMPLE 4.1   *A Cross-Tabulation of Gender and Attitudes Toward Spanking*

tabulate spanking*gender   *This appears on the command line*

favor spanking to discipline child	gender		Total
	male(0)	female(1)	
strongly agree	243	269	512
agree	388	502	890
disagree	156	201	357
strongly disagree	56	108	164
Total	843	1080	1923

Based on this table, we may compute the probability (or the odds) of male and female positions on spanking as follows:

Pr(Female, strongly agrees)	=	269 / 1,080	=	0.25
Pr(Male, strongly agrees)	=	243 / 843	=	0.29
Pr(Female, strongly disagrees)	=	108 / 1,080	=	0.10
Pr(Male, strongly disagrees)	=	56 / 843	=	0.07

Note that if we compute the probabilities for all four positions (strongly agree, agree, disagree, strongly disagree), they sum to one within each category of *gender*.

Now think about computing the odds of attitudes toward spanking. In the binary case, it was a simple matter to compute, for example, the odds of one category relative to the other. The reference category is typically the category that is coded as zero. For example, in Chapter 3 the odds of high life satisfaction (coded 1) was compared to the reference category of low life satisfaction (coded 0) in the logistic regression models. In the ordinal case, it seems a little trickier because the reference category is not clear. However, although a clear reference category is needed for a multinomial logistic regression model (see Chapter 5), it really does not apply well to the ordered logistic regression situation because the ordered logistic model assumes that the odds of one category relative to the others are roughly equal and cumulative. An example is perhaps the best way to demonstrate what this means. Suppose we wish to know the odds of falling in the various categories. For instance, if we replace the labels of the possible outcomes with SD, D, A, and SA (denoting strongly disagree, disagree, agree, and strongly agree), we might have

$$\text{Odds(Females, SD vs. SA, A, D)} \quad = \quad 108 / (269 + 502 + 201) \quad = \quad 0.11$$

$$\text{Odds(Males, SD vs. SA, A, D)} \quad = \quad 56 / (243 + 388 + 156) \quad = \quad 0.07$$

Given these odds, the next question to ask is, what is the odds ratio of females relative to males in terms of strongly disagreeing versus not strongly disagreeing? Although saying this is a mouthful, just remember that in simple odds ratio calculations with only two outcome groups, we did the same thing. The reference group was much simpler to determine in that situation, but the answer to this question is derived in the same manner.

$$\text{Odds ratio for females vs. males} \quad = \quad 0.11 / 0.07 \quad = \quad 1.57$$

Interpreting this odds ratio in plain English is formidable, but let's try anyway. The odds that females strongly disagree that spanking is appropriate are about 1.57 times higher than the odds that males strongly disagree that spanking is appropriate. Or, in simpler terms, females are less likely than males to support spanking as a way to discipline a child. This rough interpretation is also apparent by looking at the probabilities we computed previously.

The ordered logistic assumption that the odds of one category relative to the others are equal and cumulative means that we are assuming that this odds ratio is constant across gender regardless of which comparison we make. Note that, so far, we have not gone beyond our binary case; we have simply compared two possible outcomes: strongly disagreeing versus not strongly disagreeing. However, we may also compute the odds ratio for strongly disagreeing *and* disagreeing vs. agreeing *and* strongly agreeing (SD, D vs. A, SA).

$$\text{Odds(Females, SD, D vs. A, SA)} \quad = \quad (108 + 201) / (502 + 269) \quad = \quad 0.40$$

$$\text{Odds(Males, SD, D vs. A, SA)} \quad = \quad (56 + 156) / (388 + 243) \quad = \quad 0.34$$

Hence, the odds ratio for females vs. males is 0.40 / 0.34 = 1.18.

Given the assumption of cumulative comparisons, the final odds ratio is to compare SD, D, A versus SA.

$$\text{Odds(Females, SD, D, A vs. SA)} \quad = \quad (108 + 201 + 502) / 269 \quad = \quad 3.01$$

$$\text{Odds(Males, SD, D, A vs. SA)} \quad = \quad (56 + 156 + 388) / 243 \quad = \quad 2.47$$

The final odds ratio for females vs. males is 3.01 / 2.47 = 1.22.

To summarize, we now have three odds ratios that make three different (and cumulative) comparisons: 1.57, 1.18, and 1.22. The next step is to see what advantage is to be
gained by estimating a regression model. Because, by their nature, regression models are
designed to summarize information about relationships among variables, we might conclude that there should be a summary of these three odds ratios. So, at first glance, it is
reasonable to think that the ordered logistic regression model produces an odds ratio that
is the average of these three odds ratios (because it assumes they are identical irrespective
of the comparison made). The average of these three odds ratios is 1.32. But wait, there is
a problem with this approach. Notice that these three odds ratios depend on different subsample sizes, in both the numerator and denominator. The numerator for the first odds
ratio, based on only a small proportion of the sample, has too much influence on our summary odds ratio. Therefore, we need to take an alternative approach so that one of the odds
ratios, particularly if it is based on a relatively small proportion of the sample, does not
overly influence our summary measure. Ordered logistic regression solves this dilemma
by estimating the summary odds ratio using, in effect, a weighted average of the three
observed odds ratios.

The Ordered Logistic Regression Model

So let's see what the ordered logistic regression model reveals about the association between gender and attitudes toward spanking. Continuing our use of the *GSS96* data set,
Stata, and using the *ologit* command, we find the following:

EXAMPLE 4.2   *An Ordered Logistic Regression Model of Gender and Attitudes Toward Spanking*

ologit spanking gender   *This appears on the command line*

Ordered logit estimates				Number of obs	=	1923
				LR chi2(1)	=	5.87
				Prob > chi2	=	0.0154
Log likelihood = –2365.1653				Pseudo R2	=	0.0012

spanking	Coef.	Std. Err.	z	P > |z|	[95% Conf. Interval]	
gender	.206204	.085213	2.420	0.016	.039190	.373218
_cut1	–.900450	.069399		(Ancillary parameters)		
_cut2	1.107179	.070971				
_cut3	2.491789	.095768				

As with our other regression models, the table has only one coefficient associated
with the independent variable. However, implicit in this model is the fact that this coeffi-

cient is actually a summary measure. As with the binary logistic regression model in Chapter 3, we may exponentiate the coefficient to come up with an odds ratio: exp(0.206) = 1.23. Recall that our unweighted summary odds ratio is 1.32. It thus appears that the first comparison {SD vs. D, A, SA} contributed the smallest amount to the computation of the ordered logistic model's odds ratio. This is not unexpected because it was based on a relatively small numerator and a relatively large denominator.

Interpreting the odds ratio from an ordered logistic model can be a difficult task. In the binary logistic model, the reference group was clear; it is not so clear in the ordered logistic model. Without unduly complicating the interpretation, it is best to simply keep in mind the implicit comparisons that are made. Hence, one interpretation is the following: The odds of strongly disagreeing about spanking versus the other outcomes are about 1.23 times higher among females than among males. However, the odds of strongly disagreeing *or* disagreeing versus agreeing or strongly disagreeing are also 1.23 times higher among females than among males. Finally, the odds of strongly disagreeing, disagreeing, or agreeing versus strongly agreeing are 1.23 times higher among females than among males. Because we assume all these comparisons yield the same odds ratio, a simplified interpretation is that, in a general sense, females are less likely than males to report that it is sometimes necessary to discipline a child with a "good, hard" spanking.

Testing the Proportional Odds Assumption

The assumption that all of the implicit comparisons yield the same odds ratio can be stringent. However, keep in mind that our statistical models are based on samples, so we must consider the issue of statistical inference and precision of the estimates. Our point estimates are mere imprecise reflections of reality. The odds ratios are estimates of some true population odds ratio, so they come with sampling variability. Our next task, therefore, is to determine whether any of our implicit odds ratios is *significantly* different from the others. This task is simplified by direct examination of the *proportional odds* assumption (also known as the *parallel regression* or *parallel lines* assumption). Simply put, testing this assumption involves testing whether any implicit odds ratio is significantly distinct. Stata, SPSS, and SAS all provide tools for testing this assumption in the ordered logistic regression model. Stata and SAS offer a similar test for the ordered probit model. The null hypothesis is that the $q - 1$ odds ratios implied by the model are not significantly different from one another. The test is based on a χ^2 distribution. If the ordinal logistic regression model is appropriate, then we do not wish to reject the null hypothesis.

The following provides a truncated view of the results of SAS's Proc Logistic to estimate our model. SAS provides a likelihood ratio test to examine the proportional odds assumption. Recall from Chapter 2 that likelihood ratio tests are distributed χ^2, so a significant χ^2 value indicates that the assumption is violated. SPSS provides a similar test but labels it as the *test of parallel lines*. Stata will also compute this test, but you first must download from Stata's website *omodel* and then replace the command *ologit dependent independent* with *omodel logit {or probit} dependent independent*. The SAS likelihood ratio test resulted in the following:

EXAMPLE 4.2   *(Continued)*

Approximate likelihood-ratio test of proportionality of odds
across response categories:

chi2(2)   =   3.35
Prob > chi2   =   0.1874

The output indicates that the proportional odds assumption may not be rejected, so we are relatively safe in assuming that an ordinal model is appropriate. The ultimate test must rely on theory, however.

As an alternative, informal test, some observers suggest computing several cumulative logistic models. For example, suppose that we recode *spanking* into three distinct variables and then estimate three binary logistic regression models (e.g., SD vs. D, A, SA; SD, D vs. A, SA; and SD, D, A vs. SA). Informally examining the coefficients associated with *gender* might reveal differences among the odds ratios. In fact, this is what we did when we computed the three odds ratios based on the crosstabulation of *gender* and *spanking*. But then analysts must trust their judgment about whether or not the odds ratios are similar or distinct. The following Stata results demonstrate this approach (command lines and model fit information are omitted; the *logistic* command is used).

EXAMPLE 4.3   *Results of Binary Logistic Regression Models of Gender and Attitudes Toward Spanking*

SD vs. D, A, SA:

spank3	Odds Ratio	Std. Err.	z	P > |z|	[95% Conf. Interval]	
gender	1.561508	.267815	2.598	0.009	1.115717	2.185416

SD, D vs. A, SA:

spank2	Odds Ratio	Std. Err.	z	P > |z|	[95% Conf. Interval]	
gender	1.192882	.1241688	1.694	0.090	.9727356	1.462852

SD, D, A vs. SA:

spank1	Odds Ratio	Std. Err.	z	P > |z|	[95% Conf. Interval]	
gender	1.221022	.1264946	1.928	0.054	.9966471	1.495911

This set of logistic regression models confirms what we found earlier. The biggest difference is between strongly disagreeing and the other outcomes. Of course, one's raw judgment might conclude that the odds ratio are different enough to justify using a different approach to modeling attitudes toward spanking, even though the formal proportional odds test indicates that the odds ratios are not significantly distinct.

But suppose that both the formal and informal tests suggest that the proportional odds assumption is violated. In this situation, many observers recommend falling back on the multinomial logistic regression model (see Chapter 5). However, as mentioned in the conclusion to this chapter, there are some other alternatives that are beyond the scope of this presentation.

The Ordered Probit Regression Model

As shown in earlier chapters, one of the main values of regression models is their ability to control for the effects of other independent variables. If we are faced with only one independent variable, the only advantage of a regression model is its ability to show whether coefficients are significantly different from zero (or from some other constant). Nevertheless, before moving on to a model with multiple independent variables, it is useful to look at the results of the ordered probit model.

EXAMPLE 4.4   *An Ordered Probit Model of Gender and Attitudes Toward Spanking*

oprobit spanking gender   *This appears on the command line*

Ordered probit estimates

				Number of obs	=	1923
				LR chi2(1)	=	6.79
				Prob > chi2	=	0.0091
Log likelihood = –2364.7011 | | | | Pseudo R2 | = | 0.0014 |

spanking	Coef.	Std. Err.	z	P > |z|	[95% Conf. Interval]	
gender	.129667	.049761	2.606	0.009	.032137	.227197
_cut1	–.552565	.041206	(Ancillary parameters)			
_cut2	.683704	.041741				
_cut3	1.446062	.050202				

To help us understand these results a little better, let's revisit the cross-tabulation of *gender* and *spanking*, but make some modifications.

EXAMPLE 4.5   *Cross-Tabulation of Gender and Attitudes Toward Spanking Using Cumulative Probabilities*

favor spanking to discipline child	gender	
	Male(0)	Female(1)
strongly agree	0.29	0.25
agree	0.75	0.71
disagree	0.94	0.90
strongly disagree	1.00	1.00

In this table, we've replaced the frequencies with cumulative probabilities, which, by definition, must sum to one. Hence, about 25 percent of females strongly agree that spanking is appropriate, 71 percent strongly agree or agree that spanking is appropriate, and so forth. We may then use the ordered probit coefficient in the Stata output to compute predicted cumulative probabilities. (Remember that the probit link is the inverse of the standard normal so we should use a table of z scores or Stata's *normprob* function to translate z scores into probabilities.) Using the preceding coefficients and the *normprob* function we may come up with the following for males and females:

```
* Males *
display normprob(–.5525)          =   .29
display normprob(.6837)           =   .75
display normprob(1.446)           =   .93

* Females *
display normprob(–.5525 – .129)   =   .25
display normprob(.6837 – .129)    =   .71
display normprob(1.446 – .129)    =   .90
```

Unlike the ordered logistic regression model, the cut-points are very useful in the probit model; in concert with the *gender* coefficient they allow us to compute the predicted probabilities directly. Note that we have subtracted rather than added the value of the coefficient. This is because we are dealing with cumulative probabilities, so we need to backtrack from one. (More details about this issue are provided in Long (1997, Chapter 5).)

Comparing the observed and predicted probabilities, we can see that females are estimated to be about four points lower in their probability of strongly agreeing or agreeing that spanking is appropriate. Hence, they are more likely to strongly disagree with the appropriateness of spanking (Females: $1.0 - 0.90 = 0.10$; Males: $1.0 - 0.93 = 0.07$). Here are the observed and predicted probabilities.

EXAMPLE 4.6   *Observed and Predicted Cross-Tabulation of Gender and Attitudes Toward Spanking Using Probabilities*

favor spanking to discipline child	observed		predicted	
	Male(0)	Female(1)	Male(0)	Female(1)
strongly agree	0.29	0.25	0.29	0.25
agree	0.46	0.46	0.46	0.46
disagree	0.19	0.19	0.18	0.19
strongly disagree	0.07	0.10	0.07	0.10

When faced with only one independent variable, we should be able to predict the observed probabilities with a high degree of accuracy. The more interesting task, however, is to predict odds and probabilities using several independent variables.

Introducing Multiple Independent Variables

We may now generalize our ordered logistic and ordered probit models so that they include multiple independent variables. First, let's look at an ordered logistic regression model. We'll continue to use *spanking* as the dependent variable, but add the following independent variables: *gender*, *educate*, and *polviews* (political views; it ranges from very liberal {1} to very conservative {7}).

EXAMPLE 4.7   *An Ordered Logistic Regression Model with Multiple Independent Variables*

ologit spanking gender educate polviews   *This appears on the command line*

Ordered logit estimates

				Number of obs	=	1821
				LR chi2(3)	=	111.18
				Prob > chi2	=	0.0000
Log likelihood = –2198.2519				Pseudo R2	=	0.0247

spanking	Coef.	Std. Err.	z	P > |z|	[95% Conf. Interval]	
gender	.253211	.088254	2.869	0.004	.080237	.426186
educate	.115298	.015637	7.374	0.000	.084651	.145945
polviews	–.221454	.032483	–6.817	0.000	–.285120	–.157788
_cut1	–.297669	.267066	(Ancillary parameters)			
_cut2	1.784512	.270642				
_cut3	3.192660	.279290				

Keeping in mind that the coefficients represent summary measures, we may loosely interpret the odds ratios as

1. Controlling for the effects of education and political views, the expected odds of strongly disagreeing are exp(0.253) = 1.29 times higher among females than among males.
2. Controlling for the effects of gender and political views, each one-unit increase in education is associated with a {[exp(0.115) – 1] * 100} = 12 percent increase in the odds of strongly disagreeing.
3. Controlling for the effects of gender and education, each one-unit increase in political views is associated with a {[exp(–0.22) – 1] * 100} = 20 percent *decrease* in the odds of strongly disagreeing that spanking is appropriate.

We could just as easily have replaced the term *strongly disagreeing* with *disagreeing*. Keep in mind that these are adjusted odds ratios because they control for the effects of the other independent variables in the model.

Here's the same model, but using an ordered probit regression approach.

EXAMPLE 4.8   *An Ordered Probit Regression Model with Multiple Independent Variables*

oprobit spanking gender educate polviews   *This appears on the command line*

Ordered probit estimates				Number of obs	=	1821
				LR chi2(3)	=	108.21
				Prob > chi2	=	0.0000
Log likelihood = –2199.7348				Pseudo R2	=	0.0240

spanking	Coef.	Std. Err.	z	P > |z|	[95% Conf. Interval]	
gender	.151932	.051513	2.949	0.003	.050970	.252895
educate	.065095	.009079	7.170	0.000	.047300	.082890
polviews	–.125504	.018713	–6.707	0.000	–.162181	–.088833
_cut1	–.211023	.155710		(Ancillary parameters)		
_cut2	1.056828	.157069				
_cut3	1.836510	.159780				

Just as with the binary probit regression model (see Chapter 3), there are a number of ways to compute changes in the probabilities. Perhaps the easiest method is to simply compute probabilities for each of the different groups {SA, A, D, SD} and see how they differ based on gender. This is accomplished in Stata using its *predict* option after estimating the *oprobit* model, followed by a cross-tabulation of *gender* and the predicted probabilities. Note that we now have as many predicted probabilities for each observation as we have categories of the dependent variable. After estimating the model in Stata, we then use the postcommand *predict* to compute predicted probabilities.

EXAMPLE 4.8   *(Continued)*

---

predict SA A D SD   *This appears on the command line*

(option p assumed; predicted probabilities)
(166 missing values generated)

Note, however, that before asking for a list of the predicted probabilities for males and females, we need to decide on appropriate values for the other independent variables. For instance, suppose we decide to compute the predicted probabilities for *polviews* = 4 (middle of the road) and *educate* = 12 years. In Stata, we type the following commands:

table gender if polviews==4 & educate==12, contents(mean SA mean A mean D mean SD)
      This appears on the command line

gender	mean(SA)	mean(A)	mean(D)	mean(SD)
male	.312015	.469613	.158682	.059689
female	.260411	.473857	.185789	.079943

Here we have asked Stata for the predicted probability for males and females for each of the four possible outcomes, and at specific values of *polviews* and *educate*. This provides support for the patterns we saw previously, but it also shows a specific set of predicted probabilities. For example, we may now predict that for those with moderate political views and 12 years of education, about 8 percent of females are expected to strongly disagree that spanking is appropriate, but only 6 percent of males think the same way.

When faced with a dummy variable, such as *gender*, it is easy to make sense of the probabilities. But what about continuous variables? One possibility is to use the discrete change formula shown in Chapter 3 to compute changes in probabilities associated with particular changes in the independent variable. Another approach is to categorize the continuous variable, perhaps by using quartiles, quintiles, categories based on its standard deviation, or simply categories of interest. For example, the following table shown in Example 4.8 (Continued) divides the variable *educate* into low, medium, and high categories that are based on convenient and widely understood year groups. *Educ2* is coded as 1 if *educate* is less than 12 years, 2 if *educate* is between 12 years and 15 years, and 3 if *educate* is more than 15 years. Using this new variable, we then ask Stata for the average

78   Chapter 4

predicted probabilities for the four possible outcomes of *spanking*. We'll also specify particular categories for *gender* and *polviews*.

EXAMPLE 4.8   *(Continued)*

table educ2 if gender==0 & polviews==4, contents(mean SA mean A mean D mean SD)

educ2	mean(SA)	mean(A)	mean(D)	mean(SD)
0-11	.376930	.450994	.129450	.042626
12-15	.293738	.471340	.168211	.066711
16+	.202393	.463459	.219877	.114271

Perhaps the most interesting thing about these probabilities is the low likelihood that those low in education strongly disagree that spanking is appropriate; they are the most likely group to strongly agree that spanking is appropriate.

Considering the coding of *educ2*, we may derive the following interpretations:

The predicted probability of strongly disagreeing that spanking is appropriate increases by about $0.11 - 0.04 = .07$ as one moves from low education to high education, controlling for the effects of gender and political views.

Moving from a low level of education to a high level of education decreases the predicted probability of strongly agreeing by about $0.38 - 0.20 = 0.18$, controlling for the effects of gender and political views.

Finally, let's see what sense we can make of the association between political views and attitudes toward spanking. Although we have treated *polviews* as a continuous variable in the model, it is really categorical, with a manageable number of groups.

EXAMPLE 4.8   *(Continued)*

table polviews if gender==0 & educate==12, contents(mean SA mean A mean D mean SD)

think of self as liberal or conservative	mean(SA)	mean(A)	mean(D)	mean(SD)
extreme liberal	.193065	.462796	.225313	.118826
liberal	.229300	.471498	.203490	.095712
slight liberal	.269063	.473802	.181047	.076089
middle of the road	312015	.469613	.158682	.059689
slight conservative	.357689	.459103	.137009	.046198
conservative	.405499	.442694	.116535	.035273
extreme conservative	.454763	.421031	.097643	.026563

Based on these results, we may derive similar interpretations as we derived with educational level. For example, moving from middle of the road to extremely liberal is expected to increase the probability of strongly disagreeing that spanking is acceptable by about $0.119 - 0.060 = 0.059$. The expected probability of extreme conservatives strongly disagreeing that spanking is appropriate is very low (0.03). In other words, we expect only about three percent of extreme conservatives to say that they strongly disagree that spanking a child is appropriate. And, of course, these differences statistically control for the effect that gender or education might have on the association between political views and attitudes toward spanking.

Various observers recommend other ways to use these results, such as looking at the difference in predicted probabilities between minimum and maximum values of some independent variable. For example, we might wish to determine the difference between the minimum and maximum values of political views using the preceding table. However, the interpretations already shown are adequate in many situations.

Finally, don't forget to check the parallel odds assumption when conducting an ordered logistic or probit regression model. In the previous ordered logistic regression model (Example 4.7) that used *gender, educate,* and *polviews* as independent variables, the test of parallel lines in SPSS indicates the following:

EXAMPLE 4.7 *(Continued)*

Test of Parallel Lines

Model	−2 Log Likelihood	Chi-Square	df	Sig.
Null Hypothesis	1255.717			
General	1246.414	9.303	6	.157

The null hypothesis states that the location parameters (slope coefficients) are the same across response categories.

Link function: Logit.

It appears that we are safe in using the ordered logistic regression model to analyze attitudes toward spanking in the GSS data set. The chi-square test is not significant, thus suggesting that the underlying odds ratios associated with the independent variables are not significantly different as we make the various implicit comparisons.

But suppose that the assumption of proportional odds is not met. What is one to do in this situation? Some observers suggest giving up on ordered logistic or ordered probit and going directly to the multinomial logistic regression model (see Chapter 5). However, as mentioned in the opening section of this chapter, there are other regression models for ordinal dependent variables. Although these are not as widely available in statistical software, the analyst who has access to them should consider using them. For example, in the adjacent category logistic model, the comparisons are between each category of the dependent variable and the one directly below it. So, we might wish to compare the odds of strongly agreeing and agreeing that spanking is acceptable. Another model, known as the continuation ratio model, compares the odds of one category to the odds of each higher category. In our example, this could include comparing the odds of strongly agreeing to the odds of agreeing, disagreeing, or strongly disagreeing. It should be apparent that, in this example, the results of the cumulative odds model demonstrated in this chapter and the continuation ratio model should be similar. Finally, some analysts advocate the stereotype model. This is actually quite similar to the multinomial logistic regression model discussed in the next chapter. More details about these various ordinal logistic models are described in Agresti (1990, 1996), Powers and Xie (2000), and Long (1997). A slightly different approach to modeling ordinal variables based on latent class analysis is discussed in Clogg (1995), Clogg and Shihadeh (1994), and Hagenaars (1993).

Conclusion

This chapter has demonstrated two very useful regression models, ordered logistic and ordered probit. In most situations, the models yield similar results, at least in terms of rough interpretations. The preference for one model over the other is based on whether you are more comfortable with odds and odds ratios or probabilities. Nevertheless, because statistical software has developed to the point that either model will provide predicted probabilities, the use of one or the other is usually not an important decision. Issues of model specification and correct interpretation are much more important.

The utility of these ordered regression models becomes apparent when attempting to analyze variables from various data sets. In the social and behavioral sciences, in business applications, the natural sciences, engineering, epidemiology, and many other fields, an abundance of variables are measured discretely and ordinally (e.g., Dionne, Gourieoux, and Vanasse 2001; Dolsak 2001; Rhea and Otto 2001; Bolks, Evans, and Polinard 2000; Clark, Oswald, and Warr 1999; Lowery and Gray 1998; Peel and Goode 1998). Typically, this occurs because the instruments we use to measure phenomena of interest are not developed well enough to yield continuous variables. So we are stuck with variables with outcomes such as *agree completely, agree somewhat, disagree somewhat,* and *disagree completely;* or *low, medium,* and *high.* Fortunately, we now have widely available tools to predict these types of outcomes.

Our next goal is to look at another type of variable that is almost as common in applied statistics: discrete variables that cannot be ordered in a reasonable way. In this case, we must move beyond ordered logistic or probit and examine the multinomial logistic regression model.

Exercises

1. The data set *Environ* (available in Stata, SAS, and SPSS formats) contains survey data from a 1991 study of environmental attitudes among Presbyterian church members in the United States. The variable of interest in this set of exercises is based on the following

question: "The Presbyterian church should become more involved in environmental issues." The response categories are 1 = disagree completely (DC), 2 = disagree somewhat (DS), 3 = neither disagree nor agree (NDA), 4 = agree somewhat (AS), and 5 = agree completely (AC). The following table shows the frequency distribution by gender (coded 0 = male, 1 = female):

gender	Presbyterian church should become more involved in environmental issues					Total
	DC	DS	NDA	AS	AC	
male	70	156	205	382	376	1189
female	15	85	113	219	196	628
Total	85	241	318	601	572	1817

a. Using the table, compute the probabilities that males and females disagree completely or disagree somewhat that their church should be more involved in environmental issues.

b. Using the table, compute the odds ratios for females relative to males using the following comparisons: {AC vs. AS, NDA, DS, and DC}; {AC and AS vs. NDA, DS, and DC}; {AC, AS, and NDA vs. DS and DC}; and {AC, AS, NDA, and DS vs. DC}.

c. Using the *Environ* data set, estimate an ordinal logistic regression model with *env_ch* as the dependent variable and *gender* as the independent variable. Compare the odds ratio from this model to the four odds ratios estimated in 1.b. Comment on similarities or differences.

d. If available in the statistical software used, test the proportional odds assumption of this model. Interpret the test.

2. Estimate an ordinal logistic and ordinal probit model using *env_ch* as the dependent variable and *literal* (coded as 0 = not a literal belief in the Bible, and 1 = literal belief in the Bible) as the independent variable.

a. Compute and interpret the odds ratio associated with *literal* from the ordinal logistic model.

b. Compute and interpret the predicted probabilities for the two groups based on *literal* from the ordinal probit model.

3. Estimate an ordinal logistic and ordinal probit model using *env_ch* as the dependent variable and the following independent variables: *gender*, *literal*, *age* (in years), and *educate* (coded as 0 = did not graduate from college, 1 = graduated from college).

a. Compute and interpret the odds ratio for *gender*, *age*, and *educate* from the ordinal logistic model.

b. Compute the predicted probabilities that males and females fall into each of the response categories at the following levels of the other independent variables: *age* = 52, *educate* = 1, and *literal* = 0.

    c. Compare the AICs and BICs (see Chapter 2) of the two ordinal probit models estimated thus far. Comment on what these model fits statistics say about the models.

    d. If available in the statistical software used, test the proportional odds assumption of one of these models (or both). Interpret the test. Based on this test, what would you recommend as the next step in predicting *env_ch?*

5

The Multinomial Logistic Regression Model

We now know how to proceed when faced with a dependent variable that is measured in an ordinal fashion. But we made a key assumption about this ordinal model—that the odds or the probabilities shifted consistently as we moved from one category to another. This is known as the *proportional odds, parallel regression,* or *parallel lines* assumption. If this assumption is violated, there are a number of options. One is to find a model for ordinal outcomes that does not make this assumption. However, these alternative models typically make other, often more stringent, assumptions. (For a comprehensive overview of these models, see Agresti (1996).) An alternative option is to ignore the assumption that the dependent variable is ordinal and assume that it is nominal. In other words, we ignore the ordering of the categories and assume that the variable consists of a set of unordered responses. This is usually reasonable and sometimes preferable, although, as we shall see, it makes interpretation of model results more tenuous. Many variables actually are by their nature nominal. In this chapter we shall see what to do with nominal dependent variables. (Note: These are sometimes labeled *polytomous* variables because they are extensions of dichotomous variables.)

As a reminder, nominal variables are categorical, but the categories have no natural ordering. For example, occupations are often considered nominal variables. We might wish to predict which groups are more likely to fall into various occupational categories, whether they are broad categories such as professional, service, and manual labor, or more specific categories such as plumber, carpenter, secondary school teacher, and lawyer. Another example involves marital status. A goal might be to predict what type of person is more likely to be married rather than living alone or cohabiting. In a recent study, I looked at the odds that various groups of workers were exposed to different types of drug testing programs (i.e., random, preemployment, neither type, or both types). Because these categories cannot be effectively ranked, I relied on what is known as a multinomial logistic regression model to determine these odds (Hoffmann and Larison 1998).

In order to get a better sense of the distribution of these types of variables as well as the multinomial logistic regression model, it is helpful to revisit the multinomial distribution. Recall from Chapter 2 that the multinomial distribution is a more general form of the binomial distribution. Rather than computing the probability (or odds) of some category versus another, we are interested in computing the probability (or odds) of falling into one of three or more categories (remember the blue-, brown-, and green-eyed children in Chapter 2?).

Recall that the probability mass function for the multinomial distribution is

$$p\left\{X_1 = n_1, X_2 = n_2, \ldots X_r = n_r\right\} = \frac{n!}{n_1! n_2! \ldots n_r!} \, p_1^{n_1} p_2^{n_2} \ldots p_r^{n_r} \qquad (5.1)$$

Note that r is the number of outcomes possible (e.g., random test, preemployment test, or no drug testing; blue-, brown-, or green-eyed children), the p's are the probability of each outcome, and the n's are the frequency with which we observe the particular outcome.

Let's put this function to use with an example. Assume that we have a sample of 10 workers which will serve as our "trials." These workers are employed by different companies that have either random drug testing, preemployment drug testing, or no drug testing program. Note that these are mutually exclusive categories; the companies may employ only one of these three options. We know, based on previous research on the applicable population of workers from which our sample is drawn, that the probability of random drug testing is 0.05, the probability of preemployment drug testing is 0.15, and the probability of no testing is 0.80. We observe in our sample the following: One worker reports random testing, three report preemployment testing, and six report no drug testing. From Equation 5.1, we may compute the probability of this sample occurring.

$$\frac{10!}{1!3!6!} (0.05)^1 (0.15)^3 (0.80)^6 = 0.037 \qquad (5.2)$$

If the original probabilities were accurate, we would expect to find this combination about 4 times out of 100. If we worked out all other possible combinations, such as {4,4,2}, {2,6,2}, and so forth, we would come up with (many) probabilities that summed to 1. Given that there are only 3 possible drug testing outcomes, how many possible combinations of 10 workers are there? This is a combination of 10 items taken 3 at a time. Recall from Chapter 2 that this may be solved using the formula for a combination,

$$\binom{10}{3} = 120.$$

As discussed in the earlier chapters, in statistical analysis we normally do not know these predetermined probabilities. We usually have data from a sample of workers, for instance, and then determine how many report exposure to random testing, preemployment testing, or neither type of testing program. The next stage is to determine the probability (or odds) that a worker falls into one of these three categories. The final step in a regression analysis is to determine the characteristics of workers or their workplace that are associated with (or predict) the probability (or odds) of falling into one of these categories.

It turns out that although a multinomial probit regression model is possible, it is extremely difficult to program, so most software makes available only a multinomial logistic regression model. (Greene (2000) includes a brief discussion of these difficulties.) If the reader has access to SAS/ETS, it has a procedure labeled MDC (multinomial discrete choice model) that estimates a variety of logistic and probit models, including a multinomial probit model, for categorical data. The program LIMDEP also has a multinomial probit routine.

Because the multinomial logistic model is used much more widely than the multinomial probit model, we shall focus on the former. A key question to ask at this point is: What does this model do? Perhaps the simplest way to think about the multinomial logistic model is as a set of binomial logistic models. The dependent variable is assumed to be nominal, so we could simply break up the variable into a set of binomial outcomes and run a batch of binomial logistic models (e.g., preemployment vs random drug testing; no testing vs random drug testing). So why not take this route? Think about how many models we would have to run if we had, say, six categories. Even if we merely wished to compare each category to only one predetermined category, this would involve estimating five binomial logistic regression models. If we wanted to make any additional comparisons, this would quickly add up to an intractable number of models.

Another problem with running a bunch of binomial logistic models is that sampling variability would affect the results. We would be comparing a set of models with different sample sizes and a variety of binomial distributions. For some category comparisons, we would probably find larger standard errors for the regression coefficients than in others. (Don't forget that standard errors are based partly on sample size.) So this approach is quite inefficient.

To get around these problems, the multinomial logistic regression, in effect, simultaneously estimates a set of binary logistic regression models. Hence it is a far more efficient approach than a series of binomial logistic models. But continuing to think about it as a set of binomial logistic models can help aid in the interpretation (see Long 1996, pp. 149–151).

To see how this works, let's start off with a simple example involving political views (*polview1*; recoded into three groups from the variable *polviews* that was used in Chapter 4) and *race* (coded white = 0, non-white = 1) that uses the *GSS96* data file. A cross-tabulation in Stata reveals the following:

EXAMPLE 5.1 *A Cross-Tabulation of Race and Political Views*

tabulate polview1*race   *This appears on the command line*

	race		
	W	**NW**	**Total**
Liberal (1)	546	150	696
Moderate (2)	854	191	1045
Conserv (3)	844	158	1002
Total	2244	499	2743

Based on this table, we may compute a variety of odds and probabilities. For example, the probability that a white person reports being liberal is 546 / 2244 = 0.24, moderate 854 / 2244 = 0.38, and conservative 844 / 2244 = 0.38. In other words, about 24 percent of white people in the *GSS96* data set say they are liberal. As should be the case, these probabilities add up to 1.00. The probabilities that non-whites report being liberal is 0.30, moderate 0.38, and conservative 0.32.

But this chapter focuses on logistic regression, so we will also need to compute the odds. This becomes a little trickier than it might have been if we were using a binary logistic model. Recall that when we computed odds in the binary case we had only two outcome categories, so the odds were simple to compute as $[p / 1 - p]$. Thus, if the probability of marijuana use (a binomial outcome) among males is 0.3, then we can compute the odds as 0.3 / 0.7 = 0.43. A similar calculation might produce an odds among females of 0.2 / 0.8 = 0.25. Hence the odds ratio of marijuana use by gender is 0.43 / 0.25 = 1.72 (see Chapter 3).

But consider the data presented in Example 5.1. We no longer have only two outcomes; we now have three possible outcomes (liberal, moderate, or conservative). How should we compute the odds of being liberal among whites? At first glance this may seem simple: The odds are simply $[0.24 / (1 - 0.24)] = 0.32$. Similarly, the odds of being liberal among non-whites are $[0.30 / 1 - 0.30] = 0.43$. So if we wish to discover an odds ratio for non-whites versus whites, we compute 0.43 / 0.32 = 1.34. We might now feel comfortable saying that the odds of being liberal among non-whites are about 34 percent higher than the odds of being liberal among whites.

The problem with this approach is that we have computed the odds based on only two categories: liberal vs. non-liberal. By approaching the data in this way, we have lost the information we have distinguishing between moderates and conservatives. Theoretically, this distinction may be very important.

There are two solutions to this problem. First, we may simply wish to compute all the possible odds. For whites, these are 0.24 / 0.76 = 0.32; 0.38 / 0.62 = 0.61; and 0.38 / 0.62 = 0.61. For non-whites, these are 0.30 / 0.70 = 0.43; 0.38 / 0.62 = 0.61; and 0.32 / 0.68 = 0.47.

Then, to compare non-whites and whites, we compute three odds ratios and judge which are significant. Scanning the odds just computed, we probably expect to find differences across race categories in the odds of reporting conservative (0.47 / 0.61 = 0.77) and liberal (0.43 / 0.32 = 1.34), but not moderate (0.61 / 0.61 = 1.00). It appears that whites are more likely than non-whites to report being conservative, but less likely to report being liberal.

A second method that takes full advantage of the categories (which, we should remember, have no logical ordering, though some might argue otherwise when considering political views, but probably from an ideological perspective) is to select one of the categories as the comparison group. In essence this is what we did tacitly in the binomial logistic regression model.

Let's do this with the preceding example. We'll select moderates as the reference group. (Note: It is common to select the most common category as the reference group, although this may vary depending on the specific goals of the analysis.) Observe that

TABLE 5.1 *Odds of Political Views, by Race/Ethnicity*

White	Odds
Liberal/moderate	546/854 = 0.64
Conservative/moderate	844/854 = 0.99
Non-White	
Liberal/moderate	150/191 = 0.79
Conservative/moderate	158/191 = 0.83

rather than three odds, we have reduced the number to only two for each racial group. Table 5.1 presents these odds.

Looking over these odds, should we say that whites or non-whites are more likely to be liberal? Conservative? Keep in mind that, when using odds, we may only say more or less likely *relative* to the comparison group (i.e., moderates). Now, let's pull all this together by seeing the results of a multinomial logistic regression model. Recall that in the model *race* is coded as 0 = white and 1 = non-white, and *polview1* is 1 = liberal, 2 = moderate, and 3 = conservative.

EXAMPLE 5.2 *A Multinomial Logistic Regression Model of Race and Political Views*

mlogit polview1 race, basecategory(2)   *This appears on the command line*

Multinomial regression

				Number of obs	=	2743
				LR chi2(2)	=	9.16
				Prob > chi2	=	0.0103
Log likelihood = −2967.4873				Pseudo R2	=	0.0015

polview1	Coef.	Std. Err.	z	P > |z|	[95% Conf. Interval]	
liberal						
race	.205674	.122085	1.68	0.092	−.033608	.444956
_cons	−.447312	.054795	−8.16	0.000	−.554708	−.339917
conservative						
race	−.177900	.117985	−1.51	0.132	−.409147	.053347
_cons	−.011779	.048537	−0.24	0.808	−.106909	.083351

(Outcome polview1==moderate is the comparison group)

Note that in Stata, we may specify the base category. This is simply the reference or comparison group. If the category is not specified, Stata will choose the most frequent category. We may also ask for odds ratios (Stata calls these *relative risk ratios*) rather than the coefficients shown here. To do so, simply type *mlogit dependent independents, basecategory(x) rrr*. If we were to estimate the multinomial regression model in SPSS, the reference category must be coded as the highest category. So, in the preceding example, we would be required to code moderate as 3 if liberal and conservative were coded as 1 and 2.

The first thing to notice is that there are two sets of results. This should not be surprising given what we have done so far. There are two sets of comparisons that we have established and the model presents two sets of coefficients. The second thing to notice is that the variable *race* is not significant at the $p < .05$ significance level in either model. For example, in the part of the model that compares liberal and moderate, the p-value for the race coefficient is 0.092. So although it may have appeared from our original computations that there were significant differences by race, we cannot generalize this conclusion to the population of adults in the United States represented in the GSS.

Let's assume that the p values are small enough for our initial expository purposes. Just like in the binomial logistic model, we would probably wish to compute odds ratios associated with these coefficients. If the software has estimated the simple model correctly, we should recreate (with some allowance for rounding errors) the odds ratios we computed in the previous table. The following table includes the odds and odds ratios from the observed data shown in the preceding table and from the multinomial logistic regression model.

This is rather unremarkable. It tells us, for instance, that the odds of reporting conservative *relative to moderate* are about 16 percent lower among non-whites than among

TABLE 5.2   *Odds of Political Views, Table and Model Based, by Race/Ethnicity*

Non-White	Odds
Liberal/moderate	150 / 191 = 0.79
Conservative/moderate	158 / 191 = 0.83

White	
Liberal/moderate	546 / 854 = 0.64
Conservative/moderate	844 / 854 = 0.99

Odds Ratios (table)	Non-White vs. White
Liberal/moderate	0.79 / 0.64 = 1.23
Conservative/moderate	0.83 / 0.99 = 0.84

Odds Ratios (model)	Non-White vs. White
Liberal/moderate	$e^{.206} = 1.23$
Conservative/moderate	$e^{-.178} = 0.84$

whites. But we already knew this from our initial cross-tabulation. However, think once again what we would have to do if faced with multiple independent variables. How would we then go about constructing a table similar to this one? Fortunately, we will never have to do this tedious exercise because the multinomial logistic regression model will do all of the summarizing for us. It is also a simple matter to use the coefficients from the model to recreate the observed odds. For example, the odds of whites reporting liberal versus moderate are exp{−0.4473 + 0.2057(0)} = 0.64. The odds of non-whites reporting liberal versus moderate are exp{−0.4473 + 0.2057(1)} = 0.79.

Before moving on to a model with multiple independent variables, it is useful to know that the multinomial logistic regression model is not limited to computing odds and odds ratios. Just as with the binary and ordinal logistic regression models, we may also compute predicted probabilities and discrete changes in these probabilities.

We do not have to compute these probabilities ourselves because the software will do it for us (for details on the formulas to compute predicted probabilities, see Hosmer and Lemeshow 1989, pp. 217–219; or Long 1996, pp. 164–167). To do this in Stata, we simply type the following after estimating the model, keeping in mind that there are as many probabilities as there are categories of the dependent variable.

EXAMPLE 5.2   *(Continued)*

predict liberal moderate conserv, p   *This appears on the command line after the model*

Note that the labels *liberal*, *moderate*, and *conserv* are determined by the user. We could just as easily have labeled them *p1*, *p2*, and *p3*. However, experience suggests that intuitive labels are simpler to manage. The next step is usually to ask for a table of these predicted probabilities by the categories of interest: In Stata's command line type *table race, contents(mean liberal mean moderate mean conserv)*. Recall that we request the mean of the predicted values for groups based on white/non-white status. Although in this case there are only two sets of predicted values (because we entered only one independent variable in the model), when we enter multiple independent variables there will be numerous predicted values. Perhaps the most important thing to keep in mind when computing all these various probabilities is what the labels *liberal*, *moderate*, and *conserv* represent. Again, this is why labels are important. Here's what Stata produces.

EXAMPLE 5.3   *A Cross-Tabulation of Race and Predicted Percentage in Political View Categories*

table race, contents(mean liberal mean moderate mean conserv)
This appears on the command line

race	mean(liberal)	mean(moderate)	mean(conserv)
white	.243316	.380570	.376114
non-white	.300601	.382766	.316633

Based on these predicted probabilities, we may then judge (remembering to pay attention to the *p*-values) the predicted differences (in this case, discrete change) associated with the variable *race*. For instance, these results indicate that the probability of reporting conservative is about 0.06 higher (0.376 – 0.317) among whites than among non-whites. However, keep in mind that when we ask for a list of predicted probabilities following a model with multiple independent variables, we should do so at particular levels of the other independent variables. This is illustrated in the next section.

Introducing Multiple Independent Variables

Next, we may extend the model to determine whether other variables affect the odds or the probabilities of how respondents report their political views. Based on some previous literature, we'll hypothesize that gender, age, and education are important predictors of political views. We'll also drop race/ethnicity from further consideration.

EXAMPLE 5.4   *A Multinomial Logistic Regression Model with Multiple Independent Variables*

mlogit polview1 gender age educate, basecategory(2)   *This appears on the command line*

Multinomial regression

Log likelihood = –2924.3639

		Number of obs	=	2733
		LR chi2(6)	=	75.10
		Prob > chi2	=	0.0000
		Pseudo R2	=	0.0127

polview1	Coef.	Std. Err.	z	P > |z|	[95% Conf. Interval]	
liberal						
gender	.113074	.100482	1.125	0.260	–.083866	.310014
age	–.007314	.003087	–2.369	0.018	–.013365	–.001262
educate	.120085	.018082	6.641	0.000	.084646	.155524
_cons	–1.770859	.306263	–5.782	0.000	–2.371123	–1.170594
conserv						
gender	–.208564	.089547	–2.329	0.020	–.384074	–.033055
age	.003111	.002675	1.163	0.245	–.002131	.008353
educate	.072913	.016031	4.548	0.000	.041493	.104333
_cons	–1.037023	.272878	–3.800	0.000	–1.571854	–.502192

(Outcome polview1==2 is the comparison group)

Note something very interesting: Although *gender* significantly predicts reporting conservative, it does not significantly predict reporting liberal. *Age* predicts reporting liberal (older people are significantly less likely than younger people to report liberal relative to moderate) yet does not do well at predicting those who report conservative. This is a common result of multinomial logistic regression models. In this situation you might consider running another model that explicitly compares those who report liberal to those who report conservative, especially if you think that both *gender* and *age* are important for this comparison.

To take this additional step using Stata, simply change the reference group by specifying conservative (3) in the *basecategory* subcommand:

EXAMPLE 5.5 *A Multinomial Logistic Regression Model with Multiple Independent Variables and a Different Reference Category*

mlogit polview1 gender age educate, basecategory(3)   *This appears on the command line*

Multinomial regression

					Number of obs	=	2733
					LR chi2(6)	=	75.10
					Prob > chi2	=	0.0000
Log likelihood = −2924.3639					Pseudo R2	=	0.0127

polview1	Coef.	Std. Err.	z	P > |z|	[95% Conf. Interval]	
liberal						
gender	.321638	.100237	3.209	0.001	.125178	.518099
age	−.010425	.003112	−3.351	0.001	−.016524	−.004327
educate	.047172	.017858	2.642	0.008	.012172	.082173
_cons	−.733835	.306197	−2.397	0.017	−1.333970	−.133700
moderate						
gender	.208564	.089547	2.329	0.020	.033055	.384074
age	−.003111	.002675	−1.163	0.245	−.008353	.002131
educate	−.072913	.016031	−4.548	0.000	−.104333	−.041493
_cons	1.037023	.272878	3.800	0.000	.502192	1.571854

(Outcome polview1==3 is the comparison group)

Based on these two multinomial logistic regression models, we may conclude with confidence that females are more likely than males to report being liberal and moderate relative to conservative. For example, we now know that the odds of females reporting liberal relative to conservative are about exp(0.322) = 1.38 times (or 38 percent higher than) the odds of males reporting liberal relative to conservative. The odds of females reporting moderate relative to conservative are about exp(.209) = 1.23 times (or about 23 percent higher than) the odds of males reporting moderate relative to conservative.

To simplify all these comparisons, let's focus on the multinomial logistic regression model that uses conservative as the reference group. The other coefficients may be transformed in the same way to provide odds ratios. These transformations lead to the following interpretations:

Each one-unit increase in age is associated with an expected exp(−.01) = 0.99 → 1% decrease in the odds of reporting liberal relative to the odds of reporting conservative, controlling for the effects of gender and education.

Each one-unit increase in education is associated with an expected exp(.047) = 1.05 → 5% increase in the odds of reporting liberal relative to conservative, but an expected exp(−.073) → 7% decrease in the odds of reporting moderate relative to conservative, controlling for the effects of gender and age.

The education results, in particular, are strongly indicative of different processes operating to predict these three groups. It seems that more education pushes people out of the moderate category and into the liberal or conservative categories. Deciding what this and the other results mean in a practical sense, however, relies on the analyst's conceptualization of political ideology and how education, gender, and age affect it.

Although this model can become highly complex if it includes numerous outcome categories, as long as the analyst keeps the explicit comparisons being made (which should be straightforward because there is an explicit reference category) clearly in mind, the task of analysis is not too difficult. It is as if we have simultaneously computed many binomial logistic regression models and now we have the many possible odds ratios to consider.

What about using this model to determine predicted probabilities and discrete changes in these probabilities? First, let's re-estimate the model but replace age and education with their standardized versions (*zage* and *zeducate*).

EXAMPLE 5.6   *A Multinomial Logistic Regression Model with Multiple Independent Variables and Standardized Values of Age and Education*

mlogit polview1 gender zage zeducate, basecategory(3)   *This appears on the command line*

Multinomial regression						
				Number of obs	=	2733
				LR chi2(6)	=	75.10
				Prob > chi2	=	0.0000
Log likelihood = −2924.3639				Pseudo R2	=	0.0127

polview1	Coef.	Std. Err.	z	P>|z|	[95% Conf. Interval]	
liberal						
gender	.321638	.100237	3.209	0.001	.125178	.518099
zage	−.175850	.052484	−3.351	0.001	−.278717	−.072984
zeducate	.138188	.052312	2.642	0.008	.035657	.240718
_cons	−.570200	.075776	−7.525	0.000	−.718718	−.421683
moderate						
gender	.208564	.089547	2.329	0.020	.033055	.384074
zage	−.052478	.045115	−1.163	0.245	−.140901	.035946
zeducate	−.213592	.046961	−4.548	0.000	−.305634	−.121551
_cons	−.076747	.065838	−1.166	0.244	−.205787	.052292

(Outcome polview1==3 is the comparison group)

Next, we ask Stata to compute predicted values and produce a table with the means of the predicted values from each group.

EXAMPLE 5.6 *(Continued)*

predict liberal moderate conserv   *This appears on the command line*

(option p assumed; predicted probabilities)
(14 missing values generated)

table gender if age==44 & educate==13, contents(mean liberal mean moderate mean conserv)
     This appears on the command line

gender	mean(liberal)	mean(moderate)	mean(conserv)
male	.222896	.379280	.397824
female	.262220	.398491	.339289

Note that we have asked for the predicted probabilities at the approximate means of *age* and *educate* (find the means in order to verify this). Thus, the mean predicted probabilities are for males and females at convenient values of age and education. Some conclusions based on these results are that, after controlling for age and education, males are about .06 units higher (0.398 – 0.339) than females in their predicted probability of reporting conservative, while females are about .04 units higher (0.262 – 0.222) than males in their predicted probability of reporting liberal. Overall, it appears, as we previously concluded, that females are more likely than males to report liberal or moderate, but males are more likely to report conservative.

   Let's conclude this section by seeing what is going on with age.

EXAMPLE 5.6 *(Continued)*

table agecat if gender==1 & educate==13, contents(mean liberal mean moderate mean conserv)
This appears on the command line

agecat	mean(liberal)	mean(moderate)	mean(conserv)
low 1	.299754	.389715	.310531
med 2	.269066	.396874	.334061
high 3	.211877	.406085	.382038

The variable *agecat* splits age into three categories based on low, medium, and high standardized values. Looking at the distribution of age (using, perhaps, *summarize age, detail* in Stata), we find that low (1) corresponds approximately to ages 18–28, medium (2) to ages 29–60, and high (3) to ages 61 and older. Of course, we might wish to choose more precise age groups. In any event, we see that younger people are more likely to report being liberal, while older people are more likely to report being conservative. The difference for liberal appears to be the most dramatic: almost a 0.09 difference. The difference is lower in the conservative category. Determining what these results mean in a practical sense, however, requires tools beyond statistics. For example, would you interpret these results to mean that younger people are more liberal, people born in the late 1960s and 1970s are more liberal, or that young people were more likely to report being liberal in the mid-1990s only? Could it be some combination of these things? Sorting out the possibilities is one task of cohort analysis (Firebaugh 1997), but getting at the true underlying patterns requires solid conceptual tools.

Now that we have seen how to interpret the coefficients and come up with predicted values, it is useful to remind ourselves about model fit. Let's do this briefly by considering a multinomial logistic regression model that uses only *gender* as an independent variable (labeled *Model 1;* printout omitted) and the final model that uses *age, educate,* and *gender* as independent variables (labeled *Model 2;* see Example 5.5). What are the AICs for these models?

TABLE 5.3   *Model Fit Comparisons from Multinomial Logistic Regression Models*

Model	AIC
1	$\{(-2{,}966.5)(-2) + (2)(4)\} / 2{,}743 \ = \ 2.166$
2	$\{(-2{,}924.4)(-2) + (2)(8)\} / 2{,}733 \ = \ 2.146$

Recall that smaller AICs are associated with better fitting models (see Chapter 2). Therefore, the second model provides a better fit than the first model. This is not surprising when considering that the first model contains only one independent variable and the second model includes three independent variables, including some additional significant information. The pseudo-R^2 measures in the Stata printouts also show that the second model provides a better fit to the data. However, the pseudo-R^2 measures also do not provide the analyst with much confidence that either model provides a good fit.

Diagnostic Tests for the Multinomial Logistic Regression Model

Although the same diagnostic plots demonstrated in Chapter 3 for the logistic regression model may also be used for the multinomial logistic regression model (Hosmer and Lemeshow 1989), the relevant statistical software has not been developed that allows us to do this in a straightforward manner. Hence it is easier to simply run the implicit binary logistic models separately and then estimate the diagnostic plots. Here is one approach that does this in Stata. It begins with separate logistic regression models.

First, generate two new binary variables that compare conservative to liberal and conservative to moderate.

EXAMPLE 5.7 *Logistic Regression Models of Political Views*

gen conslib = polview1 (161 missing values generated)	*This appears on the command line*
recode conslib 1=1 2=. 3=0 (2047 changes made)	* This appears on the command line*
gen consmod = polview1 (161 missing values generated)	*This appears on the command line*
recode consmod 1=. 2=1 3=0 (2743 changes made)	*This appears on the command line*

Next, estimate logistic regression models for each binary variable and save the predicted probabilities and ΔD_i's (see Chapter 3 for a description of these residuals).

logit conslib gender age educate   *This appears on the command line

Logit estimates

Number of obs = 1695
LR chi2(3) = 28.88
Prob > chi2 = 0.0000
Log likelihood = −1132.855   Pseudo R2 = 0.0126

conslib	Coef.	Std. Err.	z	P > |z|	[95% Conf. Interval]	
gender	.327164	.100478	3.26	0.001	.130231	.524097
age	−.010458	.003137	−3.33	0.001	−.016606	−.004310
educate	.040136	.017216	2.33	0.020	.006393	.073878
_cons	−.638121	.302664	−2.11	0.035	−1.231331	−.044911

predict pred1, p   *This appears on the command line*
(14 missing values generated)

predict delta1, ddeviance   *This appears on the command line*
(1209 missing values generated)

logit consmod gender age educate   *This appears on the command line*

Logit estimates

Number of obs = 2038
LR chi2(3) = 28.36
Prob > chi2 = 0.0000
Log likelihood = −1398.0972   Pseudo R2 = 0.0100

(continued)

consmod	Coef.	Std. Err.	z	P > |z|	[95% Conf. Interval]	
gender	.197953	.089789	2.20	0.027	.021969	.373936
age	−.002750	.002663	−1.03	0.302	−.007969	.002468
educate	−.076643	.016612	−4.61	0.000	−.109201	−.044084
_cons	1.075941	.277546	3.88	0.000	.531961	1.619921

predict pred2, p   *This appears on the command line*
(14 missing values generated)

predict delta2, ddeviance   *This appears on the command line*
(866 missing values generated)

Next, plot the ΔD_i's by the predicted values for each model (Hosmer and Lemeshow 1989). Recall that the recommended cut-off point for the ΔD_i's is four. Anything above four should be examined as a possible influential observation. We should also look for other unusual patterns in the plot (see Figures 5.1 and 5.2).

There are clearly many observations represented in both graphs that appear to be overly influential. As a final step, we should examine these observations carefully to determine if they are part of a particular group (e.g., males, younger people, highly educated people). In many studies, we might also wish to check for coding errors that may cause outliers or other influential observations. We shall leave it with the reader as a useful exercise to take these steps.

Finally, there is an issue we will discuss only briefly, though much attention is devoted to it in other presentations of multinomial logistic regression. This involves an important assumption about the *independence of irrelevant alternatives* (IIA), a catchy phrase that addresses the fact that we have tacitly assumed that the choice of one alternative over the other (e.g., conservative vs. liberal) is unaffected by the choice of the other alternative (e.g., moderate). Yet this assumption is often an oversimplification that does not stand up in the "real" world.

Suppose we wish to model a person's clothing preferences, with the following choices available: Black dress slacks, dark blue dress slacks, blue jeans, or shorts. The person may actually have no preference for black or dark blue dress slacks (i.e., they are considered *equivalent substitutes* in the language of economics), yet the choice between dress slacks, blue jeans, and shorts may reflect important differences that are gauged by some set of independent variables. If we eliminate the choice of dark blue dress slacks altogether, then the probability (or odds) of choosing black slacks should double. Yet under the IIA assumption, if we were not given the choice of the color of slacks, we would assume a smaller probability of choosing black slacks relative to the other choices. This is typically not reasonable when choices are differentially substitutable.

The Hausman-McFadden test (Hausman and McFadden 1984; see Fry and Harris (1998) for a review) is designed to test the IIA assumption by comparing a logistic model with all the choices to a model with restricted choices. It uses a statistic that follows a χ^2 distribution to compare the models. The null hypothesis is that the coefficients from the

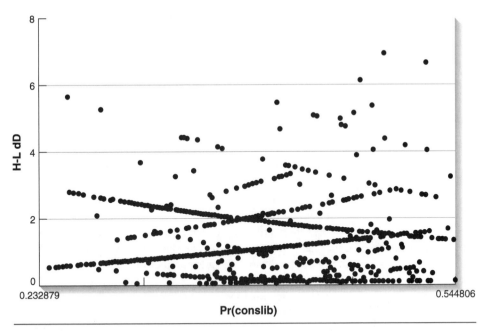

FIGURE 5.1

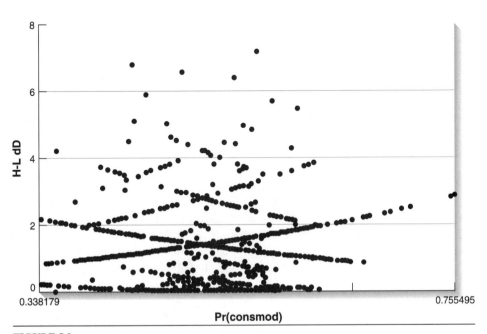

FIGURE 5.2

models are identical. This test is implemented in Stata via a downloadable file titled *iia.ado*. Details of the test and the IIA assumption are provided in many econometrics textbooks (e.g., Greene 2000; Kennedy 1992).

Alternatives to the Multinomial Logistic Regression Model

The multinomial logistic model is very useful and highly flexible. Even when faced with ordinal dependent variables, many analysts prefer the multinomial logistic model. Some types of categorical variables are often viewed as containing more interesting information than continuous variables, especially when there is no natural continuity in their underlying concepts. The multinomial logistic model allows explicit comparisons among discrete variables even when there are many categories. However, there are numerous situations when the multinomial logistic model discussed in this chapter is not suitable.

A common example that arises in economics and other disciplines is when the categories are considered alternative choices, such as when a commuter has the choice of taking the bus, a car, or the train to work. She may choose different alternatives depending on various factors such as the weather, the travel time, or other variables. Note that the variables may be different not only across people in a sample, but also within people. Hence each sample member can contribute up to three "observations" to the analysis. In this situation the conditional logistic model is used. Stata and SAS/ETS will estimate this type of model (see Powers and Xie (1998) and Greene (2000) for details).

There is a similar yet subtly different situation when respondents on a survey are allowed to choose more than one option ("choose your favorite flavors of ice cream from the following list"). In this situation, Agresti and Lui (2001) describe a marginal logit model that allows for multiple selections of some dependent variable. They also supply SAS code that may be used to estimate this and related models.

Another situation involves dependent variables that may appear as nominal or ordinal, but that are also sequences, as in a decision tree. For instance, suppose the analyst wishes to analyze condom use among a sample of adolescents. This may seem simple: Take sample of adolescents and ask them (privately!) whether or not they used condoms during their last sexual encounter. However, this seemingly simple exercise masks an important issue: It assumes that the adolescents are sexually active, yet many may not be. A more reasonable approach is to model sexual activity as an outcome, followed by condom use as an outcome for those who are sexually active. Hence the odds or probability of condom use follows the odds or probability of sexual activity. Another example involves decisions to use drugs. Many studies indicate that drug use follows a sequential pattern, with alcohol an initial stage followed by a limited group of people who go on to use marijuana, cocaine, and other illicit drugs. In these situations a sequential or nested logistic regression model is appropriate. As with the standard multinomial logistic model, there is a separate set of coefficients for each sequential outcome. Fox (1997), Powers and Xie (1998), and Greene (2000) provide concise discussions of this model.

Finally, many analysts prefer to use log-linear analysis when confronted with variables that follow a multinomial distribution. This seems to be the preferred alternative when all the variables are categorical, when there are many proposed interaction terms in the model, or when the distinction between the independent and dependent variables is not clear. Sobel (1995) provides a thorough introduction and Christensen (1990) presents a comprehensive treatment of log-linear models.

Conclusion

This chapter has presented a brief introduction to multinomial logistic regression models. Multinomial logistic regression is used when the dependent variable is measured as a nominal random variable. However, it is also often used when ordinal logistic regression models fail the proportional odds test. Although it can get rather "messy" and overwhelming when the dependent variable has many categories, multinomial logistic regression provides an efficient approach to modeling discrete dependent variables. Nevertheless, there are many situations when the IIA assumption is violated, when the categories are sequential, or when the choices represented by the categories are not mutually exclusive. In these and related situations, there are other models for discrete dependent variables that lack a natural ordering. More information about multinomial logistic regression and related techniques, such as log-linear models, is available in Borooah (2001), Powers and Xie (2000), Lloyd (1999), Retherford and Choe (1993), and Knoke and Burke (1990). Examples of multinomial logistic models from various disciplines are provided in Duncombe, Robins, and Wolf (2001), Sherkat (2000), Coley and Chase-Lansdale (1999), Hoffmann and Larison (1998), Holloway (1998), Johnson (1997), Pagan and Davila (1997), Sigelman, Wahlbeck, and Buell (1997), Haynes and Jacobs (1994), Nownes (1992), Park and Kerr (1990), and Weiler (1987).

Exercises

1. The data set *Drugtest* (available in Stata, SAS, and SPSS) contains information from more than 9,000 adult respondents who participated in the 1994 National Household Survey on Drug Abuse (NHSDA). A key concern in this set of exercises is the distribution of drug testing programs to which adult workers are exposed. A cross-tabulation of drug testing programs by whether respondents report marijuana use in the past year reveals the following:

	Type of Drug Testing Program				
Marijuana use in past year	*No Testing*	*Preemployment testing only*	*Random testing only*	*Preemployment and random testing*	*Total*
No	4,875	1,242	244	1,120	7,481
Yes	1,144	236	50	186	1,616
Total	1,609	1,478	294	1,306	9,097

    a. Compute the probability of exposure to each type of drug testing program for those who report marijuana use in the past year and for those who report no use.

    b. Using *No Testing* as the reference category, estimate the odds of exposure to each of the three types of testing programs for those who report marijuana use in the past year relative to those who report no use in the past year.

    c. Estimate a multinomial logistic regression model that includes type of drug testing program (*drugtest*) as the dependent variable and past-year marijuana use (*mjuser*) as the independent variable. Use *No Testing* as the reference category. Compute and interpret the odds ratios for each category of drug testing.

2. Extend the multinomial logistic regression model in 1.c. by including the following independent variables: *mjuser, age, educate, gender, income, south, construc,* and *sales*. Based on this model,

    a. Compute and interpret the odds ratios associated with *mjuser, south, construct,* and *sales*.

    b. Compute and interpret the predicted probabilities of each type of drug testing program for the two marijuana use groups.

    c. Compute the Deviance, AIC, BIC, and the McFadden adjusted R^2 for the model.

3. Estimate a multinomial logistic regression model with *drugtest* as the dependent variable and the following independent variables: *mjuser, gender, income, south, construc,* and *sales*. Based on this model,

    a. Compute the Deviance, AIC, BIC, and the McFadden adjusted R^2 for the model.

    b. Compare these fit statistics to those in 2.c. and discuss what this comparison reveals about the models.

4. Using the same model as in 2. (but with the modifications discussed in this chapter), save the ΔD_i's and plot them against the predicted values.

    a. Comment on what these plots indicate about the model.

    b. Based on all you have learned about predicting *drugtest* thus far, discuss what additional steps you might take to improve the model.

6

Poisson and Negative Binomial Regression Models

It is now time to leave the land of odds and probabilities and return to the world of predicting something a bit more tangible. There are many examples of variables in the social, behavioral, and health sciences, in educational research, in business applications, in the natural sciences, and in many other fields that are not precisely continuous but are also not precisely categorical (e.g., Flowerdew and Geddes 1999; Beck and Tolnay 1995; Land 1992; Knudsen 1990; Hsu 1980). These variables frequently include counting some event: how many times a person has visited a medical doctor; how many cases of measles occur in a particular town; how often hurricanes hit Miami, Florida; and many other outcomes. In the social and behavioral sciences there are many examples of count variables: how many delinquent acts adolescents commit in a year (Hoffmann and Cerbone 1999), the number of political protests in a nation (Kasler 1996), the number of lynchings that occurred per county per year in the postbellum South (Tolnay, Deane, and Beck 1996), a count of mortgage prepayments and defaults (Schwartz and Torous 1993), and the number of retirements per year that occur on the U.S. Supreme Court (Hagle 1993).

Fortunately, many of these types of outcomes occur frequently enough that their distributions closely mimic a normal distribution. For example, Figure 6.1 shows a histogram that represents a simulated distribution of the count of monthly traffic accidents on Interstate 15 in an area of central Utah known as "Point of the Mountain" during the past 10 years ("Point of the Mountain" is notorious for its strong cross-winds and blowing snow during winter months).

A normal distribution curve is superimposed on this histogram. Note that the distribution of the count variable is not too far off from a normal distribution. If we are faced with a count variable with this type of a distribution and a large sample, then a linear regression model may be acceptable.

Unfortunately, more often than not we find that count variables have distributions with means much closer to zero. One way of thinking about this is to realize that these variables often measure "rare" events. Look back over the list of examples that opened this chapter. Variables such as the number of delinquent acts or the number of Supreme

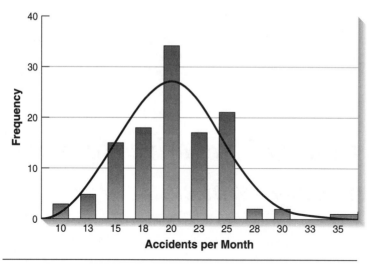

FIGURE 6.1

Court retirements are typically rare events. Now, think about what happens when the mean approaches zero. One consequence is that the distribution will usually be cut off at zero because, by most definitions, counts are nonnegative (e.g., there cannot be –3 accidents in a month; a person cannot have –2 arrests in his or her lifetime). To get a picture of what this means, let's continue to look at the frequency of traffic accidents. Figure 6.2 shows a histogram that also represents monthly traffic accidents, but switches location from our busy interstate to a side street in Springville, Utah (2000 population 20,424).

Notice that a normal distribution curve does not fit this distribution very well. Monthly traffic accidents are a rare event on this street. A large proportion of the distribution's mass is now located at zero and one accident per month, with relatively little at two or more accidents. This type of distribution is commonly known as a *Poisson distribution*. It was developed originally to study jury decisions in early 1800s France, but became well known when it was used by Von Bortkiewicz to examine the distribution of Prussian soldiers killed by horse kicks in the late 1800s (Stigler 1986). Hopefully, this was a rare event.

The probability mass function for the Poisson distribution was shown in Chapter 2. To repeat, it is

$$p(i) = e^{-\lambda} \frac{\lambda^i}{i!} \tag{6.1}$$

Equation 6.1 indicates that the probability of observing some count (i) equals the exponentiated value of the negative value of *lambda* (the upside down y, also known as the *rate*; note that it must be a positive number) multiplied by *lambda* to the ith power divided by i factorial.

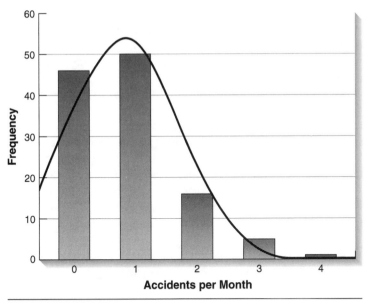

FIGURE 6.2

For instance, if the rate of traffic accidents along that side street in Springville, Utah, is 0.8 (or, the average number of monthly traffic accidents is 0.8; in other words, λ may be thought of as the mean of the Poisson distribution), then the probability of observing three traffic accidents in any month is

$$p(3) = e^{-0.8} \frac{0.8^3}{3!} = 0.038 \qquad (6.2)$$

Hence, if we have followed the rate of accidents for ten years, we'd expect to find three accidents in about (0.038 * 120) = 4.6 months. This is slightly larger than the frequency shown in Figure 6.2, but close enough for most analyses. We could similarly compute the number of months we expect to see zero accidents, one accident, and so forth.

Some readers may recognize that these types of variables share a common characteristic: They may be thought of as rates of events either across time or across geographic units (other levels of abstraction are also possible). For example, the Poisson distribution is often used to model rates of disease, such as tuberculosis, across geographical units, such as cities (see Chapter 24 in Kleinbaum et al. (1998) for several examples). Typically, these rates are adjusted for the size of the relevant population, so that we may be interested in rates of some disease in a city per 100,000 population. The Poisson distribution is also used often to model events over time, such as the traffic accidents per month example just discussed. We shall focus on this latter type of rate, although the methods discussed may be used to model rates across geographical units as well.

There are two rather unique, yet interrelated, characteristics of the Poisson distribution. The first is that the Poisson distribution assumes that the mean equals the variance. (In the normal distribution, as well as in many others, the mean and variance may have a variety of relationships. For instance, the standard normal distribution has a mean of zero and a standard deviation (and variance) of one.) The second characteristic is that the events that make up a Poisson distribution are assumed to be independent. This is usually a rather restrictive assumption to make. For instance, the fact that a person is arrested one time may make the likelihood of additional arrests higher (for some poor uncontrollable sod; perhaps he likes police stations) or lower (perhaps due to deterrence). One consequence of a lack of independence is that the variance often exceeds the mean in distributions of count variables. This situation is known as *overdispersion*. The converse, in which the mean is larger than the variance (a much rarer situation), is known as *underdispersion*. Some observers lump these two conditions together and label them *extradispersion*. The Poisson distribution assumption of mean = variance is known as *equidispersion*.

Suppose we are faced with a count variable—for example, the *GSS96* data set includes a variable that is labeled *volteer*. It is a count variable that sums the number of volunteer activities that a person says he or she was involved in during the past year. Here is the frequency distribution of *volteer* in Stata.

EXAMPLE 6.1   *Frequency Distribution of Volunteer Work*

tabulate volteer   *This appears on the command line*

number of volunteer activities	Freq.	Percent	Cum.
0	2377	81.85	81.85
1	286	9.85	91.70
2	133	4.58	96.28
3	64	2.20	98.48
4	19	0.65	99.14
5	11	0.38	99.52
6	7	0.24	99.76
7	6	0.21	99.97
9	1	0.03	100.00
Total	2904	100.00	

You can probably guess simply by looking at this that it does not resemble a normal distribution. The distribution shows a large majority of people reporting that they did not volunteer for any activity in the past year (81.9 percent). Hence, volunteering might be considered a "rare" event. Moreover, this distribution clearly has a long tail. But does this variable appear to be distributed as a Poisson random variable? First, let's look at its summary statistics.

EXAMPLE 6.2   *Summary Statistics of Volunteer Work*

. summarize volteer   *This appears on the command line*

Variable	Obs	Mean	Std. Dev.	Min	Max
volteer	2904	.333333	.885706	0	9

The variable *volteer* has a mean of 0.33 and a variance of $0.886^2 = 0.78$. So it is actually overdispersed because its variance exceeds its mean.

Nevertheless, it is often also useful to compare graphically a distribution of "rare" events to a Poisson distribution with the same mean. The two histograms (see Figures 6.3 and 6.4) compare the actual distribution of *volteer* to a simulated Poisson variable with a mean (i.e., λ) of 0.333. SPSS was used to simulate the Poisson distribution, although other programs may be used in a similar manner.

It should be apparent that the variable that measures the actual number of volunteer activities is overdispersed because its maximum value is nine whereas the maximum value of the simulated Poisson variable is only four. Note also that there are more zero counts in

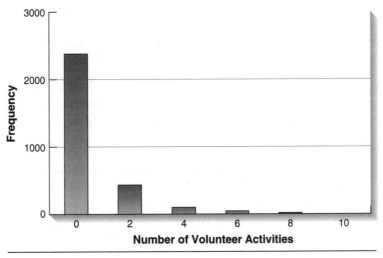

FIGURE 6.3

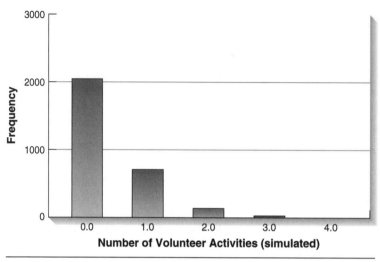

FIGURE 6.4

the observed variable than predicted by a Poisson distribution. Many count variables have an overabundance of zero values and a long-tailed distribution.

The Poisson Regression Model

Although we will learn about an alternative modeling strategy for overdispersed count variables, let's ignore this issue for now and see what we might discover from a Poisson regression model. Like any other regression approach, we are interested in determining something about the dependent variable. In an OLS regression model one goal is to compute the predicted value of the dependent variable based on information from an independent variable. For instance, we might be interested in predicting mean family income based on parents' education. But another goal is to estimate slopes that indicate the expected change or difference in the dependent variable based on changes in the independent variables. In a logistic regression we are interested in determining odds ratios or adjusted odds ratios. In both logistic regression and the probit model, we may compute predicted probabilities. In the Poisson regression model we are back to something a bit more tangible. One aim is to predict expected counts for various groups.

Because the Poisson regression model is a generalized linear model, we have to choose some way to transform the expected values. Fortunately for us, the transformation involves something we have seen before—the log link. When the log link is used the transformation back to the expected values is simple: We use the regression equation to come up with the expected log-number of events and then exponentiate this quantity to obtain the predicted count. The interpretation of the coefficients in terms of differences or changes is derived in a similar manner.

To keep things relatively straightforward, let's begin with a model with a single independent variable. Based on some previous literature with which we have become familiar, we posit that females are involved in more volunteer activities than are males. Before running the Poisson regression model, let's summarize *volteer* by gender. After sorting the *GSS96* data file by *gender* (in Stata this is simple; on the command line type *sort gender*), we type the following:

EXAMPLE 6.3 *Summary Statistics of Volunteer Work, By Gender*

by gender: summarize volteer   *This appears on the command line*

-> gender=   0 (male)

Variable	Obs	Mean	Std. Dev.	Min	Max
volteer	1285	.316732	.849267	0	7

-> gender=   1 (female)

Variable	Obs	Mean	Std. Dev.	Min	Max
volteer	1619	.346510	.913641	0	9

It appears that the mean number of volunteer activities among males is less than among females, but at this point we don't know if this difference is significant statistically. A Poisson regression model will help us answer this question.

To run a Poisson regression model in Stata we type *Poisson dependent variable independent variable(s)*.

EXAMPLE 6.4 *A Poisson Regression Model of Gender and Volunteer Work*

poisson volteer gender   *This appears on the command line*

Poisson regression

Log likelihood = –2460.4143

				Number of obs	=	2904
				LR chi2(1)	=	1.91
				Prob > chi2	=	0.1666
				Pseudo R2	=	0.0004

volteer	Coef.	Std. Err.	z	P > |z|	[95% Conf. Interval]	
gender	.089858	.065112	1.380	0.168	–.037759	.217474
_cons	–1.149701	.049568	–23.194	0.000	–1.246853	–1.052549

As usual, our hypothesis is incorrect. (Note the *p*-value for the gender coefficient is larger than 0.05.) But let's pretend that the *p*-value is close enough for our initial purposes. Can we reproduce the differences found in the above variable summary? First, let's exponentiate the gender coefficient and see what we get: exp(0.0899) = 1.094. What does this mean? Keeping in mind that we have a log-linear model (because we used the log link), one way to interpret this is to say that being a female is associated with about {100 * (exp(0.0899) − 1)} = 9.4% more volunteer activities. Another name for the exponentiated coefficient is the incidence rate ratio (IRR), because it compares the rate of occurrence (λ) of the dependent variable for the groups identified by the independent variable. Similar to the comparison of odds in logistic regression, rates are compared using ratios. Moreover, we may use the information provided by this model to come up with the expected number of volunteer activities by females and by males:

Expected number among males: exp(−1.150)   = 0.317

Expected number among females: exp(−1.150 + 0.0899) = 0.346

Now, let's use these expected values to compute the percent difference between males and females in terms of volunteer activities: {0.346 − 0.317} / 0.317 = 0.09, or about 9 percent. This agrees with the gender difference computed directly from the Poisson regression model's *gender* coefficient. The expected values also agree with our gender-specific summary statistics in Example 6.3. As should be the case, we have confirmed what we learned from our simple example of summary statistics by gender with our semi-sophisticated Poisson regression analysis.

Although this simple model doesn't do us much good, we can extend the Poisson model to include a larger number of independent variables. Based on previous studies, we shall hypothesize that race, education, and respondent's income predict volunteer activities. Just for fun, we'll leave gender in the model.

EXAMPLE 6.5   *A Poisson Regression Model of Volunteer Work with Multiple Independent Variables*

poisson volteer gender race educate income   *This appears on the command line*

Poisson regression

Number of obs   =   1944
LR chi2(4)   =   101.33
Prob > chi2   =   0.0000
Log likelihood = −1685.4299   Pseudo R2   =   0.0292

volteer	Coef.	Std. Err.	z	P > |z|	[95% Conf. Interval]	
gender	.261322	.077849	3.357	0.001	.108741	.413903
race	−.280377	.108379	−2.587	0.010	−.492795	−.067959
educate	.102802	.014432	7.123	0.000	.074516	.131088
income	.056828	.015664	3.628	0.000	.026128	.087528
_cons	−3.158300	.244792	−12.902	0.000	−3.638082	−2.678517

We've stumbled (bumbled?) onto an important result: The gender coefficient becomes significant after adding race, education, and income to the model. This is known as a *suppressor effect*. At this point, we probably don't know why such a suppressor effect occurs, so we'll save this result for our substantive publications (see Smith, Ager, and Williams (1992) for a general discussion of suppressor effects in regression analysis).

The results indicate that females, whites, those with more formal education, or those with more personal income are expected to be involved in more volunteer activities than their counterparts. To put a bit more meat on this bony interpretation, we may say such fascinating things as:

Females are involved in $\{100 * (\exp(0.2613) - 1)\} = 29.9$ percent more volunteer activities than are males, controlling for the effects of race, education, and income.

Each one-year increase in education increases the expected number of volunteer activities by a factor of $\exp(0.1028) = 1.11$ or about 11 percent, holding all other variables constant. The education effect appears to be particularly powerful in this model. (Think about why.)

What else might we do with this model? With other regression models, we computed predicted values, sometimes probabilities. However, we have now returned to numbers with a much clearer meaning. So what type of expected values might we want? How about expected counts? Stata makes it easy to determine expected counts. Just as with other models, after running the Poisson model we use the *predict* postcommand.

EXAMPLE 6.5 *(Continued)*

predict volunt1, n   *This appears on the command line*

(960 missing values generated)

table gender if race==0 & educate==13 & income==10, contents (mean volunt1)

gender	mean(volunt1)
Male	.285475
Female	.370731

This table shows us the predicted or expected counts (or means, if you prefer) of males and females in terms of number of annual volunteer activities at particular values of race/ethnicity, education, and income. Notice that we specified the predicted values as **n,** rather than **p.** This provides counts because *p* (for probability) does not make sense here. We may also run similar tabulations for race, education, and income, keeping in mind that continuous variables need to be categorized or particular sensible values chosen. To keep it simple, let's look at education only.

EXAMPLE 6.5 *(Continued)*

table educ2 if race==0 & gender==1 & income==10, contents(mean volunt1)
   This appears on the command line

educ2	mean(volunt1)
1	.259042
2	.391977
3	.661218

The effects of education are clearly important. *Educ2* divides education into low (more than one standard deviation below the mean), medium (one standard deviation below to one standard deviation above the mean), and high (more than one standard deviation above the mean, or those who have spent far too much time in school). Those in the high education group are involved, on average, in more than twice as many volunteer activities as those in the low education group.

If this education effect is not clear enough, try standardizing *income*, rerunning the model, and then computing predicted counts for those with 10, 12, 14, 16, and 18 years of education (remember you must choose convenient categories for the dummy variables, such as female and non-white). You should see an increasing step function that is indicative of how education is related to the mean number of volunteer activities. I came up with the following adjusted counts:

           0.270   0.332   0.408   0.501   0.615

Fun stuff (and pretty easy, too), but we noticed at the start of this analysis that the distribution of *volteer* appears to violate a key assumption of the Poisson regression model. That is, the variance of this variable exceeds its mean by a pretty substantial margin. Let's learn what to do in this situation.

The Extradispersed Poisson Regression Model

If the variance of the dependent variable exceeds the mean there are several alternatives. We will discuss two of them. The extradispersed Poisson model is relatively simple to estimate with SAS's *Proc Genmod* or with Stata's *glm* command. The extradispersed Poisson model takes into consideration that the variance of the dependent variable differs from the mean. An interesting thing about this model is that the extradispersion affects only the standard errors; the point estimates are the same in the regular and extradispersed Poisson models. Using Example 6.5 as a baseline, here's what the extradispersed Poisson regression model looks like in Stata.

EXAMPLE 6.6 *An Overdispersed Poisson Regression Model of Volunteer Work*

glm volteer gender race educate income, family(poisson) link(log) scale(dev) irls
   This appears on the command line

			No. of obs	=	1944
Generalized linear models					
Optimization	: MQL Fisher scoring		Residual df	=	1939
	(IRLS EIM)		Scale param	=	1
Deviance	= 2465.513855		(1/df) Deviance =		1.271539
Pearson	= 4349.279397		(1/df) Pearson =		2.243053
Variance function	: V(u)	= u	[Poisson]		
Link function	: g(u)	= ln(u)	[Log]		
Standard errors	: EIM				
BIC	= 2427.65134				

volteer	Coef.	EIM Std. Err.	z	P > |z|	[95% Conf. Interval]	
gender	.261322	.087784	2.98	0.003	.089269	.433375
race	−.280377	.122210	−2.29	0.022	−.519904	−.040851
educate	.102802	.016273	6.32	0.000	.070907	.134697
income	.056828	.017663	3.22	0.001	.022210	.091446
_cons	−3.158302	.276031	−11.44	0.000	−3.699313	−2.617291

(Standard errors scaled using square root of deviance-based dispersion)

As shown in Chapter 1, when using Stata's *glm* option we must specify the family and the link function, both of which should be familiar by now. But note the command after the comma, *scale(dev)*. This subcommand asks for an estimate of the dispersion parameter and adjusts the standard errors based on this parameter. The assumption in the regular Poisson regression model is that the dispersion is one. In this model, we have asked the program to estimate the value of this parameter. A value greater than one indicates that the distribution of the expected value of the dependent variable is overdispersed. The dispersion parameter of interest here appears to the right in the Stata printout and is labeled *Deviance*. It should not be confused with the deviance of the model (see Chapter 2), which is shown on the left side of the printout. (Moreover, the BIC presented in Stata's *glm* command is computed differently than our BIC from Chapter 2, even though smaller is better is still the rule-of-thumb.) Although we already know that *volteer* is extra-dispersed based on its simple distribution, we now may take this extradispersion into account when estimating our Poisson regression model. Comparing Example 6.6 to the previous Poisson model, we see that the standard errors from the extradispersed model are larger than those from the model that does not account for extradispersion. (If in doubt, it is best to use the model that allows over- or underdispersion—unless you just can't live without significant effects!) The dispersion parameter is used to adjust the standard errors using the following formula: SE(unadjusted model) $* \sqrt{\text{dispersion}}$. For example, the standard error for *gender* in the preceding model is $.0778 * \sqrt{1.27} = .088$.

A final point about the extradispersed Poisson model: Just as with the regular Poisson regression model, we may use Stata to come up with predicted counts. However, following this model we would type *predict volunt2, mu*. Note that the postcommand asks for *mu* rather than *n* (*mu* is the general command for asking for predicted values following Stata's *glm* command). But think about what these predicted counts indicate and whether or not they are different from the predicted counts estimated earlier. As mentioned previously, the extradispersed Poisson regression model differs from the regular Poisson regression model in its standard errors, not its point estimates. Therefore, the predicted counts are identical.

The Negative Binomial Regression Model

The second alternative to the regular Poisson regression model is the negative binomial regression model. As mentioned in Chapter 2, some observers note that the negative binomial model is not a true generalized linear model because its underlying distribution is not derived from the exponential family of distributions (Lindsey 1997). Nevertheless, it is often used as a substitute for the Poisson model because, as we saw when we investigated its probability function, the negative binomial distribution frequently assumes that the variance is larger than the mean. The negative binomial model is more appropriate than the Poisson model in the common situation where the events of interest are not independent (Cameron and Trivedi 1998).

Recall that the probability mass function of the negative binomial distribution is

$$P(n) = \binom{n-1}{r-1} p^r (1-p)^{n-r} \tag{6.3}$$

This function comes in handy when we wish to calculate how many trials (n) it will take to get a fixed number of successes (r). A simple example (see Chapter 2) involves determining the number of people we must approach to get 10 signatures if the probability (p) is 0.60 that any person we approach will sign. Of course, in a practical situation we know only the number of trials and successes based on the sampling scheme. The key goal is to determine something about the p's or, more directly, something about the expected number of "successes."

Let's try a negative binomial regression model using the same variables as those in the Poisson regression model designed to predict volunteer work in the past year. In Stata this model is estimated as follows:

EXAMPLE 6.7 *A Negative Binomial Regression Model of Volunteer Work*

nbreg volteer gender race educate income	*This appears on the command line*

Negative binomial regression		Number of obs	=	1944
		LR chi2(4)	=	42.71
		Prob > chi2	=	0.0000
Log likelihood = −1419.7818		Pseudo R2	=	0.0148

volteer	Coef.	Std. Err.	z	P > |z|	[95% Conf. Interval]	
gender	.284408	.124065	2.29	0.022	.0412463	.527570
race	−.311073	.162237	−1.92	0.055	−.629052	.006906
educate	.111995	.024269	4.61	0.000	.064429	.159562
income	.051931	.022410	2.32	0.020	.008008	.095855
_cons	−3.247383	.376887	−8.62	0.000	−3.986067	−2.508699
/lnalpha	1.362715	.097951			1.170735	1.554695
alpha	3.906786	.382673			3.224362	4.733642

Likelihood ratio test of alpha=0:   chibar2(01) = 531.30 Prob>=chibar2 = 0.000

Comparing the three models we have estimated, it appears that the negative binomial regression model is the most conservative. For example, note that the *race* coefficient is not significant in the negative binomial model, even though it was significant in each of the Poisson models. Note also that the z-value for education is lower in this model than in the others. In this situation, we should probably opt for the most conservative approach, unless we have some strongly compelling theoretical reason for thinking that race, for example, is especially important for understanding the number of volunteer activities in which a person is engaged.

The *alpha* and *lnalpha* (which is the natural logarithm of alpha) provide estimates of the overdispersion parameter (although it is on a different scale than the dispersion parameter in the extradispersed Poisson model already estimated). If there is no overdispersion in the outcome variable, then alpha is expected to equal zero. Stata provides a likelihood ratio test for alpha = 0. Recalling that likelihood ratio tests are distributed χ^2, this test indicates clearly that alpha is not equal to zero. One very general way to interpret this result is to say that the Poisson model is inappropriate for these data. So we have compelling evidence that a negative binomial model is more appropriate than a Poisson model that does not consider extradispersion. Unfortunately, there is no generally accepted rule of thumb about how much extradispersion is allowable before one should switch from a Poisson regression model to a negative binomial regression model. Some authorities recommend estimating both the Poisson model and the negative binomial model and then comparing the results. If the alpha is significantly greater than zero and the results differ, then the negative binomial model is preferred (Cameron and Trivedi 1998).

Just as with the Poisson model, we may use the results of the negative binomial regression model to compute expected counts for the various groups. The steps in Stata for doing this are identical to those we saw previously.

EXAMPLE 6.7   *(Continued)*

---

predict volunt3, n   *This appears on the command line*
(960 missing values generated)

table gender if race==0 & educate==12 & income==10, contents (mean, volunt3)

gender	mean(volunt3)
male	.250542
female	.332964

The gender discrepancy according to the negative binomial model is slightly greater than the gender discrepancy according to the original Poisson model (32.9 percent vs. 29.9 percent). If we ask Stata to estimate the differences by education, we will find a similar discrepancy between models. But keep in mind that the key difference of the Poisson and negative binomial regression models tends to show up in the standard errors rather than the estimated counts. Other useful ways to interpret results from a negative binomial regression model are described in Cameron and Trivedi (1998). A word of warning, however: The negative binomial model is not appropriate in the rare case when the expected value of the dependent variable is underdispersed. In this situation, an extradispersed Poisson model is an option. This model may be estimated using Stata's *glm* or SAS's *Proc Genmod*.

Diagnostic Tests for the Poisson Regression Model

The diagnostic tests for the Poisson regression model are very similar to tests that we learned about in earlier chapters. Residual analysis, in particular, follows a familiar route—we ask the software to compute residuals, in particular deviance residuals, and predicted values and then plot them against one another, looking for areas where the fit is poor, such as when influential observations are present. Although other types of residuals may be computed, such as Pearson or Anscombe, deviance residuals are appropriate for most situations (Cameron and Trivedi 1998; Pierce and Schafer 1986). We can also compute ΔD_i's and use them as we use deviance residuals (see Chapter 3), but experience indicates that the deviance residuals and ΔD_i's are almost indistinguishable in the Poisson model, especially in large samples.

Another diagnostic test that is often useful is to plot the deviance residuals against the independent variables, assuming, of course, that the latter are continuous random variables. This might indicate whether there is a different functional form of the independent variable that should be included in the model. For instance, in the previous Poisson regression example, perhaps personal income and volunteer activities have a nonlinear relationship that is not captured in the estimated model.

Finally, it is useful to use the deviance residuals in a normal probability (Q-Q) plot to ensure that the distributional assumptions are met. If they are met, we should find that the residuals fall on a diagonal line (Davison and Gigli 1989).

Unfortunately, when faced with a small sample size, deviance residuals and predicted values can be influenced by various conditions of model specification, including influential observations and other empirical issues (see Cameron and Trivedi (1998), pp. 145–151). In this case, Pierce and Schafer (1989) recommend the following adjusted deviance residuals for the Poisson model:

$$adjusted\,dev_i \,=\, d_i + \frac{1}{6\sqrt{\hat{y}_i}} \tag{6.4}$$

Let's explore some of these diagnostic issues using the Poisson model that predicts the number of volunteer activities based on *gender, race, educate,* and *income.* First, we'll re-run the model, ignoring for now the fact that the negative binomial actually provides a more appropriate fit.

EXAMPLE 6.8 *A Poisson Regression Model of Volunteer Work*

glm volteer gender race educate income, family(poisson) link(log)   *This appears on the command line*

Generalized linear models				No. of obs	=	1944
Optimization	: ML: Newton-Raphson			Residual df	=	1939
				Scale param	=	1
Deviance	=	2465.513855		(1/df) Deviance	=	1.271539
Pearson	=	4349.349483		(1/df) Pearson	=	2.243089
Variance function	: V(u)	= u		[Poisson]		
Link function	: g(u)	= ln(u)		[Log]		
Standard errors	: OIM					
Log likelihood	=	−1685.429933		AIC	=	1.739125
BIC	=	2427.65134				

volteer	Coef.	Std. Err.	z	P > |z|	[95% Conf. Interval]	
gender	.261322	.077849	3.36	0.001	.108741	.413903
race	−.280377	.108379	−2.59	0.010	−.492795	−.067959
educate	.102802	.014432	7.12	0.000	.074516	.131088
income	.056828	.015664	3.63	0.000	.026128	.087529
_cons	−3.158302	.244792	−12.90	0.000	−3.638084	−2.678519

Note first that we have estimated the model in Stata using the *glm* command. This is because the *Poisson* command does not allow postcommand residuals to be predicted. Nevertheless, the models are identical (within rounding error).

Next, we ask Stata to save the predicted values (counts) and the deviance residuals, and we also compute the adjusted deviance residuals using Stata's *generate* command. Note that the deviance residuals and adjusted deviance residuals are very similar given our large sample size. (Compute their correlation to verify this.)

EXAMPLE 6.8   *(Continued)*

---

predict count, mu   *This appears on the command line*
(960 missing values generated)

predict dev1, deviance   *This appears on the command line*
(960 missing values generated)

generate adjdev = dev1 + (1/(6*sqrt(count)))   *This appears on the command line*
(960 missing values generated)

We may now use these predicted values and residuals to check for model misspecification and influential observations. For example, a plot of the residuals by the predicted counts is shown in Figure 6.5.

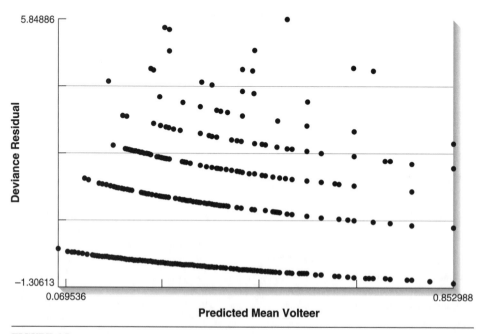

FIGURE 6.5

It appears that there are some observations found at the top of the plot that should be checked carefully. These may represent influential observations. A normal probability plot of the deviance residuals, shown in Figure 6.6, also illustrates serious problems with model specification that the analyst should address. Of course, these problems may simply indicate that the Poisson model is incorrect because there is such substantial extra-dispersion in the distribution of the dependent variable *volteer*.

Finally, although it might be tempting to use Stata, SAS, or some other statistical software to compute deviance residuals and other predicted values for diagnosing problems in the negative binomial regression model, Cameron and Trivedi (1998) advise against this approach (except under very specific circumstances) because the negative binomial model is not a true generalized linear model. Hence there are clearly trade-offs when it comes to using the Poisson versus the negative binomial regression model. However, in our situation, a review of all the evidence provides a clear case that the negative binomial regression model is more appropriate for predicting the number of volunteer activities reported by *GSS96* sample members. However, the analyst may also wish to explore other related regression models for count variables, some of which are described in the next section, in order to develop the most appropriate model for predicting volunteer activities.

Other Models for Count Variables

The few models we have discussed for count variables share some problems. Both the Poisson and negative binomial regression models fail to account for a couple of common

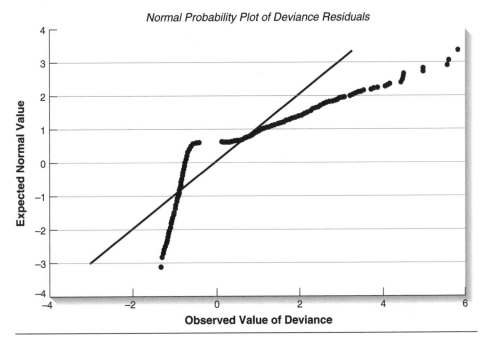

FIGURE 6.6

phenomona: neither engages until a certain number of events have occurred and counting stops after some maximum number has been reached. An example of the former is if we observed only one traffic accident along that Springville, Utah, street in a six-month period and then recorded zero for those months (our patience is limited, after all). An example of the latter may be found in the *GSS96* survey. The *GSS96* allows a maximum count of children as eight (labeled "eight or more"), so that a person with, say, twelve children is given a value of eight. Hence we find the value truncated "from above." In both of these cases the analyst may use truncated models (Cameron and Trivedi 1998, Chapter 4). Cameron and Trivedi (1998) provide a thorough discussion of many other models for count variables.

Two other related types of count models are known as zero-inflated and hurdle models. Zero-inflated models are appropriate when an excess of zeros occurs in the distribution. The underlying rationale for the excess of zeros is that some observations in the population may actually have zero probability of experiencing the event, yet others may differ in the count of events they experience. These two processes are governed by different mechanisms. For instance, Long (1997) provides an example of publications among scientists with PhDs in the United States. He argues that some scientists have a zero probability of publication, yet, for others, a set of variables affects the predicted number of publications. In effect, we must model both the probability of any publication and then the probability of the number of publications. Zero-inflated Poisson and negative binomial models are designed to estimate both processes simultaneously.

A similar yet subtly different model is known as a hurdle model. The hurdle model actually models the two-part process that leads to observation of any event and the observation of multiple events if any occur. For example, we may wish to model a two-part decision-making process involving drinking alcoholic beverages. The first part is the hurdle: whether people drink any alcoholic beverages. This decision may be governed by a particular set of variables. The second part is the number of alcoholic beverages a person among the subsample of drinkers consumes per day. A similar hurdle process might involve doctor's visits or even the number of children among a sample of couples. Zorn (1998) shows that the zero-inflated and hurdle models are actually special cases of the more general extradispersed Poisson model and that the results of these two models may be interpreted similarly. A thorough discussion of these and other models is provided in Cameron and Trivedi (1998); simplified discussions may be found in Long (1997), Land, McCall, and Nagin (1996), and Gardner, Mulvey, and Shaw (1995). Technical details are provided in Lambert (1992). Long and Freese (2001) describe how to estimate and interpret zero-inflated models in Stata.

Conclusion

This chapter has discussed a useful set of regression models that are appropriate for count variables. Count variables are found throughout the research community, from health studies to explorations of the cosmos. Poisson, extradispersed Poisson, and negative binomial models are useful when one is faced with such count variables, especially those that measure rare events. They are also very useful when estimating models concerned with rates in populations, such as the rate of disease or crime per 100,000 population across cities, counties, states, or other geographical units. If the strict assumptions of the Poisson model are met, in particular equidispersion and independence of events, then the Poisson regression model is appropriate. However, experience and an emerging body of literature suggest that independence is rare and an abundance of zeros is common. This usually means that variables of interest to the research community are overdispersed. In this situation, it is tempting (and often appropriate) to turn to the negative binomial regression model. An advantage of this model is that it leads to more precise coefficients and standard errors, and it allows an explicit test of overdispersion.

Nonetheless, it is becoming routine to reevaluate the assumptions of the Poisson and negative binomial models. These models, in their regular form, assume that the same process governs the counting of the dependent variable. Some argue that such an assumption is naive. More often than not, a different process dictates a zero count versus some positive count. Hurdle models and zero-inflated models are useful in this situation because they explicitly separate the two processes and allow the analyst to use different sets of variables to predict these separate processes (Zorn 1996). Given that these models are not widely available in the software (although they are available in Stata and LIMDEP), we have not discussed them in detail in this chapter. But they should be considered as suitable companions to the regular Poisson and negative binomial regression models.

Exercises

1. The following exercises use the data set *Stress* (available in Stata and SAS formats). The data set includes information from about 650 adolescents in the United States who were asked various questions about the number of stressful life events (*stress*) they had experienced in the past year and about other issues. The data set also includes the following family- and school-related variables, which are assumed to be continuously distributed: family cohesion (*cohes*, a measure of how well the adolescents get along with their families, coded low to high), self-esteem (*esteem*, coded low to high), past-year school grades (*grades* from low to high), and how much they like their schools (*sattach*, coded low to high).

   a. Estimate a histogram and summary statistics for the variable *stress*. What do you think is its most likely probability distribution? Explain.

   b. Plot a normal probability (Q-Q) plot of the variable *stress*. Comment about its departure from a normal distribution.

2. Estimate a Poisson regression model, an overdispersed Poisson regression model, and a negative binomial regression model with *stress* as the dependent variable and the following independent variables: *cohes*, *esteem*, *grades*, and *sattach*.

   a. Interpret the coefficients (from the Poisson *and* negative binomial models) associated with the variables *cohes* and *sattach* using the percent change formula we have seen in this and earlier chapters.

   b. Based on both the Poisson and negative binomial regression models, compute the predicted count of *stress* for those whose levels of family cohesion are less than one standard deviation below the mean (low), between one standard deviation below and one standard deviation above the mean (medium), and more than one standard deviation above the mean (high).

    c. What is the expected percent difference in the number of stressful life events for those at high and low levels of family cohesion in each model?

3. Compute the AICs and BICs from the Poisson, the overdispersed Poisson, and the negative binomial regression models estimated in exercise 2. Discuss which model you prefer and why.

4. Using the Poisson regression model estimated in exercise 2, plot the deviance residuals by the predicted values. Discuss what this plot indicates about the regression model.

7

Event History and Survival Models

We have been concerned thus far with might be called "static" variables. These are variables that measure some "current" condition: scores on a depression scale, current attitudes toward corporal punishment, or political ideology. Although these types of variables would seem to exhaust the possibilities, there is another type of variable that is hinted at by the use of the term "static." These are variables that explicitly address some time dimension. But what about a measure of activities or behaviors over the past year, such as our look at the number of volunteer activities a person has been involved in? Although this might be thought of as having a time dimension, we still tend to measure it by grouping time so that it has only a tangential role in our models.

There are generally two types of models that explicitly address a time dimension. The first type involves models that use change scores or estimate change in some statistical way. Often, researchers simply use a linear regression model (although others could also be used) and examine the impact of time one variables (t_1) on changes from time one to time two (t_2) in some dependent variable. For example, we might be interested in determining the impact of stressful life events on changes in adolescent self-esteem over time, perhaps by measuring change with a difference score ($t_2 - t_1$) or by including the lagged value of the dependent variable as an independent variable in the model (e.g., $Y_2 = \alpha + \beta_1 Y_1$). Most books on structural equation models have some discussion of this type of analysis. The interested reader may also wish to consult Allison (1990) or Finkel (1995) for additional information. I also include under this first type *time series models* because they are often concerned with predicting the value of some variable based on a series of past values and a set of independent variables (Bowerman and O'Connell 1993; Greene 2000).

The second type of model concerns the timing of events. For instance, medical researchers are often interested in the effects of certain drugs on the timing of death (or recovery) among a sample of patients. In fact, these statistical models are known most commonly as survival models because they are used often by biostatisticians, epidemiologists, and other medical researchers to study the time between diagnosis and death, or between therapeutic intervention and death or recovery (Kleinbaum 1996; Lee 1992).

Social and behavioral scientists have adopted these models for a variety of purposes. Under the term *event history analysis* (Yamaguchi 1991) or *duration analysis* (Amemiya 1985), sociologists, psychologists, political scientists, economists, and other researchers are interested in issues such as the following: Among those who have divorced, what is their average length of marriage? What is the average length of a war (from declaration to cessation) and can we predict this quantity based on some set of determinants? What is the average duration of one's first job? Does this affect the average duration of one's second job or the probability that one will change jobs in the future? Many other outcomes are conceivable in a variety of disciplines (e.g., Sherer and Lee 2002; Snell et al. 2001; Luke and Homan 1998; Box-Steffensmeier and Jones 1997; Leiter and Johnsen 1997; Hill and Perry 1996; Heaton and Call 1995; Willett and Singer 1993; Shpayer-Makov 1991).

Event history models have been developed to explicitly address these and other similar questions. According to Allison (1995, p.2), "[event history analysis] was designed for longitudinal data on the occurrence of events." Events include transitions such as those just mentioned (e.g., job change) as well as death, birth, heart transplant, marriage, one's first delinquent act, and many other outcomes. Many events, birth and death being notable exceptions, may occur more than once. An adolescent could commit delinquent acts each month continuously; a person might get married several times; or a person may have several jobs over a forty-year employment career. In fact, statisticians often distinguish survival models and event history models by focusing on how many events are allowed to occur. If only one event occurs, then we have a survival model; if multiple events may occur, then we have an event history model. In this sense, survival models may be thought of as a special case of event history models where only one event occurs (Lindsey 1997). We will not make this distinction so precise in this chapter (mainly because the social and behavioral sciences seem to prefer the term "event history"), but it is a useful distinction nevertheless.

Continuous- versus Discrete-Time Models

A key for survival and event history models is knowing when the event(s) occurred. Sometimes one can be very precise (Sam died on January 14 at 2:32 p.m.), although we often have to place an event into a particular time interval (Sally contracted scarlet fever some time in May of 1962). This distinction is important because it gives rise to two types of models: *Continuous-time models* and *discrete-time models*. In continuous-time models the researcher assumes that the event may occur at any time, but, as with most continuous variables, we often have to approximate the time. Discrete-time models assume that the event may occur only within distinct time units. Practically speaking, discrete-time models are often used to approximate continuous-time models, such as if we wished to determine what predicted the length of time until one's first marriage, but we had only annual data on a set of individuals (see Yamaguchi 1991, Chapters 2–3). We'll return to this issue later. The first part of the chapter addresses continuous-time models; the second part discusses discrete-time models.

You might be tempted to ask what seems an obvious question at this early point—Why not simply create a continuous variable that measures the time until some event (e.g., it's 15 months from Joe and Lana's marriage to the birth of their first child) and then plug this variable into a linear regression model? After all, time until something happens seems to be a continuous variable. Even if this type of variable is not normally distributed (typically it is not), we could simply transform it using some function, such as the square root or natural logarithm, and then use OLS regression. We'll examine why this approach is unwise.

Censoring and Time-Dependent Covariates

There are two major impediments to using OLS regression when faced with event histories. First, suppose we were involved in a study designed to sort out factors that predicted first births among a sample of women. We collected a sample over a five-year period but found that 30 percent of the respondents had not had a child by the time we completed the study. What should we do? Should we drop them from the analysis? This is unwise because it leaves us with a biased sample and ultimately leads to biased parameter estimates. Considering the expense it takes to collect data over a five-year period, this would be most unfortunate.

The general issue of sample members who have not experienced the event during the "observation" period is known as *censoring*. Censoring includes "right" censoring, such as the situation just described. Right censoring also involves subjects who drop out of a study (due to death or utter exhaustion from answering all our questions). There is also "left" censoring, wherein the sample member experienced the event of interest (e.g., first marriage) before we began observing her, and "interval" censoring, wherein the sample member experienced the event, but we cannot determine precisely when it occurred. (Censoring may be described in more detail, but we will limit our discussion and presentation of models to right censoring only.) Censoring is very common in longitudinal data and must be addressed in the statistical model if we wish to come up with accurate estimates. A concise description of censoring and a related phenomenon, *truncation* (events are observed for only a portion of the observation period), is found in Yamaguchi (1991).

The second impediment concerns the variables we wish to use to predict the event. Suppose we had monthly measures from a sample of married couples and wished to predict the length of time from marriage to first child. Ignoring for now the censoring issue (i.e., some may not have a child), suppose that our monthly measurements included questions about use of contraceptive devices. This variable may very well change over time, thus involving what is known as a *time-varying coefficient* (also called a *time-dependent covariate*). If we wished to stick to the tried-and-true OLS regression approach, it would be virtually impossible to include this variable in the model, even though it seems that most reasonable (and many unreasonable) persons would suspect that contraceptive use affects the timing of the birth of one's first child.

In both of these situations, the best approach is to use a statistical model that is designed explicitly to deal with these issues. This is where event history models come into play.

The Basics: Survivor and Hazard Functions and Curves

There are a variety of event history models from which to choose. We have already distinguished continuous-time and discrete-time models. At a more finely tuned level, there are exotic things such as univariate models, exponential models, Weibull models, Gompertz models, gamma models, competing risk models, proportional hazard models, and many other types. Yamaguchi (1991), Allison (1995), and Lee (1992) provide thorough overviews. Cleves, Gould, and Gutierrez (2002) discuss how to estimate most of these models in Stata; Allison (1995) does the same in SAS. We'll focus our interest on only a few of the more popular of these. Several of these models fall under the topic of generalized linear models because they either involve a transformation to normality (via a link function and a specific parametric family) or, in the case of discrete-time models, we may use the same old logistic, probit, or multinomial logistic regression approaches we've seen in earlier chapters. The key distinction for discrete-time models is in the way the data are set up, rather than in the estimation and interpretation of the models.

Before seeing how to estimate some of these models, it is helpful to have a minimum understanding of survivor and hazard functions. Consider the event of marriage. If you imagine time until marriage as continuously distributed over some time interval (e.g, ages 15–75), then the survivor function gives the probability of "surviving" unmarried (we'll use that term loosely) beyond some specific time point (e.g., beyond 30 years of age). The survivor curve associated with this function is rarely normally distributed; it may have a variety of shapes.

The hazard function is the instantaneous probability of an event at some specific time point, t, divided by the probability of not having experienced the event prior to that specific time point, or divided by the survivor function. So, it's the conditional probability of experiencing the event given that you have not experienced it before this time. More formally, this relationship may be expressed as

$$h(t) = \frac{f(t)}{S(t)} = \lim_{\Delta t \to 0} \frac{P(t \leq T < t + \Delta t \mid T \geq t)}{\Delta t}$$

(7.1)

$$\text{Average hazard rate} = \frac{\text{number of failures}}{\text{sum of observed survival times}}$$

In the first part of Equation 7.1, $f(t)$ is the probability density function (*pdf*) of the times to the event and $S(t)$ is the survivor function. This also shows that the hazard is a conditional measure. Hence it is often called the *conditional failure rate*. Less formally, the hazard may be thought of as the expected number of events per unit of time (or within some small interval of time). In this respect, the hazard is very similar to the *lambda* (λ) in Poisson regression (see Chapter 6). An important difference is that the hazard is conditional on the person "surviving" until the particular time point. A key similarity is that the hazard and λ are both interpreted based on the measurement of time. For instance, someone may have a predicted count (λ) of 1.2 delinquent events per year. Similarly, if the hazard of committing a delinquent act during age 16 is 1.2, then a 16-year-old is expected to commit 1.2 delinquent acts during the course of that year. If we switched the time frame to months, both the λ and the hazard would change.

If you're not confused yet, you probably will not be at all confused by event history models. Assuming this is the case, let's get our hands dirty with some real data.

As a first step, we'll take a look at what survivor and hazard functions and curves look like. We'll do this two ways, numerically and graphically. Perhaps the most common approach to estimating survival functions and curves is the Kaplan-Meier method (KM). The simplest way to understand the KM approach is with a data set that has no censored observations. When there is no censoring, KM provides the percentage of observations with event times greater than some time point, *t*. In order to see this, we'll use a random subsample of people who married from the National Survey of Family Growth (NSFG). The data structure (see the data set *event1*) looks like the following:

TABLE 7.1   *Event History Data of Time Until Marriage*

marriage	*attend14*	*cohab*	*educate*	*race*
43	1	1	1	1
170	1	1	1	0
77	0	1	1	1
1	1	0	1	0
987	0	1	0	0
80	1	0	1	0
1	1	0	1	0
19	0	0	0	1
23	1	1	1	0

Table 7.1 shows nine observations from the data set. The variable *marriage* shows the length of time in days from when the respondent moved out of his or her parent's home to the time of marriage. The other variables include *attend14* (attended religious services at age 14, coded as 1 = yes, 0 = no), *cohab* (1 = cohabited prior to marriage, 0 = did not), *educate* (1 = graduated from high school, 0 = did not), and *race* (1 = non-white; 0 = white).

In order to begin our analysis we'll use Stata and tell the program that these are event history data using the *stset* command (see Cleves, Gould, and Gutierrez 2002). Because marriage gauges the "time" variable, we use it in the command structure.

EXAMPLE 7.1   *Setting Event History Data in Stata*

---

stset marriage   *This appears on the command line*

---

　　failure event: (assumed to fail at time=marriage)
obs. time interval: (0, marriage]
exit on or before: failure

　59　　total obs.
　 0　　exclusions

　59　obs. remaining, representing
　59　failures in single record/single failure data
5635　total analysis time at risk, at risk from t　=　　　0
　　　earliest observed entry t　　　　　　=　　　0
　　　last observed exit t　　　　　　　=　　1071

　　　We can see the assumptions made by Stata. It notices that every observation "failed": We don't yet have any censoring. (We'll get to this later.) The total analysis time is derived by adding together all the days in the variable *marriage*. The printout also shows that the minimum time until marriage is 0 and the maximum is 1,071 days. Next, let's look at a graphical representation of this variable. Figure 7.1 shows what Stata's *sts graph* gives us.

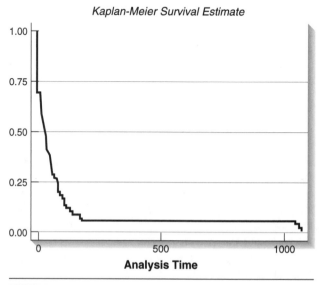

FIGURE 7.1

This is the estimated survivor distribution function represented as a curve. We may see that almost all of this random subsample married within what appears to be about 200 days from the time they moved out of their parents' home. Of particular interest is the median "failure" time; in this sample it is the point at which 50 percent got married (look at where the line drops below 0.50). It appears to be at fewer than 100 days, but it is difficult to tell from the graph.

If we wish to see the actual median and other statistics, we may use *sts list* and *stsum* in Stata. Be warned, though, that with large data sets we will get a lot of printout if we specify *sts list*. Here is an abbreviated version of what we get from *sts list*.

EXAMPLE 7.2 *Listing Event History Data in Stata*

sts list   *This appears on the command line*

Time	Beg. Total	Fail	Net Lost	Survivor Function	Std. Error	[95% Conf. Int.]	
1	59	18	0	0.6949	0.0599	0.5604	0.7955
11	41	1	0	0.6780	0.0608	0.5428	0.7810
12	40	1	0	0.6610	0.0616	0.5254	0.7663
14	39	2	0	0.6271	0.0630	0.4910	0.7363
17	37	2	0	0.5932	0.0640	0.4572	0.7058
21	35	1	0	0.5763	0.0643	0.4405	0.6903
24	34	1	0	0.5593	0.0646	0.4240	0.6747
28	33	1	0	0.5424	0.0649	0.4076	0.6590
29	32	1	0	0.5254	0.0650	0.3914	0.6431
30	31	1	0	0.5085	0.0651	0.3753	0.6270
34	30	1	0	0.4915	0.0651	0.3593	0.6109
36	29	1	0	0.4746	0.0650	0.3435	0.5946
37	28	1	0	0.4576	0.0649	0.3278	0.5782
39	27	2	0	0.4237	0.0643	0.2969	0.5449
40	25	1	0	0.4068	0.0640	0.2817	0.5280
47	24	1	0	0.3898	0.0635	0.2666	0.5111
53	23	1	0	0.3729	0.0630	0.2517	0.4939
55	22	1	0	0.3559	0.0623	0.2369	0.4767
59	21	1	0	0.3390	0.0616	0.2223	0.4592

Notice that many sample members "failed" at time one; within one day of leaving their parent's home they were married (perhaps you can hear the ghost of parental cheering). The median survival time is found looking at the column labeled survivor function. At 0.50 the value of marriage is between 30 and 34. Therefore, in Figure 7.1, if we had a better labeling system, we would have seen that the line dropped below 0.50 at some value between 30 and 34. We may also use the values in this printout to make some interpretations. For instance, we may say "The estimated probability that a sample member will not get married for at least 40 days is 0.41." The printout also provides standard errors and confidence intervals, which are interpreted in the usual manner.

Let's see if we can gain any additional information from *stsum*.

EXAMPLE 7.3   *Summary Statistics for Event History Data in Stata*

---

stsum   *This appears on the command line*

---

failure _d: 1 (meaning all fail)
analysis time _t: marriage

| | time at risk | incidence rate | no. of subjects | —— Survival time —— | | |
				25%	50%	75%
total	5635	.010470	59	1	34	86

Notice that our estimate of the median was close. The table shows it to be 34 days (look directly underneath the *Survival time 50%*). The incidence rate is the hazard rate, or the "rate of marriage" per one unit of time (days). The reciprocal of this number is 1 / .010470 = 95.5, so the average sample member is expected to "survive" about 96 days before marriage takes over his or her life. Note that this "mean" length of time and the "median" length of time until marriage differ by a substantial margin. This occurs frequently because the lengths of time measured by the survival curves are rarely distributed normally. In the rare case when these lengths of time are distributed normally, the median and the mean are equal. When the distribution is not normal, the median is the preferred measure of average survival time.

So far, these results are not very interesting (although they may be rather frightening to the average single person living with his or her parents). As we have seen in earlier chapters, looking at distributions of dependent variables is rarely exciting. Therefore, the next step is to explore differences by potential explanatory variables. For example, we might suspect that those who cohabited before marriage will have a shorter length of time from leaving Mom and Dad to marital bliss, especially if an uncomfortable parent got wind of the arrangement. On the other hand, it may be more reasonable to suspect that cohabitation delays marriage. In Stata we may ask for separate survivor curves by independent variables (of course, these should be discrete variables). Figure 7.2 shows the results of asking Stata for these curves.

sts graph, by(cohab)   *This appears on the command line*

Note that all of those who cohabited were married by around 250 days, but many of those who did not remained unmarried for a pretty lengthy period of time. So it may appear that cohabitation is more likely to lead to marriage. But looking at the graph this way can be deceiving. A better method is to look at the median (the point 0.50): Notice that

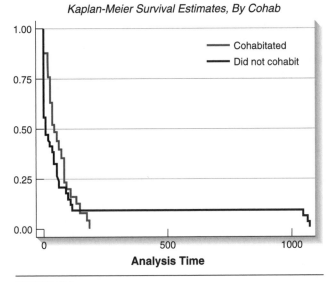

FIGURE 7.2

those who cohabited appear to have a higher median than those who did not (i.e., their curve at 0.50 is to the right of the other curve), thus indicating longer (on average) "survival" times. The next question to ask is whether these differences are significant.

There are two basic tests for comparing survival curves: the log-rank test and the Wilcoxon test. Both are based on ranks, so they are nonparametric. (Note: Nonparametric tests do not assume a particular probability distribution and thus are often considered more flexible than parametric tests.) Both tests are implemented using Stata's *sts test* command. The key difference is that the Wilcoxon test is less sensitive to differences that occur later in time, as in our example. For such a case, I prefer using the Wilcoxon test.

EXAMPLE 7.4 *Comparing Survival Curves in Stata*

sts test cohab, wilcoxon   *This appears on the command line*

```
         failure _d:   1 (meaning all fail)
     analysis time _t:   marriage
```

Wilcoxon (Breslow) test for equality of survivor functions

cohab	Events observed	expected	Sum of ranks
no	34	31.54	267
yes	25	27.46	−267
Total	59	59.00	0

```
         chi2(1)  =      4.27
         Pr>chi2  =      0.0389
```

It appears that there are differences in the likelihood of "survival" until marriage. But the direction of difference is still not entirely clear. One way to tell the difference is to look at the events observed versus those expected. Notice that those who cohabited had fewer events than expected; in other words, they lasted longer than expected. We may also use *stsum, by(cohab)* to provide additional information about which group lasts longer.

EXAMPLE 7.5 *Comparing Survival Times in Stata*

stsum, by(cohab)   *This appears on the command line*

> failure _d: 1 (meaning all fail)
> analysis time _t: marriage

cohab	time at risk	incidence rate	no. of subjects	── Survival time ──		
				25%	50%	75%
no	4056	.008383	34	1	12	61
yes	1579	.015833	25	24	47	88
total	5635	.010470	59	1	34	86

It seems that those who cohabited do last longer before marriage (look at the median survival times) and we now know that the difference between the two groups is statistically significant. So the second, perhaps more reasonable, hypothesis is supported.

Much of what we have done so far is rather unrealistic. Looking at the original data indicates that a substantial proportion of sample members never married. So there is obviously some censoring going on in these data. Moreover, we have not yet controlled for any other variables. The effects of cohabiting could be due to a censoring issue (many of those who cohabited in the sample may not get married at all; *event1* includes only those who were married by the conclusion of the observation period) or it could be due to other variables such as education or race.

Parametric Event History Models

In order to conduct a more thorough analysis, we will now turn to some parametric and semiparametric event history models. All of them allow us to enter numerous explanatory variables in the model. We'll focus on the most common of these models: the *log-normal*, the *exponential*, the *Weibull*, and the *Cox proportional hazards regression model*. The first three are known as parametric models because we make a distinct assumption about the distribution of the error term. This section addresses parametric models, and the next describes the Cox model, a semiparametric model that is used widely throughout the research community. Because the presentation of parametric and semiparametric models initially focuses on continuous time models, we'll save a discussion of discrete-time models for a later section of this chapter.

The log-normal model is actually almost identical to an OLS regression model. The probability density function of a log-normal variable is similar to that of the standard normal distribution (see, e.g., the probit function in Chapter 3), except that the random variable in the *pdf* is replaced by its natural logarithm (*ln(y)*; Lindsey 1995). Note, however, that because we assume that its logarithm is normally distributed, the random variable may only take on non-negative values. An advantage of the log-normal event history model is that we may allow censoring of observations. Another advantage is that it is a generalized linear model with a log link, so we may exponentiate its coefficients and come up with something tangible—the estimated ratio of the expected (predicted) survival times for two groups.

Let's first see how Stata estimates a log-normal event history model using the data set *event2.dta*. Unlike *event1*, it includes censored values for marriage (denoted by 1500 days). The variable *evermarr* indicates whether the respondent ever married. A quick review of these data will show that all of those with a value of 1500 on *marriage* have a value of 0 on *evermarr*. (Note: SAS's *Proc Lifereg* may also be used to estimate these parametric models; see Allison 1995.) We first tell Stata that these are event history data using *stset* and then use *streg* to estimate the model.

EXAMPLE 7.6   *A Log-Normal Event History Model of Time Until Marriage*

---

stset marriage, failure(evermarr)   *This appears on the command line*

streg educate age1sex attend14 cohab race, dist(lognormal)   *This appears on the command line*

Log-normal regression -- accelerated failure-time form

No. of subjects	=	1506			Number of obs =	1506
No. of failures	=	1048				
Time at risk	=	754457				
					LR chi2(5) =	127.43
Log likelihood	=	−3268.9873			Prob > chi2 =	0.0000

_t	Coef.	Std. Err.	z	P > |z|	[95% Conf. Interval]	
educate	.122973	.036260	3.391	0.001	.051905	.194041
age1sex	−.073423	.035085	−2.093	0.036	−.142188	−.004657
attend14	1.089191	.239525	4.547	0.000	.619733	1.558653
cohab	.382928	.200681	1.908	0.056	−.010401	.776265
race	2.325504	.248290	9.366	0.000	1.838862	2.812142
_cons	2.775972	.728887	3.809	0.000	1.347378	4.204564
/ln_sig	1.290994	.023768	54.316	0.000	1.244409	1.337579
sigma	3.6364	.086431			3.470884	3.809808

The coefficients may be exponentiated to come up with expected ratios of "survival" times. For example, the coefficient for *race* (coded as 0 = white, 1 = non-white) indicates that non-whites are expected to "survive" about exp(2.32) = 10 times longer than whites, controlling for the effects of the other variables in the model. Each additional year of education is expected to increase time to marriage by about {exp(0.123) – 1} * 100 = 12.3 percent. For each one year increase in age at first sexual experience (*age1sex*), time to marriage is expected to decrease by about 7 percent, holding all the other variables constant. The sigma value shown at the bottom of the printout is an estimate of the variance of the disturbance (error) term. Note that it is pretty large, thus indicating substantial variability in the error distribution.

Next, let's see what an exponential model looks like. Obviously, it is based on the exponential distribution. This probability distribution is normally designated as gauging the time until some event occurs (e.g., a lightbulb burns out). So it clearly cannot be used with negative numbers. Its probability density function is

$$f(y) = \lambda \exp\{-\lambda y\} \text{ if } y \geq 0 \qquad (7.2)$$

Note that this function has a λ, which we called a *rate* in Poisson regression. It serves a similar purpose here. It gauges the (hazard) rate at which "failures" (i.e., events) are expected to occur. An important assumption to keep in mind is that the exponential model assumes that the hazards are proportional over time. In other words, in our model it assumes that the hazard rate of getting married is the same at 5 days and at 500 days. So the coefficients measure only the expected difference in the hazard rate. Simply looking at Figure 7.2 shows that this is not a wise assumption to make. Nevertheless, in the interests of seeing all the models we mentioned, we'll estimate the exponential model.

EXAMPLE 7.7   *An Exponential Event History Model of Time Until Marriage*

stset marriage, failure(evermarr)   *This appears on the command line*

streg educate age1sex attend14 cohab race, dist(exponential) nohr   *This appears on the command line*

Exponential regression -- log relative-hazard form

No. of subjects	=	1506		Number of obs =	1506
No. of failures	=	1048			
Time at risk	=	754457			
				LR chi2(5) =	323.16
Log likelihood	=	−5188.0854		Prob > chi2 =	0.0000

_t	Coef.	Std. Err.	z	P>|z|	[95% Conf. Interval]	
educate	−.009935	.010503	−0.946	0.344	−.030521	.010652
age1sex	.058551	.009171	6.385	0.000	.040577	.076526
attend14	−.686906	.073263	−9.376	0.000	−.830498	−.543314
cohab	.279140	.062499	4.466	0.000	.156646	.401635

(continued)

EXAMPLE 7.7   *(Continued)*

race	−1.045976	.086467	−12.097	0.000	−1.215447	−.876505
_cons	−6.787822	.209157	−32.453	0.000	−7.197762	−6.37788

Unlike the log-normal model, which was interested in survival time, the exponential model is interested in the "hazard" of marriage. Therefore, if we wish to make the results of these models roughly comparable, we may simply flip the signs of the coefficients. We may also derive what are known as *hazard ratios* from the coefficients by exponentiating them. These are similar to odds ratios (see Chapter 3): A value greater than 1 indicates a positive relationship between increasing values of the independent variable and the hazard of the outcome; a value between 0 and 1 indicates a negative relationship.

For example, the "hazard" of marriage is about exp(.279) = 1.32 times higher among those who cohabited than among those who did not, controlling for the effects of the other variables in the model. Unfortunately, we should not trust this model because it assumes a constant hazard rate across the timespan measured.

A good way to determine whether or not the hazard is constant is with the Weibull model. This model assumes that the error term has a shape similar to the exponential model, but it does not assume the hazard rate is constant. In the notation shown in Equation 7.2, it does not assume that λ is a constant. The probability density function of the Weibull distribution is

$$f(y) = \alpha y^{\alpha-1} \exp\left\{-y^a\right\} \text{ if } y \geq 0 \tag{7.3}$$

Although this appears to be a complicated function, note its similarity to the *pdf* for the exponential distribution. The main difference is that it allows the hazard rate to vary based on the parameter α. If $\alpha = 1$, then the function becomes the exponential distribution (Lindsey 1995). In the Weibull regression model estimated in Stata, the changes in the hazard rate parameter are based on values of p (rather than α). In order to make this parameter useful, however, it is normal to take its inverse, $1/p$. A $1/p$ estimate in the Weibull model greater than 1 indicates that the hazard is decreasing over time. If it is between 0.5 and 1, the hazard is increasing, but at a decreasing rate. If it is between 0 and 0.5, the hazard is increasing at an increasing rate. Here's what Stata estimates.

EXAMPLE 7.8 *A Weibull Event History Model of Time Until Marriage*

stset marriage, failure(evermarr)   *This appears on the command line*

streg educate age1sex attend14 cohab race, dist(weibull) nohr   *This appears on the command line*

Weibull regression -- log relative-hazard form

No. of subjects	=	1506	Number of obs =	1506
No. of failures	=	1048		

(continued)

EXAMPLE 7.8   *(Continued)*

Time at risk   =   754457

			LR chi2(5)	=	145.93
Log likelihood	=	−3409.4673	Prob > chi2	=	0.0000

_t	Coef.	Std. Err.	z	P > |z|	[95% Conf. Interval]	
educate	−.020707	.010796	−1.918	0.055	−.041866	.000452
age1sex	.035150	.009820	3.580	0.000	.015904	.054397
attend14	−.419766	.073335	−5.724	0.000	−.563501	−.276032
cohab	.077014	.062841	1.226	0.220	−.046153	.200181
race	−.780810	.086657	−9.010	0.000	−.950653	−.610966
_cons	−1.787937	.220763	−8.099	0.000	−2.220625	−1.355249
/ln_p	−1.179021	.025801	−45.697	0.000	−1.229592	−1.128453
p	.307580	.0079358			.292413	.323533
1/p	3.251191	.0838829			3.090872	3.419827

There are substantial differences between the exponential and Weibull models. The $1/p$ estimate is well above one, so we may conclude that the hazard of marriage is decreasing substantially over time. Hence it seems that the Weibull model is clearly preferable to the exponential model in this situation.

This may all seem rather overdone. Often we may simply assess the distribution of the "raw" survival or hazard curves and decide on which distribution is most appropriate. As a more rigorous alternative, because these models are estimated with maximum likelihood techniques, we may also rely on AICs and BICs, or, in the preceding three models, compare them through estimating differences in deviance measures. Let's see what the AICs and BICs tell us.

TABLE 7.2   *Model Fit Comparisons for Parametric Event History Models*

Model	AIC	BIC
Log-normal	4.35	−4,430.5
Exponential	6.80	−739.7
Weibull	4.53	−4,149.5

It appears that the log-normal model provides the best fit of the three. However, graphical techniques that are useful for assessing the fit of these models indicate that none of the three works very well. Recall that in past chapters we plotted some form of the

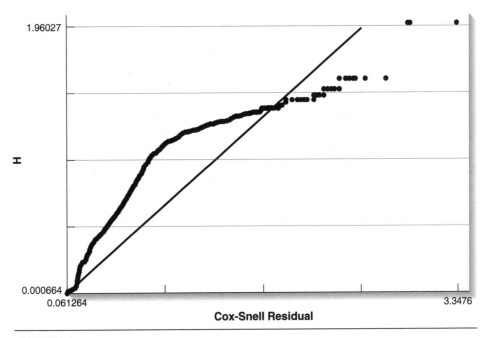

FIGURE 7.3

residuals against the predicted values or against a normal distribution. In these survival models, we may plot what are known as the Cox-Snell residuals against the empirical survival curve (the KM estimator). If the assumptions of the model are met, the residuals should fall on a 45° line. For example, Figure 7.3 provides this plot from the Weibull model. It should be clear that the points do not fall along a 45° line. A plot from the log-normal model shows a similar result. (Try this. The Cox-Snell residuals may be obtained by specifying *predict cs, csnell* after running the event history model. Note that *cs* is an arbitrary name specified by the user.)

In a similar manner, we may also save the deviance residuals, perhaps through the *predict* postcommand in Stata, and plot them against the survival curve or simply look at their summary statistics to determine if there are influential observations. For more information on the use of residuals in these models, see Therneau, Grambsch, and Fleming (1990). A thorough treatment of parametric survival models is provided in Lee (1992). Blossfeld and Rohwer (1995) discuss how to include time-dependent covariates in parametric models. We shall look at time-dependent covariates, but only in the context of discrete-time event history models.

The Cox Proportional Hazards Model

The final alternative, and perhaps the most widely used event history approach for these "time-to-failure" data, is known as the *Cox Proportional Hazards (PH) model*. The Cox

PH model has some distinct advantages over the models we've discussed so far. First, it does not require the user to choose a particular distributional form for the survival times. It is known as a *semi-parametric model* because the full parametric form of the model does not need to be specified *a priori*. The Cox model uses an approach known as partial likelihood to estimate the model parameters (see Allison 1995, pp. 114–117, 122–126, for straightforward examples). Second, the Cox PH model accommodates both continuous- and discrete-time models. Given the first advantage, we should probably opt to use the Cox PH model for our analysis of time to marriage. None of the parametric models seems to fit the data very well.

An important assumption the Cox PH model makes is known as the *proportional hazards assumption*. This is similar to the assumption we make with dummy variables in linear regression: We assume that the slopes are the same; only the intercepts differ. As with the exponential model, the Cox model assumes that the hazard ratios are constant over time. Nonetheless, we may relax this assumption if needed. Without further ado, here is what Stata gives us for its Cox PH model.

EXAMPLE 7.9 *A Cox PH Model of Time Until Marriage*

stset marriage, failure(evermarr)   *This appears on the command line*

stcox educate age1sex attend14 cohab race, efron   *This appears on the command line*

Cox regression -- Efron method for ties

No. of subjects	=	1506		Number of obs =	1506
No. of failures	=	1048			
Time at risk	=	754457			
				LR chi2(5) =	118.63
Log likelihood	=	−7106.8978		Prob > chi2 =	0.0000

_t _d	Haz. Ratio	Std. Err.	z	P > |z|	[95% Conf. Interval]	
educate	.967644	.010422	−3.054	0.002	.947432	.988287
age1sex	1.023473	.010185	2.332	0.020	1.003705	1.043632
attend14	.695673	.050994	−4.950	0.000	.602575	.803155
cohab	.950732	.060038	−0.800	0.424	.840050	1.075996
race	.479483	.041558	−8.481	0.000	.404573	.568264

Rather than specifying no hazard ratios, I allowed Stata to provide them (note that the *nohr* subcommand that appeared in the exponential and Weibull models is not on the command line for the Cox model). These are exponentiated coefficients and may be interpreted in terms of percent change following our usual transformation. Before doing this, however, compare the results of the Weibull model and the Cox model. The results are quite similar in terms of exponentiated coefficients and significance levels. One exception is that education was only borderline significant in the Weibull model, but it is highly significant in the Cox model. Note also that cohabitation, which was significant in the exponential model and in our baseline model that compared survival curves, is not significant in the Weibull or Cox models. Thus, it appears one or more of the other independent variables in the model explains the association between cohabitation and the "hazard" of marriage. Some interpretations from this model include the following (remember, we don't have to exponentiate):

> The "hazard" of marriage is expected to decrease by about $[(.968 - 1) * 100] = 3$ percent for each one-year increase in education, controlling for the effects of the other variables in the model.

> Attending religious services at age 14 (*attend14*) is associated with about a 30 percent decrease in the "hazard" of getting married, holding the effects of the other variables constant.

The final step we'll take with the Cox model is checking the proportional hazards assumption. Stata provides a simple approach for testing this assumption. It involves saving another type of residual (known as *Schoenfeld residuals*) and then using a specialized command labeled *stphtest*. The steps are as follows (note that the Cox model output is omitted):

EXAMPLE 7.10   *Checking the Proportional Hazards Assumption in a Cox PH Model*

---

stcox educate age1sex attend14 cohab race, efron schoenfeld(sch*) scaledsch(sca*)
    This appears on the command line

stphtest, rank detail   *This appears on the command line*

Test of proportional hazards assumption

Time: Rank(t)

	rho	chi2	df	Prob > chi2
educate	0.25785	62.40	1	0.0000
age1sex	0.13899	16.74	1	0.0000
attend14	−0.02638	0.73	1	0.3914
cohab	0.38091	149.51	1	0.0000
race	0.07837	6.53	1	0.0106
global test		223.00	5	0.0000

The null hypothesis is that the hazards are proportional. We can see that we may reject this hypothesis for each variable except *attend14*. In this situation, we should explore the data further in order to examine some of these nonproportional hazards more explicitly. For instance, suppose that we suspect that the hazard ratio for whites versus non-whites changes over time. To test this hypothesis, we'll compute an interaction term between *race* and our time variable, *marriage* (labeled *wmarr*), and place it in the Cox model. Just to make the situation more interesting, we'll also include an interaction term between *cohab* and *marriage* (labeled *cmarr*).

EXAMPLE 7.11   *A Cox PH Model with Interaction Terms to Test Nonproportional Hazards*

stcox educate age1sex attend14 cohab race wmarr cmarr, efron   *This appears on the command line*

Cox regression -- Efron method for ties

No. of subjects	=	1506		Number of obs =	1506
No. of failures	=	1048			
Time at risk	=	754457			
				LR chi2(7)	=	1071.99
Log likelihood	=	−6630.2143		Prob > chi2	=	0.0000

_t _d	Haz. Ratio	Std. Err.	z	P > |z|	[95% Conf. Interval]	
educate	.946331	.010441	−5.000	0.000	.926087	.967018
age1sex	1.027816	.010507	2.684	0.007	1.007428	1.048617
attend14	.786139	.057831	−3.271	0.001	.680584	.908064
cohab	2.488567	.236670	9.587	0.000	2.065369	2.998479
race	1.684202	.161815	5.426	0.000	1.395123	2.033182
wmarr	.996528	.000504	−6.877	0.000	.995541	.997516
cmarr	.993372	.000953	−6.934	0.000	.991507	.995241

The results are compelling. Both interaction terms are significant. Moreover, a significant positive effect of *cohab* emerges. It appears that the hazard of marriage is actually higher for non-whites in the early going, but then decreases over time relative to whites. Similarly, early on, those who cohabit are highly likely to get married, but over time this "hazard" tends to decrease. We may use Stata's *stphplot* to check what is happening with cohabitation. This command produces the plot shown in Figure 7.4.

EXAMPLE 7.12   *A Proportional Hazards Plot to Examine Survival Curves*

stphplot, by(cohab)   *run after the original Cox model (Example 7.9)*

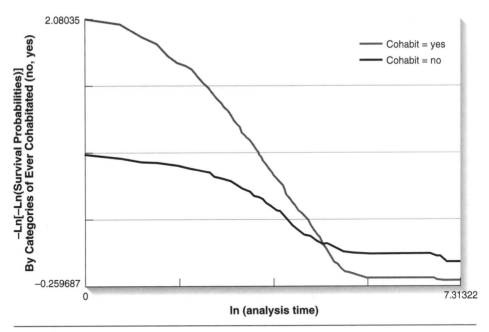

FIGURE 7.4

This plot represents what is known as a *log cumulative hazard function*. It shows that the hazard over time is changing substantially for the two groups. As suggested by the Cox model in Example 7.11, the hazard of marriage for those who cohabited begins high, but then, proportionally speaking, it decreases much more rapidly than among those who have not cohabited. In fact, the estimated hazards cross at some point late in the time distribution. Therneau and Grambsch (2000, Chapter 6) discuss various ways to adopt the Cox model when faced with nonproportional hazards. Including interaction terms with the time variable (as we did) is one approach. However, they also point out that nonproportional hazards often do not affect the overall utility of the model, especially when it is based on a large sample.

There are many other optional analyses that a Cox model provides. A very useful option is its easy ability to include time-dependent covariates. For example, suppose we had measures of relationship satisfaction from prospective grooms and brides in our data set. If these were collected over time, we could test whether satisfaction influences the length of time until marriage. Similarly, if we had measures of the strength of the relationship between those at home and their parents over time, we might wish to throw this in a model of time to marriage. It should be clear that event history models can quickly become highly complex, so a solid understanding of the conceptual processes underlying the hypothesized model is needed. Therneau and Grambsch (2000) provide a comprehensive treatment of the Cox model, including a discussion of residuals, additional tests for the proportional hazards assumption, and many other issues. Kleinbaum (1996) also provides a thorough treatment of the Cox model, but in a much less technical style.

Discrete-Time Event History Models

We are now going to turn back to some familiar methods to estimate event history models with time-varying covariates. Do not take this to imply that the Cox model is second rate when it comes to these models. Many analysts argue that it offers a superior approach to conducting event history models with time-varying covariates. We are changing course in order to discuss discrete-time models. It turns out that our familiarity with Stata's *glm* and *logit* commands (or SAS's *Proc Genmod*; or SPSS's *Binary Logistic*) comes in very handy in this context. The only trick to using our generalized linear models for event history analysis is to set up the data so that we may analyze multiple episodes taken from each individual.

In these models we assume that each person's involvement in the event of interest occurs within some discrete time period. For instance, longitudinal data are often collected on an annual basis using questionnaires that ask respondents about events that occurred in the previous year. The data set-up for a discrete-time event history analysis requires us to treat each year (or whatever time period we are using) as a separate observation for each individual. Whether or not the event occurred in any particular year is then estimated with a logistic regression model, a multinomial logistic regression model (if an event takes on more than two values), or a complementary log-log model. Although we haven't discussed this last option, it comes in handy if we are willing to assume that events occur in continuous time (Allison 1995). Moreover, it is one of the options in Stata's *glm* and SAS's *Proc Genmod*.

The set-up should be clear from the data shown in Table 7.3. The data are from a longitudinal study of adolescent behavior. Each year, adolescents filled out a questionnaire that asked about their drug use, delinquency, life events, family relations, and many other things. Delinquency (*delinq1*) is coded as 0 = no delinquent acts that year and 1 =

TABLE 7.3 *Discrete-Time Event History Data*

newid	year	age	stress	cohes	delinq1
13	1	11	0	61	1
14	1	14	0	49	0
14	2	15	0	50	0
14	3	16	1	39	1
23	1	14	1	35	0
23	2	15	3	41	0
23	3	16	4	27	0
23	4	17	3	26	1

the respondent's first delinquent activity occurred in that year. As described, the data are structured so that an individual contributes multiple observations across years. The data show that not only does initial delinquency vary by individual, but also that stress and family cohesion (*cohes*) vary over time. In other words, stress and family cohesion are time-dependent covariates. These data may be found in the data set *event3*.

The data indicate that person with *newid* number 13 committed his first delinquent act in year one at age 11; person 14 committed his first delinquent act in year three at age 16, and so forth. Once the data are read into Stata (or SAS or SPSS), it is very easy to estimate a discrete-time event history model. In this situation, we simply ask for a *logit* model (or a *glm* model with log link and binomial distribution) and include year as an independent variable. A practical way to do this is with Stata's *xi* command, which automatically creates dummy variables. Here's one model of adolescent delinquency using the *event3.dta* data set and Stata.

EXAMPLE 7.13   *A Discrete-Time Event History Model of First Delinquency*

---

xi: logit delinq1 stress cohes i.year   *This appears on the command line*

---

i.year   Iyear_1-4   (naturally coded; Iyear_1 omitted)

Logit estimates

					Number of obs	=	2604
					LR chi2(5)	=	238.43
					Prob > chi2	=	0.0000

Log likelihood = −995.98366   Pseudo R2   =   0.1069

delinq1	Coef.	Std. Err.	z	P > |z|	[95% Conf. Interval]	
stress	.122445	.030631	3.997	0.000	.062409	.182482
cohes	−.028894	.004971	−5.813	0.000	−.038637	−.019151
Iyear_2	−.952427	.142497	−6.684	0.000	−1.231716	−.673138
Iyear_3	−1.535232	.164199	−9.350	0.000	−1.857054	−1.213407
Iyear_4	−1.865752	.184343	−10.121	0.000	−2.227057	−1.504446
_cons	.386481	.300420	1.286	0.198	−.202331	.975293

The year variables show the effects of years 2–4 on the odds of delinquency. Hence the intercept, following an exponential transformation, indicates the odds of initial delinquency in year one for those who experienced no stressful life events and who scored 0 on the family cohesion scale. Each year the odds of initial delinquency decrease significantly.

The *stress* coefficient indicates that each one-unit increase in stressful life events is associated with an exp(0.122) = 1.13 unit increase in the odds of delinquency (or a 13 percent increase), controlling for the effects of year and family cohesion. Similarly, a one-unit increase in family cohesion is associated with a 100 * (exp(−.029) − 1) = 2.9 percent decrease in the odds of delinquency, holding the effects of *year* and *stress* constant.

This model may also be estimated with the Cox PH model. First, we must tell Stata that the data set consists of event histories with *year* as the time variable, *newid* as the id variable, and *delinq1* as the "failure" variable.

EXAMPLE 7.14   *A Discrete-Time Cox PH Event History Model of First Delinquency*

stset year, id(newid) fail(delinq1) * This appears on the command line *

id:	newid
failure event:	delinq1 ~= 0 & delinq1 ~= .
obs. time interval:	(year[_n-1], year]
exit on or before:	failure

2604	**total obs.**
858	**obs. begin on or after (first) failure**

1746	obs. remaining, representing
651	subjects
399	failures in single failure-per-subject data
1746	total analysis time at risk, at risk from t = 0
	earliest observed entry t = 0
	last observed exit t = 4

Then we may run the Cox PH model as we did earlier in the chapter.

. stcox stress cohes, efron   *This appears on the command line*

failure _d:	delinq1
analysis time _t:	year
id:	newid

Cox regression -- Efron method for ties

No. of subjects	=	651	Number of obs =	1746
No. of failures	=	399		
Time at risk	=	1746		
			LR chi2(2) =	122.39
Log likelihood	=	−2364.3714	Prob > chi2 =	0.0000

_t _d	Haz. Ratio	Std. Err.	z	P > |z|	[95% Conf. Interval]	
stress	1.156793	.029285	5.753	0.000	1.100793	1.215637
cohes	.965997	.003977	−8.402	0.000	.958233	.973824

Notice that the hazard ratios for stress and cohesion are very similar to the exponentiated coefficients in the logistic model. This is normally the case, so that either model may be used to estimate the associations between the independent variables and the dependent variable. An advantage of the logistic regression approach is that it may be used to estimate the effects of discrete time explicitly. For the present model, we may observe clearly that the hazard of first delinquency decreases over the four years of observation.

To check the proportional hazards assumption, we follow the same steps as those outlined in Example 7.10: Ask for Schoenfeld residuals in the Cox model and then ask Stata to test the PH assumption with the *stphtest* command.

EXAMPLE 7.15   *Testing the Proportional Hazards Assumption of a Cox Discrete-Time Event History Model*

stcox stress cohes, efron schoenfeld(sch*) scaled(sca*)   *This appears on the command line*

Cox PH results omitted

stphtest, rank detail   *This appears on the command line*

Test of proportional hazards assumption

Time: Rank(t)

	rho	chi2	df	Prob > chi2
stress	−0.01150	0.05	1	0.8157
cohes	−0.05334	0.91	1	0.3391
global test		0.91	2	0.6331

From these results we should have little concern that the proportional hazards assumption is violated. Neither the relationship involving stressful life events nor that involving family cohesion includes nonproportional hazards.

However, these data offer a lurking problem—think about the way we measured delinquency over the four-year span. We assumed that the earliest a delinquent act could occur was in year one. Yet many of these adolescents, especially the older ones, may have committed their first delinquent act prior to year one. This is one example of the left censoring issue that we referred to at the beginning of this chapter. To be precise, left censoring means you know the event occurred before the observation period began; you just don't know when. At this point we can only assume that some of our adolescents were delinquent earlier than the study period, but we cannot identify them. There are techniques to use when you encounter left censoring, but a discussion is beyond our goals. A description of how to handle left-censored data in the context of parametric models using SAS's *Proc Lifereg* and Cox proportional hazards models using *Proc PHReg* is provided in Allison (1995).

As a final step, we may extend this model to include multiple episodes of delinquency, rather than just the first episode. The data set *event4* includes the same variables as those we used previously, with one important exception. That is, rather than the first delinquent episode during the four years, this data set includes multiple episodes or events. For instance, an adolescent can score a one (indicating one or more delinquent acts) in from zero to four years. This is often a more realistic picture of events that are repeatable. Once the data are set up, the commands are identical to those already shown. In Stata these commands are as follows:

EXAMPLE 7.16   A Discrete-Time Event History Model of Repeated Delinquency

xi: logit delinq stress cohes i.year   *This appears on the command line*

i.year   Iyear_1-4   (naturally coded; Iyear_1 omitted)

Logit estimates

					Number of obs	=	2604
					LR chi2(5)	=	252.53
					Prob > chi2	=	0.0000
Log likelihood = −1552.5174					Pseudo R2	=	0.0752

delinq	Coef.	Std. Err.	z	P > |z|	[95% Conf. Interval]	
stress	.198296	.025226	7.861	0.000	.148854	.247738
cohes	−.042866	.003870	−11.078	0.000	−.050451	−.035282
Iyear_2	.315657	.124454	2.536	0.011	.071731	.559582
Iyear_3	.263384	.124976	2.107	0.035	.018437	.508332
Iyear_4	.349564	.125628	2.783	0.005	.103339	.595790
_cons	.888677	.238682	3.723	0.000	.420868	1.356490

The *year* variables show the effects of years 2–4 on the odds of delinquency over time. Hence the intercept, following our exponential transformation, indicates the odds of delinquency in year one of the survey for those who experienced no stressful life events and who scored 0 on the family cohesion scale. Each year the odds of delinquency increase significantly. Note that this differs from what we saw in Example 7.13. Year is associated with a decreasing odds of initial delinquency (Example 7.13), yet an increasing odds of repeated delinquency (Example 7.16).

The *stress* coefficient indicates that each one-unit increase in stressful life events is associated with an $\exp(0.198) = 1.22$ unit increase in the odds of delinquency (or a 22 percent increase), controlling for the effects of year and family cohesion. A one-unit increase in family cohesion is associated with an $\{\exp(-.043) - 1\} * 100 = 4.2$ percent decrease in the odds of delinquency, holding the effects of year and stress constant. Compare these results with those found in Example 7.13.

This model may also be estimated with the Cox PH model. We first set up the data the same way we did in Example 7.14 with *year* as the time variable, *newid* as the id variable, and *delinq* as the "failure" variable.

EXAMPLE 7.17   A Cox PH Event History Model of Repeated Delinquency

stset year, id(newid) fail(delinq)   *This appears on the command line*

id:	newid
failure event:	delinq ~= 0 & delinq ~= .
obs. time interval:	(year[_n-1], year]
exit on or before:	failure

2604	total obs.
858	obs. begin on or after (first) failure

1746	obs. remaining, representing
651	subjects
399	failures in single failure-per-subject data
1746	total analysis time at risk, at risk from t = 0
	earliest observed entry t = 0
	last observed exit t = 4

Then we simply run the Cox PH model as we did in Example 7.14:

stcox stress cohes, efron   *This appears on the command line*

failure _d:	delinq
analysis time _t:	year
id:	newid

Cox regression — Efron method for ties

No. of subjects	=	651	Number of obs	=	1746
No. of failures	=	399			
Time at risk	=	1746			
			LR chi2(2)	=	122.39
Log likelihood	=	−2364.3714	Prob > chi2	=	0.0000

_t _d	Haz. Ratio	Std. Err.	z	P > |z|	[95% Conf. Interval]	
stress	1.156791	.029285	5.753	0.000	1.100793	1.215637
cohes	.965997	.003977	−8.402	0.000	.958233	.973824

Once again, the hazard ratios for stress and cohesion are similar to the exponentiated coefficients (odds ratios) in Example 7.16's logistic regression model.

A key problem with this approach is that it does not consider that there is dependence among the observations. After all, the fact that adolescents are involved in delinquency one year probably influences their involvement in subsequent years. Therefore, we have violated a key assumption of regression analysis. We should reasonably expect some unknown degree of bias in the parameter estimates. Perhaps the best method for addressing this problem involves a random- or fixed-effects regression model, and its generalization—generalized estimating equations (GEEs). A discussion of these models is beyond the scope of this presentation (see, however, Diggle, Liang, and Zeger 1994), but a brief description is provided in Chapter 8.

Another problem, one that may affect the results of our repeated event model as well as most other types of event history models, concerns what is called *unobserved heterogeneity*. This concept involves, in a very basic sense, the fact that people bring all sorts of baggage along with them when they "decide" to engage in some type of event or perhaps simply experience some event. Take adolescent drug use as an example. Many personal, interpersonal, biological, and environmental factors influence an adolescent's decision to use drugs. We cannot expect to include all, or even a substantial fraction, of these factors in a statistical model that is designed to predict or explain drug use. In the linear regression model, all of these extraneous factors are absorbed into the error term, with the assumption that the "unobserved" factors are not correlated with explanatory variables that are included in the model. If these factors are correlated with some of the explanatory variables, then we have the common problem of omitted variable bias.

The problem is often complicated in event history models because there are likely to be omitted variables that affect the likelihood of entering and exiting some "state" (e.g., marriage), but that also affect (obviously) the hazard of the event (Yamaguchi 1991). Unobserved heterogeneity tends to bias estimates of the hazard rate. People with truly high hazards tend to drop out of the study earlier than others (because they experience the event quickly), so the remaining low-hazard people make it seem as if the hazard rate is low. This is especially problematic when the event of interest can occur only once. For instance, in our time-to-first-marriage example, we found a strongly decreasing hazard for those who cohabited, but this may be due to some unmeasured trait—common among some of those who cohabit—that led some to marry quickly (revisit Figure 7.4). Hence our estimate of the hazard rate among this group may be biased. This problem is most acute when hazard rates are decreasing. When they increase we may rest comfortable that the true hazard is increasing for at least some group (Allison 1995). It is somewhat reassuring that although the hazard rate coefficients tend to be biased toward zero, the standard errors are not biased. Once again, most observers recommend that we use random- or fixed-effects regression models to control for unobserved heterogeneity. Stata provides a full course of these models. An emerging set of alternative models that are designed to control for unobserved heterogeneity, known as frailty models, are described in Therneau and Grambsch (2000). Frailty models in Stata are discussed in Cleves, Gould, and Gutierrez (2002).

Conclusion

This chapter has provided a brief introduction to event history (survival) models. Although many presentations of event history models are divorced from discussions of other regression techniques, event history models share some interesting characteristics with the other models discussed in earlier chapters. Moreover, most statistical treatments of generalized linear models include a discussion of event history and survival models. The key "linking" characteristic is that event history models often use distributions that are drawn from the exponential family (e.g., exponential, log-normal, gamma) and thus are often, in a general sense, generalized linear models (Lindsey 1996; Dobson 1990). Other event history models, in particular the frequently used Cox proportional hazards model, are not generalized linear models. The Cox proportional hazards model is included in this chapter mainly because it provides such a flexible alternative to other event history models.

Nevertheless, there are many complicated issues when it comes to event history models. This chapter discusses some of them, such as censoring and time-varying covariates, in a simplified fashion. Other important issues, such as unobserved heterogeneity, have been described only briefly. But these and other issues are complicated enough to deserve more thorough treatment, hence the market for the many excellent textbooks devoted to event history and survival models (e.g, Cleves, Gould, and Gutierrez 2002; Therneau and Grambsch 2000; Kleinbaum 1996; Allison 1995; Blossfeld and Rohwer 1995; Lee 1992; Yamaguchi 1991).

Exercises

1. The data set *Firstsex* (available in Stata, SAS, and SPSS formats) includes a sample of more than 1,700 young men from the National Survey of Adolescent Males (NSAM, 1988–95). The variable *firstsex* measures the number of months from the respondent's 12th birthday until first intercourse. The data were collected until 1995, at which time about 10 percent of the respondents said they had never had intercourse. Hence they are censored observations. Censoring may be identified with the variable *eversex*, which is coded as 0 = never had intercourse, 1 = has had intercourse. We shall use these data to conduct the following exercises.

   a. Determine the following statistics: The total time at risk, the median survival time until first intercourse, and the average hazard rate per month.

   b. Construct a graph of the survival curve.

   c. Construct a graph of the survival curve stratified by *pstudent* (poor student, coded as 0 = no, 1 = yes). Comment on what the graph indicates about differences between poor students and others.

   d. Determine the median survival time for the two groups distinguished by *pstudent*. Is this difference statistically significant? What do you conclude about this difference?

2. **a.** Estimate two event history (survival) models, a log-normal and a Weibull, using the following independent variables: *famsize, pareduc, momdad, black, othrace, reborn,* and *pstudent.* Compare these two models statistically to determine which fits the data better.

   b. From your best fitting model, interpret the coefficients (transformed if you prefer) associated with the following independent variables: *momdad, black,* and *pstudent.*

   c. Discuss why an exponential model is not appropriate for this analysis.

3. **a.** Estimate a Cox PH model using the same set of independent variables as in 2.a.

   b. Interpret the coefficients associated with the following independent variables: *famsize, religvi,* and *pstudent.*

   c. Test the proportional hazards assumption. Indicate which, if any, variables do not follow this assumption. If you find any, discuss what might be going on with these variables. Use primarily a conceptual approach, but feel free to use graphical or other techniques to support your answer.

4. The data set *Drugprob* (available in Stata, SPSS, and SAS formats) contains repeated measures data from 750 adolescents and young adults who participated in 7 consecutive years of a study of family life. The Composite International Diagnostic Inventory (CIDI) was used to diagnose drug and alcohol problems among the participants. The CIDI is designed to render diagnoses of mental health disorders consistent with the Diagnostic and Statistical Manual (DSM IV) of the American Psychiatric Association. The following exercises are designed to predict a diagnosis of drug abuse (*drabuse,* coded as 0 = no, 1 = yes). Note the data structure of the file; there is one record for each person-year and once a diagnosis has occurred (say, for a person in the fourth year of data collection), the variable is coded as missing in subsequent years.

   a. Use a discrete-time event history model to predict *drabuse* using the following independent variables: *stress, fattach, depress, esteem, efficacy,* and *gender.*

   b. Interpret the coefficients (transformed if you prefer) associated with *esteem* and *gender.*

5. Extend the model in 4.a. by including *frdrug* (friend's drug use, logged to attenuate skewness) as an independent variable.

   a. Interpret the coefficient associated with *frdrug.*

   b. Compute the Deviance, AIC, and BIC for the two discrete-time event history models estimated thus far. Discuss what these statistics reveal about the two models.

6. Estimate the model in 4.a. using a Cox PH model.

   a. Interpret the coefficient associated with the variable *frdrug.*

   b. Test the proportional hazards assumption and discuss what this test reveals.

8

Where Do We Go from Here?

The seven substantive chapters of this book have discussed a powerful and widely applicable set of regression models. Under the general rubric of generalized linear models, we have learned when these models are applicable, how to use them, how to check some key model assumptions, and even, in some cases, when they are inappropriate. To review briefly, the generalized linear models discussed in the previous chapters are frequently appropriate when the dependent variable is measured continuously or discretely. There are models that are suitable when the dependent variable takes on two or more categories, when it is a count, or when it measures the time until some event occurs. And let's not forget the widely used linear regression model—it applies in many situations when we are faced with a continuous, normally distributed dependent variable. Even when a continuous dependent variable is not normally distributed, there is often a suitable transformation (e.g, natural logarithm, square root) that results in a variable that does follow a normal distribution. For the analyst who is confronted with a single dependent variable and multiple independent variables, the generalized linear models we have covered offer many appropriate options.

However, as noted, there are a number of situations when the generalized linear models that comprise the bulk of the examples break down. For example, many analysts now realize that some count variables contain conceptual nuances that violate key assumptions of the Poisson and negative binomial regression models. The processes that determine a count of zero and some positive count are often distinct (see Chapter 6). But we may also generalize this situation: The processes that determine a zero versus some other outcome often differ conceptually. A simple example involves income. Many analysts have tried to identify the determinants of personal income using a linear regression model. Personal income is typically transformed, perhaps using the natural logarithm (income is normally positively skewed). However, what might predict zero personal income? How about being out of the workforce? It is easy to think of numerous examples that follow this same route. We'll return to this issue when we discuss sample selection.

This chapter briefly introduces additional topics that we often face when attempting to predict or explain some outcome. Our time is almost spent, so the following topics are discussed quickly, with a recommendation that the interested reader track down the references cited to obtain additional information. Several of these topics are on the cutting edge of statistical research. So, in some cases, the software has not yet caught up to the ultimate needs of the analyst. It is important, nonetheless, to be aware of these issues and, assuming there are sufficient software tools available, to consider some of them statistically. Tipping our respective hats to the econometricians, we'll continue to discuss a topic that has already been introduced: Sample selection.

Sample Selection

Sample selection bias has been a long-running area of interest for econometricians. It was introduced in Chapter 6 when we discussed zero-inflated Poisson and negative binomial models. The conceptualization of sample selection bias is rather simple, although understanding how to overcome it is challenging.

Let's begin by extending the example from the last section. Although personal income may be measured in a number of ways, suppose that we treat it as a continuous variable and our goal is to identify a set of variables that predict it. Many studies, for example, predict personal income based on gender, education, race/ethnicity, job searching, and parental income and education. But think a little bit more carefully about personal income. Typically, a person must be employed in order to earn personal income. Yet many adults in the United States are not employed, at least in a formal sense (with all due respect to homemakers). Some do not even participate in the workforce. But potentially they could earn an income if they were working. Now suppose that we wished to predict personal income among a sample of adults in the United States, so we collected information on income and other characteristics (recall our Example 1.1 in Chapter 1). Then we constructed a regression model with personal income as the dependent variable. We should realize that our relevant sample is adults who are employed or otherwise earn an income; those who do not would be left out of the relevant sample. This makes our sample of those employed a non-random subsample of adults. Hence we may no longer use statistical significance tests in the same way (they are usually based on the assumption of random samples).

This problem may not seem to be overly taxing, but it often is. Now, you might be thinking that there is a simple solution. We'll code observations with no personal income as zero and then run the linear regression model. Unfortunately, this does not solve the *conceptual* problem: Those with zero income are a different group from those with positive income. We first must determine what makes them different before we can even think about predicting the positive values.

Many variables follow a similar pattern. In Chapter 6 we discussed problems with analyzing a count variable such as drinking alcohol beverages. If we wish to use a Poisson or a negative binomial regression model to predict counts of drinks in, say, a week, then we must also consider those who have not had a drink during our observation period. Conceptually, we are confronted with two subsamples within our overall sample: those who have values of interest to us (e.g., positive income dollars, positive counts of drinks) and those who do not engage in the behavior or otherwise are left out of the subsample. This problem is very similar to the censoring issues discussed in Chapter 7. For example, if analytic interest involves time to marriage, then those who do not marry are of little interest. Any way it is cut, we are left with analyzing a nonrandom subsample of our data.

Fortunately, there has been substantial attention to this issue. Hence there are many models that are suitable when faced with a sample selection problem. The choice of the model depends partly on whether the analyst wishes to model explicitly the selection process or leave it unanalyzed and simply analyze the subsample of interest. For example, if the variable of interest is continuous and normally distributed (or transformable to normality), the two most common sample selection models are tobit and Heckman's two-step approach. The tobit model is usually specified when the continuous dependent variable is unobserved below a certain threshold; in other words, it is left censored. It may also accommodate right censored variables. The tobit model does not attempt to model the selection process explicitly; rather, it takes into account the censoring of observations below (or above) a certain point. So the analyst may treat income as censored at or below zero dollars, but normally distributed (with an appropriate transformation) above zero dollars. Assuming the error term is normally distributed, tobit may then be used to estimate the impact of independent variables on personal income (see Roncek (1992) for a guide to interpretation). Even when the error term is not normally distributed, the tobit model may be adapted for use with censored distributions (Flood and Grasjo 2001; Fry and Orme 1998).

The Heckman two-step approach is often used when the analyst wishes to model both the selection component (e.g., in or out of workforce) and the "selected" component (e.g., personal income) of the distribution. The first step is typically a probit model to answer the "in-or-out of the subsample" question (see Chapter 3), followed by a linear regression model of the "selected" component of the dependent variable. Hence one may specify a different set of independent variables for the selection equation and the "selected" equation. Yet one may also use similar sets of independent variables in both equations. For example, one could use gender and race/ethnicity to predict any income and then use education, gender, and race/ethnicity to predict positive values of income.

As discussed in Chapter 6, the conceptual approach of these models has been generalized for use in Poisson and negative binomial models. One may predict zero counts and then predict positive counts using two distinct equations with zero inflated models (Zorn 1998). Moreover, the Heckman approach has also been modified for use with dichotomous dependent variables. Suppose that one is interested in a binary outcome such as whether or not sample members volunteer to work for their religious groups. Clearly, only those who belong to religious groups may report whether or not they volunteer, so we have a selection problem. The Heckman probit model takes a similar two-step procedure as that just outlined. But the second equation uses a probit model to estimate the "selected" portion of the dependent variable. Again, different sets or similar sets of independent variables may be used in the two equations. Stata, SAS/ETS, and LIMDEP contain routines for estimating sample selection models. Because the tobit model assumes censoring at either the left or right end of the distribution, SAS's *Proc Lifereg* may also be adapted to fit a tobit model. For technical details and examples from economics of these various sample selection procedures, see Greene (2000). Long (1997) and Breen (1996) provide concise overviews of these models. Stolzenberg and Relles (1997) and Winship and Mare (1992) review these models, discuss limitations of the Heckman two-step approach, and discuss emerging solutions to sample selection problems.

Endogeneity

Another issue that plagues many regression models involves specifying the correct dependent variable. We typically begin with the assumption that our dependent variable follows temporally the set of independent variables. Yet, in numerous situations, especially when analyzing cross-sectional data, it is not clear which came first. We also assume that our independent variables are not "caused" in some way by other independent variables, even though they may be correlated. A similar situation involves a hypothesized two-directional relationship between two variables. We may propose, for instance, that peer alcohol use leads adolescents to use alcohol, but perhaps adolescents who drink alcohol are more likely to make friends with others who also drink alcohol. Hence we are left with a bidirectional hypothesis or what some term a *reciprocal relationship* between two variables. The term *endogeneity* is often employed to characterize the general situation when the endogenous (dependent) variable is not specified well. To clarify the endogeneity issue, let's discuss two examples and their solutions.

First, suppose that we wish to analyze the impact of marijuana use on wages among a sample of adult workers in the United States. In the interests of tackling one problem at a time, we'll ignore the sample selection bias problem in this example. We'll also assume that wages are normally distributed, although the issues addressed here are problematic regardless of the distribution of the presumed dependent variable. The model we come up with is the following:

$$\text{Wages}_{(i)} = \alpha + \beta_1(\text{marijuana use}) + \beta_2(\text{education}) + \beta_3(\text{gender}) + \varepsilon_i \qquad (8.1)$$

The regression model represented in Equation 8.1 states that the three independent variables affect wages; wages are determined in a probabilistic sense by marijuana use, education, and gender. However, the equation does not recognize that marijuana use may also be affected by education and gender. Perhaps females and better educated people are less likely to use marijuana, and the effect of these variables on wages is, in part, routed through marijuana use. In the words of the economists, marijuana use is endogenous in this conceptualization. Figure 8.1 provides a picture of these possible relationships.

A second endogeneity issue involving Equation 8.1 is that not only might marijuana use affect wages, but wages may also affect marijuana use. Perhaps as people earn more money they realize that they cannot take the risk of using illegal drugs, so their probability of marijuana use decreases. On the other hand, those with more wages tend to have more disposable income, so they are better able to afford illegal substances such as marijuana. Higher wages may therefore increase the probability of marijuana use. In either case, both wages and marijuana use are endogenous. Figure 8.2 shows the endogencity of wages and marijuana use.

Note that all of the models discussed in previous chapters include a single dependent variable. In the endogeneity situation, there are two (or even more) dependent variables.

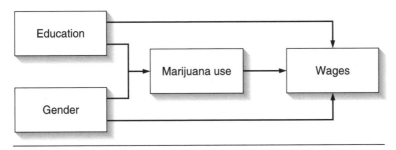

FIGURE 8.1

Fortunately, there are several solutions to this problem. Unfortunately, although there are few statistical roadblocks to finding solutions for any type of generalized linear model, the software has advanced to cover only a few.

The most common approach when the analyst hypothesizes that there are two or more endogenous variables is to estimate a set of simultaneous equations, one for each endogenous variable. Sociologists, psychologists, and education researchers often rely on structural equation models (SEMs; e.g., LISREL, EQS, AMOS) to estimate systems of simultaneous equations (Kline 1998). Some of these models have been expanded for use with binary or multinomial endogenous variables (Muthen 2001; the statistical software MPlus includes several of these models). An advantage of SEMs is that they allow the analyst to include measurement models and estimate them in the same set of equations. Hence one may presumably control for measurement error as well as endogeneity. Economists and political scientists tend to use two- or three-stage least squares or a maximum likelihood approach to simultaneous equations when estimating models with multiple dependent variables (Kennedy 1992). By making some (oftentimes stringent) assumptions, these approaches may be used to estimate models with bidirectional paths between endogenous variables, such as between wages and marijuana use (see Figure 8.2). Such models are much simpler to estimate if the analyst has access to longitudinal data.

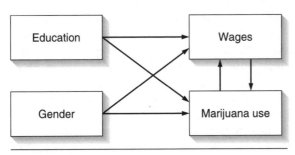

FIGURE 8.2

Longitudinal Data

We came across longitudinal data in Chapter 7. Event history models are designed for one type of longitudinal data. Other types include time series data, where aggregate-level observations (e.g., companies, counties, states), are collected repeatedly over time, and repeated cross-sectional data, such as the General Social Survey (GSS) or the National Election Survey (NES), cross-sectional surveys conducted in the United States about every two years. There are several good guides to analyzing these types of data (e.g., Firebaugh 1997; Bowerman and O'Connell 1993). Perhaps the most common type of longitudinal data is panel data, a term that economists use to identify data collected from individuals over time (Hsiao 1989). In fact, this type of data is so common and of so much concern in applied statistics that *panel data* and *longitudinal data* are often considered synonymous terms (Diggle, Liang, and Zeger 1994).

The advantages of longitudinal data over cross-sectional data should be obvious. First, as suggested in the previous section, the causal order of variables is much easier to ascertain in longitudinal data. Second, sticky issues such as age, period, and cohort effects are simpler to sort out with longitudinal data. Suppose we have cross-sectional data collected in 2002 and we wish to predict political affiliation: Democrat, Republican, or Independent. Using a multinomial logistic regression model, we find that 18–24 year olds are more likely to report being Democrat and those 60 and older are more likely to report being Republican. How do we interpret this pattern? Does it mean that when people are younger we expect them to be Democrats, but as they age they move to the Republican party? This implies an *age* effect. Or are those who were born between 1978 and 1984 more likely to be Democrats because they came of age during a period when Democrats controlled the Executive Branch of the U.S. government? This implies a *cohort* or *period* effect. Cross-sectional data are not helpful for sorting out these effects. Longitudinal data are better designed for determining these effects because we may measure *changes within individuals* and distinguish them from *differences across individuals* (Bijleveld and van der Kamp 1998). The ability to distinguish these *within-unit* and *between-unit* differences also gives us an opportunity to control for unobserved heterogeneity, which, as discussed in Chapter 7, often plagues the interpretation of regression models (Hamerle and Ronning 1995).

Most of the models described in previous chapters are amenable to longitudinal analysis. We have seen a couple of examples of this in Chapter 7 when we explored the use of discrete-time event history models to analyze repeated events. However, as mentioned in that section, using logistic regression or multinomial logistic regression (or any of our generalized linear models) to analyze longitudinal data forces us to make a strong assumption. We must assume that the observations are independent. However, it is clear that data collected from individuals over time violate this assumption. An observation at time one from person 116 is not likely to be independent from an observation at time two from this same person. This problem is compounded many times over as we collect data from the same individuals repeatedly over time.

Various solutions to this problem have been developed. The most frequently used regression solution, at least in the last couple of decades, involves random-effects and fixed-effects models. The statistical underpinnings of these models are described in Hamerle and Ronning (1995) and Hsiao (1989). The choice between these two models is primarily conceptual. The fixed-effects model is normally used when the analyst wishes to generalize only to the sample members in the data set. The random-effects model is appropriate when the members are drawn from a larger population. A disadvantage of the random-effects model is that it assumes that individual-specific effects are uncorrelated with the other independent variables (Greene 2000). So, for example, when studying the impact of marijuana use on wages, the random-effects model assumes that physiological or environmental factors that are constant within persons are not correlated with marijuana use. Such an assumption may be unrealistic.

A statistical test known as the Hausman test is often used to adjudicate between the fixed-effects and random-effects models. The test's null hypothesis is that the individual-specific effects are not correlated with the independent variables, and therefore the random-effects model is appropriate. Stata implements several of these models using its set of *xt* commands, such as *xtreg* (for continuous, normally distributed dependent variables), *xtlogit* and *xtprobit* (for binary dependent variables), and *xtpois* and *xtnbreg* (for count dependent variables). All of these allow the estimation of fixed-effects or random-effects models. LIMDEP also has routines that estimate these models. Chen and Kuo (2001) show how to estimate a random-effects multinomial logistic regression model using SAS.

An extension of these models that is somewhat more flexible falls under a class known as generalized estimating equations (GEEs). GEEs may be used to estimate most generalized linear models, such as those represented in Stata's *glm* or SAS's *Proc Genmod* commands. An advantage of GEEs over other methods of longitudinal data analysis is that they allow different correlation structures to be assumed within units in the model. To see what this means in a practical sense, let's return to our model from Chapter 7 of multiple episodes of delinquency across years. Recall that some adolescents reported no involvement in delinquency, but some reported involvement in one year, others in two years, and so forth. We analyzed these data (*event4*) using a logistic regression model. However, at that time we realized that the model assumed that the observations were uncorrelated within individuals over time. Clearly this is an unrealistic assumption. Delinquency is bound to be correlated over time within individuals. The GEE approach allows us to consider several possible correlation structures. Now we'll analyze the data set *event4* using Stata's *xtgee* command. Before estimating a GEE model in Stata, we first must tell it the individual-level identifier and the time identifier:

EXAMPLE 8.1   *GEE Model of Delinquency Using Longitudinal Data*

---

iis(newid)   *This appears on the command line*

tis(year)   *This appears on the command line*

We may then use the *xtgee* command to specify the model.

```
xtgee delinq stress cohes, family(binomial) link(logit) corr(independent)
   *This appears on the command line*
```

GEE population-averaged model			Number of obs	=	2604
Group variable:	newid		Number of groups	=	651
Link:	logit		Obs per group:	min =	4
Family:	binomial			avg =	4.0
Correlation:	independent			max =	4
			Wald chi2(2)	=	216.43
Scale parameter:	1		Prob > chi2	=	0.0000
Pearson chi2(2604):	2592.09		Deviance	=	3114.66
Dispersion (Pearson):	.995427		Dispersion	=	1.196116

delinq	Coef.	Std. Err.	z	P > |z|	[95% Conf. Interval]	
stress	.185797	.024757	7.50	0.000	.137274	.234320
cohes	−.043407	.003855	−11.26	0.000	−.050962	−.035851
_cons	1.179169	.217787	5.41	0.000	.752314	1.606024

```
xtcorr     *This appears on the command line after the xtgee model runs*
```

Estimated within-newid correlation matrix R:

	c1	c2	c3	c4
r1	1.0000			
r2	0.0000	1.0000		
r3	0.0000	0.0000	1.0000	
r4	0.0000	0.0000	0.0000	1.0000

This model is very similar to the model estimated in Chapter 7. The coefficients are different mainly because this is a population average model (see Diggle, Liang and Zeger (1994) for an explanation of this model) and we do not explicitly include the *year* variable in the model set-up. Note also that the command structure in *xtgee* is very similar to Stata's *glm*, with family and link functions specified. A key difference is that we also specify a correlation structure. The subcommand *correlation(independent)* specifies that the correlation of the observations within individuals is zero. This results in the estimated correlation matrix that follows the *xtcorr* postcommand. As mentioned previously, zero correlations are unlikely, especially when modeling delinquency.

There are several alternative correlation structures allowed in Stata. These may also be implemented in SAS using *Proc Genmod*. We'll limit this presentation to three of the most common: exchangeable, autoregressive(1), and unstructured. We'll continue the example using an exchangeable correlation structure.

EXAMPLE 8.2 *A GEE Model of Delinquency Using Longitudinal Data—Exchangeable Correlation*

xtgee delinq stress cohes, family(binomial) link(logit) corr(exchangeable)
   This appears on the command line

GEE population-averaged model		Number of obs	= 2604
Group variable:	newid	Number of groups	= 651
Link:	logit	Obs per group: min =	4
Family:	binomial	avg =	4.0
Correlation:	exchangeable	max =	4
		Wald chi2(2)	= 118.79
Scale parameter:	1	Prob > chi2	= 0.0000

delinq	Coef.	Std. Err.	z	P > |z|	[95% Conf. Interval]	
stress	.149926	.024867	6.03	0.000	.101187	.198665
cohes	−.034311	.004113	−8.34	0.000	−.042373	−.026250
_cons	.790010	.231322	3.42	0.001	.336627	1.243394

xtcor   *This appears on the command line after the xtgee model runs*

Estimated within-newid correlation matrix R:

	c1	c2	c3	c4
r1	1.0000			
r2	0.3458	1.0000		
r3	0.3458	0.3458	1.0000	
r4	0.3458	0.3458	0.3458	1.0000

Note that the coefficients and z-values are smaller in the second GEE model. Also notice that the correlation structure differs. We have now estimated an exchangeable structure, which assumes that the correlations are identical irrespective of the year. A correlation of 0.35 is substantial and suggests that delinquency is related within individuals over time. However, assuming the same correlation across years may also be unrealistic. Perhaps we should assume that the correlations decay over time. This is shown in the autoregressive model:

EXAMPLE 8.3   *A GEE Model of Delinquency Using Longitudinal Data–Autoregressive Correlation*

xtgee delinq stress cohes, family(binomial) link(logit) corr(ar1)   *This appears on the command line*

GEE population-averaged model				Number of obs	=	2604
Group and time vars:	newid year			Number of groups	=	651
Link:	logit			Obs per group: min =		4
Family:	binomial			avg =		4.0
Correlation:	AR(1)			max =		4
				Wald chi2(2)	=	119.54
Scale parameter:	1			Prob > chi2	=	0.0000

delinq	Coef.	Std. Err.	z	P > |z|	[95% Conf. Interval]	
stress	.145876	.025004	5.83	0.000	.096870	.194883
cohes	−.034577	.004110	−8.41	0.000	−.042631	−.026522
_cons	.797724	.231539	3.45	0.001	.343916	1.251532

xtcorr   *This appears on the command line after the xtgee model runs*

Estimated within-newid correlation matrix R:

	c1	c2	c3	c4
r1	1.0000			
r2	0.4181	1.0000		
r3	0.1748	0.4181	1.0000	
r4	0.0731	0.1748	0.4181	1.0000

First, notice that the coefficients and z-values in this model and in the model with an exchangeable correlation structure are not much different. Therefore, we seem to be converging to a solution (if other assumptions are not violated; see, generally, Diggle, Liang, and Zeger 1994). Second, the estimated within-unit correlation matrix differs from the matrix in the last model. This is because we have assumed that the correlation decays over time. The decay follows what is known as an autoregressive(1) pattern which is $\{(t-1)^{q+1},$ $(t-2)^{q+2}, ...\}$. In Example 8.3, the correlations are $0.418^2 = 0.175$ and $0.418^3 = 0.073$. Note that the presumed within-unit correlations diminish as the time periods become further apart. This seems realistic in the delinquency example since within-person correlations are likely to be stronger for, say, times 1 and 2 than for times 1 and 3 or 1 and 4.

Finally, there is the unstructured correlation, which allows the correlations to be freely estimated from the data. In models with many time periods, or with a small number of units, we can easily run out of degrees of freedom trying to estimate so much information. In this model, however, we don't have a problem.

EXAMPLE 8.4 *A GEE Model of Delinquency Using Longitudinal Data–Unstructured Correlation*

xtgee delinq stress cohes, family(binomial) link(logit) corr(unstructured)
  This appears on the command line

GEE population-averaged model				Number of obs	=	2604
Group and time vars:	newid year			Number of groups	=	651
Link:	logit			Obs per group:	min =	4
Family:	binomial				avg =	4.0
Correlation:	unstructured				max =	4
				Wald chi2(2)	=	112.79
Scale parameter:	1			Prob > chi2	=	0.0000

delinq	Coef.	Std. Err.	z	P > |z|	[95% Conf. Interval]	
stress	.146634	.024992	5.87	0.000	.097650	.195617
cohes	−.033436	.004125	−8.11	0.000	−.041520	−.025351
_cons	.738189	.232348	3.18	0.001	.282796	1.193582

xtcorr   *This appears on the command line after the xtgee model runs*

Estimated within-newid correlation matrix R:

	c1	c2	c3	c4
r1	1.0000			
r2	0.3858	1.0000		
r3	0.2851	0.4589	1.0000	
r4	0.2159	0.3233	0.4118	1.0000

We seem to have converged to a consistent set of results. All three models that relax the assumption of no correlation within units display very similar results in terms of coefficients and z-values. There is some decay in the correlations, although not as dramatic as the autoregressive(1) pattern implies. In the final analysis, therefore, any of the correlation structures, with the exception of the independent structure, would lead to similar conclusions about the associations between stressful life events, cohesion, and delinquency. However, we would overestimate these effects if we assumed that there was no correlation within adolescents over time. Moreover, comparing these models to a random-effects regression model indicates that the latter also overestimates the coefficients by a substantial degree. Hence, in this situation, the GEE models seem preferable.

GEE models are becoming ever more popular among those who analyze longitudinal data. As shown in the preceding examples, GEEs offer substantial flexibility. Not only do they allow the estimation of different correlation structures within units, they also allow the estimation of several generalized linear models, including logistic, probit,

Poisson, and negative binomial. Duncan et al. (1995) provide a nice example that applies GEEs in the social and behavioral sciences. Horton and Lipsitz (1999) describe and show examples from statistical software, including SAS and Stata, designed to estimate GEEs. Bijleveld and van der Kamp (1998, Chapter 4) and Duncan et al. (1999) report how to estimate longitudinal models in a structural equation modeling framework. These latter models are often termed *growth curve models*.

Multilevel Models

A set of models that may be used in a similar manner is known generally as *multilevel models* (also termed *hierarchical models*). Before briefly describing how these are used to analyze longitudinal data, we will discuss multilevel data and why they are so useful in applied statistics. Recall (again) that our typical regression model assumes that observations are independent. Although we showed how GEE models relax this assumption, most of our generalized linear models implicitly made this assumption. Now think about data that are not independent, but rather are nested. For example, Table 8.1 shows data that are nested: Students are sampled within particular schools.

Looking over the table, notice that the data set includes test scores of fifteen students who are nested within three schools. Evidently, then, the observations (students) are not independent. Students in the same school are probably more likely to share characteristics than students who attend different schools. Multilevel models are designed to take this dependence into account and allow the analyst to come up with unbiased estimates of standard errors (Goldstein 1995). However, they also have other advantages.

Think about what else might be of interest in these types of data. Perhaps the analyst is interested in whether the average test scores differ across schools, after controlling for

TABLE 8.1 *An Example of Nested (Multilevel) Data*

School number	Student number	Test Score
101	1	91
101	2	76
101	3	88
101	4	82
101	5	79
433	6	98
433	7	91
433	8	85
433	9	79
433	10	80
433	11	66
676	12	95
676	13	75
676	14	87
676	15	88

the fact that students who attend these schools differ in terms of family income, parents' education, and other *individual-level attributes*. Hence, one is interested in whether there are differences by schools that are not accounted for by individual-level differences. Another area of interest is determining whether these differences are due to school-level characteristics, such as the average number of pupils per teacher, the average teacher salary, and other factors. Plewis (1997) provides a review of several topics of interest to the educational community. He also gives a concise description of multilevel models and how they are used to investigate these topics.

We may generalize this situation widely to many issues of interest to the social and behavioral sciences, business research, educational studies, and many other disciplines. Some examples include ecologists studying organism–environment interaction, economists examining labor markets and job turnover, criminologists investigating prison culture and inmate dissatisfaction, historians and political scientists comparing peasant rebellions in various nation-states, marketing researchers studying satisfaction with product layout in various types of retail establishments, geographers analyzing land use patterns in different climatic regions, or even astronomers observing black hole formation across quadrants of space. In each of these situations, analysts encounter multilevel data.

A simple example of a multilevel model is represented in Equation 8.2.

$$
\begin{aligned}
\text{(1) Individual-level:} \quad Y_{ij} &= \alpha_j + \beta_{lj} X_{lj} + \varepsilon_{ij} \\
\text{(2) Group-level:} \quad \alpha_j &= \gamma_0 + v_{0j} \\
\beta_{lj} &= \gamma_l + v_{lj}
\end{aligned}
\tag{8.2}
$$

Suppose that Y represents an individual-level dependent variable such as personal income in dollars and X represents an individual-level independent variable such as education in years. Note that unlike the regression models we saw in earlier chapters, Y includes not only the subscript i (denoting individuals) but also a subscript j. This indicates that the dependent variable varies not only across *level one units* (individuals), but also across *level-two units* (e.g., neighborhoods, counties). Notice also that we permit the effects in the model to be disaggregated: Both the intercept and the regression coefficient are allowed to vary across the j-units. In the single-level regression model, these quantities are fixed. The equation $\alpha_j = \gamma_0 + v_0$ indicates that the intercept equals some average value across level-two units (γ_0) plus a random component (v_0), so that it varies in some fashion across the level-two units. If only the intercept is allowed to vary, we have what is known as a *random intercept model*. This is similar to the random-effects model described in the section on longitudinal data. If the regression coefficient is also allowed to vary, as in the second group-level equation in 8.2, we have a *random coefficients model*. For example, perhaps we hypothesize that not only does income vary across individuals, but it also varies across neighborhoods—a random intercept. Moreover, we could hypothesize that the impact of education on income varies across neighborhoods—a random coefficient model.

Multilevel models may be extended to more than two levels. For instance, analysts might be interested in students nested in classrooms, with classrooms nested in schools. This implies a three-level model. Numerous other data structures are possible. These models may also be used to determine whether level-two characteristics, such as neighborhood poverty, affect the associations among the level-one variables. For example, we might question whether neighborhood poverty affects the association between education and personal income at the individual level. This involves what is termed a *cross-level interaction effect*.

Multilevel models offer a straightforward way to analyze longitudinal data. If we envision level one as time periods and level two as individuals, then we have a two-level multilevel model: Time periods are nested within individuals. There are many other issues involved in multilevel models. Most important for our purposes is that multilevel models have been developed for each of our generalized linear models, from the linear model to Poisson and event history models.

Goldstein (1995) provides the technical details of multilevel models; Plewis (1997) shows their utility in educational research; Steenbergen and Jones (2002), Hoffmann (2001), and Ringdal (1992) furnish elementary overviews, and Singer (1998) presents a concise description of how to estimate multilevel models using SAS's *Proc Mixed* routine. Littell et al. (1996) provide a thorough presentation of the *Proc Mixed* routine, including how to use it to estimate GEE models for longitudinal data. Bijleveld and van der Kamp's (1998) book contains a chapter on using multilevel models to analyze longitudinal data. Stata has a downloadable command file, *gllamm* (generalized linear latent and mixed models), that is appropriate for fitting multilevel models to a variety of generalized linear models. There is also specialized statistical software designed to estimate a variety of multilevel models; the most prominent examples are HLM and MlwiN. Use of multilevel models in substantive research may be found in Jones and Jorgensen (2003), Hoffmann (2002), Crosnoe (2001), Hoshino (2001), Ramamurti (2000), Hoffmann and Cerbone (1999), Gilbert and Shultz (1998), Rountree and Land (1996), and Rumberger (1995).

Nonparametric Regression

Most of the models presented in the preceding chapters share a common characteristic: They are based on a parametric approach. In other words, we assume a particular shape or form for the dependent variable (actually for the residuals) that is represented by a member of the family of distributions (e.g., logistic, Gaussian, Poisson). However, making such an assumption may overly simplify a complex distribution of the variable or a complicated relationship among some set of variables. Recent advances in nonparametric regression allow greater flexibility for determining relationships among variables.

Many readers have probably been introduced to nonparametric methods in introductory statistics courses. Statistical techniques based on ranks rather than parametric distributions are a common class of nonparametric methods. The median test, the Wilcoxon rank-sum test, and the Kruskal-Wallis test are often used as alternatives to parametric tests such as *t*-tests or ANOVA models to compare treatments in populations (Lehman 1998). However, a different class of nonparametric models has recently been developed to analyze data in a regression context.

Early nonparametric regression models were limited primarily to two variables. Kernel regression and loess (locally weighted regression) models were designed initially to determine bivariable relationships by taking a subset of the joint distribution, estimating the relationship, taking another subset, estimating the relationship, and so forth (hence the term *locally*). The subset, also known as the *neighborhood* or *span*, is determined by the analyst, but it typically spans no more than 50 percent of the data. Figure 8.3 provides a graphical representation of a simple loess regression. Recall from Chapter 1 that the *USdata* data set contains several variables that measure state-level characteristics in 1995. The figure shows the bivariable relationship between the violent crime rate and per capita income. The straight line demonstrates the linear relationship represented in an OLS regression; the curve shows the nonparametric relationship represented by a loess smoother using a 50 percent span.

The linear association implies a positive association between per capita income and the violent crime rate. But note that the loess smoother indicates that the relationship turns negative at high values of per capita income. Of course, this may simply represent an influential observation or two. Also notice the bump in the loess line toward the right end of the distribution; it is influenced by several states with high crime rates. These are worth exploring further. In fact, loess regression often forces us to consider relationships in more detail.

There is no longer an impediment to estimating nonparametric regression models with multiple independent variables. A class of models known as Generalized Additive Models (GAMs) has been developed and implemented in several software packages (including SAS and Stata). These models allow multiple independent variables, but do so by using a smoothing function one variable at a time (Hastie and Tibshirani 1990). They also allow various distributions and link functions as starting points for the analysis, so their tie to generalized linear models is easy to recognize. A word of warning, however: The GAM

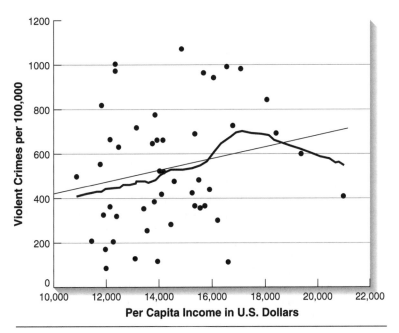

FIGURE 8.3

approach to nonparametric regression is heavily data driven, especially in this early stage of its evolution. Theory tends to play little role in the use of these models. Moreover, they can rapidly become highly complex, with multiple parameters swamping the analyst, thus making interpretation difficult. If, however, parametric approaches prove unsatisfactory or if there is little theory to guide model building, GAMs provide a welcome alternative (Myers, Montgomery, and Vining 2002; Fox 2000).

To see a GAM in action, let's return to the example shown in Figure 8.3. It depicts a nonparametric regression model with the violent crime rate as the dependent variable and per capita income as the independent variable. There appears to be a nonlinear association between these two variables. Assuming that there is little theory to guide our conceptualization of violent crime rates at the state level, we'll extend the model in a GAM context to search for additional predictors of this dependent variable. Admittedly, this is a poor assumption; there is actually substantial research on state-level crime rates (see, e.g., Kawachi, Kennedy, and Wilkinson 1999; Johnson 1996). But for our interests, we'll pretend to be on the cutting edge of research on this topic.

Example 8.5 uses SAS's *Proc GAM* in the following way. First, the GAM is used to explore nonparametrically the association between violent crime rates (*violrate*) and per capita incomes (*perinc*), unemployment rates (*unemprat*), and gross state products (GSP; *gsprod*). Then, as suggested by Xiang (2002), we'll use this information to model the predictors of violent crime rates using *Proc Genmod*. The GAM is specified using the following SAS code:

EXAMPLE 8.5   *A Generalized Additive Model of Violent Crime Rates in the U.S.*

This set of commands asks SAS for a GAM model

```
proc gam;
    model violrate =    spline(unemprat, df=3)
                        spline(gsprod, df=3)
                        spline(perinc, df=3)
                        / dist=gaussian;
    output out=estimate p uclm lclm;
run;
```

The following is the SAS output

The GAM Procedure
Dependent Variable: VIOLRATE
Smoothing Model Component(s): spline(UNEMPRAT) spline(GSPPROD) spline(PERINC)

Summary of Input Data Set	
Number of Observations	49
Number of Missing Observations	2
Distribution	Gaussian
Link Function	Identity

Iteration Summary and Fit Statistics	
Final Number of Backfitting Iterations	8

(continued)

EXAMPLE 8.5 *(Continued)*

Final Backfitting Criterion	3.107855E-9
The Deviance of the Final Estimate	1701498.2031

The local score algorithm converged.

Regression Model Analysis
Parameter Estimates

Parameter	Parameter Estimate	Standard Error	t	Value Pr > │t│
Intercept	157.01604	241.08476	0.65	0.5187
Linear(UNEMPRAT)	80.11259	25.58369	3.13	0.0033
Linear(GSPROD)	0.00077	0.00021	3.69	0.0007
Linear(PERINC)	−0.00644	0.00972	−0.66	0.5119

Smoothing Model Analysis
Fit Summary for Smoothing Components

Component	Smoothing Parameter	DF	GCV	Num Unique Obs
Spline(UNEMPRAT)	0.997596	3.000000	32973	32
Spline(GSPROD)	0.998988	3.000000	41172	49
Spline(PERINC)	0.999393	3.000000	41172	49

Smoothing Model Analysis
Analysis of Deviance

Source	DF	Sum of Squares	Chi-Square	Pr > ChiSq
Spline(UNEMPRAT)	3.00000	44765	1.0261	0.7949
Spline(GSPROD)	3.00000	466346	10.6891	0.0135
Spline(PERINC)	3.00000	112128	2.5701	0.4628

The output shows the GAM results. Note that we ask for the *spline* of each independent variable. This is a shorthand way of asking for a number of "bends" in the proposed associations implied in the model. For example, in Figure 8.3 it appears that there are at least two bends in the association between violent crime rates and per capita income. By asking for three degrees of freedom, we are asking for two bends in the data. This may be increased to more bends, but two is often a useful starting point. Note also that we are assuming a Gaussian (normal) distribution (with identity link) for the initial estimates.

The output shows the initial estimates from a linear regression model using MLE. From this model we may see that unemployment rates and GSPs have a significant linear association with violent crime rates. The next part of the output shows the smoothing parameter followed by the Analysis of Deviance table. This table is useful to determine whether our independent variables are associated nonparametrically with violent crime rates (Xiang 2002). Note that only the GSPs are associated significantly with violent crime rates. We'll use this information to develop a linear regression model with a quadratic term for GSP. This is what follows:

EXAMPLE 8.6   *A Linear Regression Model of Violent Crime Rates in the U.S.*

This set of commands asks SAS for a GLM model

```
proc genmod;
    model violrate = gsprod gsprod*gsprod / link=identity dist=normal;
run;
```

The following is the SAS output

The GENMOD Procedure
Model Information

Data Set	WORK.ESTIMATE	
Distribution	Normal	
Link Function	Identity	
Dependent Variable	VIOLRATE	violent crime rate per 100,000
Observations Used	49	

Criteria for Assessing Goodness of Fit

Criterion	DF	Value	Value/DF
Deviance	46	2459770.3002	53473.2674
Scaled Deviance	46	49.0000	1.0652
Pearson Chi-Square	46	2459770.3002	53473.2674
Scaled Pearson X2	46	49.0000	1.0652
Log Likelihood		−334.7101	

Analysis of Parameter Estimates

Parameter	Estimate	Standard Error	Wald 95% Confidence Limits		Chi-Square	Pr > ChiSq
Intercept	350.3841	56.0832	240.4630	460.3052	39.03	<.0001
GSPROD	0.0018	0.0005	0.0007	0.0028	10.88	0.0010
GSPROD*GSPROD	−0.0000	0.0000	−0.0000	0.0000	3.44	0.0637
Scale	224.0522	22.6327	183.8082	273.1075		

NOTE: The scale parameter was estimated by maximum likelihood.

The results of *Proc Genmod* provide modest evidence that there is a nonlinear association between state-level GSPs and violent crime rates. The relationship, based on the coefficients, appears to follow an inverted U-shaped pattern. Again, it is important to emphasize the exploratory nature of this analysis. We began with the assumption that we knew little theoretically about violent crime rates at the state level. If we had checked the literature on crime rates carefully, we might have discovered that a nonlinear association between economic activity and crime has been found in the past. Moreover, we probably would have also discovered that studying the association between unemployment rates and crime rates is a common endeavor in criminology. Thus, there would have been little need to resort to the GAM approach.

Even though there are several cautionary tales to tell about them, GAMs are useful in a number of ways. GAMs provide a powerful way to analyze relationships, especially for exploratory work or when the distribution of the dependent variable appears highly unusual. We should always pursue the simplest model to predict or explain our dependent variable, but sometimes nature does not cooperate and we find the search for good models tortuous. GAMs provide another statistical tool that makes research a little bit easier. Examples of and suggestions about using GAMs to model data may be found in Fox (2000), Lee et al. (2000), Beck and Jackman (1998), Yatchew (1998), Chilcoat and Schutz (1996), and Jones and Wrigley (1995).

Conclusion

This chapter has quickly reviewed several issues that are slightly beyond the objectives of this book. Its goal is to provide an introduction to these issues, with no claim that we have exhausted the possibilities or thoroughly reviewed them. Moreover, there are many other topics germane to generalized linear models that we have not addressed, such as model selection procedures, Bayesian analysis, missing data, generalized least squares (GLS), partial least squares (PLS), robust regression, quantile regression, bootstrapping, data mining, latent variables, generalized method of moment (GMM) estimators, weighting, and alternative probability distributions (e.g., inverse Gaussian, gamma, Pareto, extreme value). We must limit the presentation in some way, and issues involving sample selection bias, endogeneity, longitudinal data, multilevel data, and nonparametric regression can be thorny enough. Fortunately, additional statistical tools are constantly being developed that will help the analyst discover the best model when faced with the problems created by these and other issues. The reader who confronts problems that are not solved by the typical generalized linear model will, hopefully, be able to use the information in this chapter as a starting point. The references cited in each section should be consulted for additional information about these issues. They will also send the reader on the way toward mastering techniques that are well beyond the scope of this book.

Appendix

SPSS, SAS, and Stata Programs for Examples in Chapters

The following programs are designed to allow interested users to replicate the analyses found in the chapter examples using as many of the three common programs as apply. Please be aware, however, that statistical software packages often come with unique options and output, so that output based on the three types of programs may differ. Some of the examples may provide only partial replication. However, all three software packages are updated routinely, so users are encouraged to check the most recent software documentation to determine if conventions have changed, new features hae been added, and so forth. In some cases, the producers may have updated their software so that it now allows full replication of the examples.

Chapter 1

Example 1.1

SPSS Syntax

```
REGRESSION
  /MISSING LISTWISE
  /STATISTICS COEFF OUTS R ANOVA
  /CRITERIA=PIN(.05) POUT(.10)
  /NOORIGIN
  /DEPENDENT income
  /METHOD=ENTER educate gender race pasei .
EXECUTE .
```

SAS Code

```
libname glm '[place data subdirectory here]';
data one; set glm.gss96;
```

```
PROC REG;
  model income=educate gender race pasei / stb;
run;
```

Example 1.2

SPSS Syntax

```
REGRESSION
  /MISSING LISTWISE
  /STATISTICS COEFF OUTS R ANOVA
  /CRITERIA=PIN(.05) POUT(.10)
  /NOORIGIN
  /DEPENDENT violrate
  /METHOD=ENTER unemprat gsprod
  /SAVE COOK .
EXECUTE .
```

SAS Code

```
libname glm '[place data subdirectory here]';
data one; set glm.usdata;

PROC REG;
  model violrate=unemprat gsprod / stb;
  output out=new cookd=c;
run;
```

Example 1.3

SPSS Syntax

At the time of writing, SPSS did not include a robust regression routine.

SAS Code

SAS/IML includes several robust regression routines. Check the SAS/IML documentation for more information.

Example 1.4

SPSS Syntax

```
COMPUTE gen_educ = gender * educate .
EXECUTE .

REGRESSION
  /MISSING LISTWISE
  /STATISTICS COEFF OUTS R ANOVA COLLIN TOL
  /CRITERIA=PIN(.05) POUT(.10)
```

```
/NOORIGIN
/DEPENDENT income
/METHOD=ENTER gender educate gen_educ .
```

```
COMPUTE c_educ = educate - 13.3648 .
EXECUTE .
```

```
COMPUTE gen_cedu = gender * c_educ.
EXECUTE.
```

```
REGRESSION
 /MISSING LISTWISE
 /STATISTICS COEFF OUTS R ANOVA COLLIN TOL
 /CRITERIA=PIN(.05) POUT(.10)
 /NOORIGIN
 /DEPENDENT income
 /METHOD=ENTER gender c_edu gen_cedu .
EXECUTE .
```

SAS Code

```
libname glm '[place data subdirectory here]';
data one; set glm.gss96;
```

```
gen_educ=gender*educate;
proc reg;
  model income=gender educate gen_educ / stb vif;
run;
```

```
data two; set one;
```

```
c_educate=educate - 13.3648;
```

```
gen_ceduc=gender*c_educate;
```

```
proc reg;
  model income=gender c_educate gen_ceduc / stb vif;
run;
```

Chapter 2

Example 2.1

SPSS Syntax

At the time of writing, SPSS did not include a straightforward way to estimate a linear regression model using maximum likelihood estimation.

SAS Code

```
libname glm '[place data subdirectory here]';
```

```
data one; set glm.gss96;

proc genmod;
  model attend= / dist=normal
                  link=identity lrci;
run;

proc genmod;
  model attend=gender race educate / dist=normal
                                      link=identity lrci;
run;

proc genmod;
  model attend=gender race educate prayer / dist=normal
                                            link=identity lrci;
run;
```

Chapter 3

Example 3.1

Stata Code

```
tabulate satlife gender
```

SAS Code

```
libname glm '[place data subdirectory here]';
data one; set glm.depress;

proc freq;
  tables satlife*gender;
run;
```

Example 3.2

Stata Code

```
logit satlife gender, or
predict p
```

SAS Code

```
libname glm '[place data subdirectory here]';
data one; set glm.depress;

proc freq;
  tables satlife*gender;
run;
```

```
proc genmod descending;
  model satlife=gender / dist=bin
                         link=logit lrci;
run;
```

[or]

```
proc logistic descending;
  model satlife=gender / expb rsq;
  output out=predict1 pred=p1;
run;
```

Example 3.3

Stata Code

```
logit satlife gender iq age weight, or
predict p
```

SAS Code

```
libname glm '[place data subdirectory here]';
data one; set glm.depress;

proc genmod descending;
  model satlife=gender / dist=bin
                         link=logit lrci;
run;
```

[or]

```
proc logistic descending;
  model satlife=gender iq age weight / expb rsq;
  output out=predict2 pred=p2;
run;
```

Example 3.4

SPSS Syntax

```
LOGISTIC REGRESSION VAR=volrelig
  /METHOD=ENTER zeducate zage gender
  /CRITERIA PIN(.05) POUT(.10) ITERATE(20) CUT(.5) .
EXECUTE .
```

SAS Code

```
libname glm '[place data subdirectory here]';
data one; set glm.gss96;
```

```
proc logistic descending;
     model volrelig=zeducate zage gender / expb rsq;
     output out=predict3 pred=p3;
run;
```

[or]

```
proc genmod descending;
  model volrelig=zeducate zage gender / dist=bin
                    link=logit lrci;
run;
```

Example 3.5

SPSS Syntax

SPSS's probit routine is not used in the same way as those of Stata or SAS. Check the SPSS documentation for more information.

SAS Code

```
libname glm '[place data subdirectory here]';
data one; set glm.depress;
```

```
/* reverse code satlife so that the model will predict the probabilty of 1 not 0 */
satlife1 = 1 - satlife;
```

```
proc probit;
  class satlife1;
  model satlife1=gender;
run;
```

Example 3.6

SPSS Syntax

SPSS's probit routine is not used in the same way as those of Stata or SAS. Check the SPSS documentation for more information.

SAS Code

```
libname glm '[place data subdirectory here]';
data one; set glm.depress;
```

```
/* need to compute the standardized values for this model */
/* newage is standardized age and newiq is standardized iq */
/* check the SAS documentation to determine how to */
/* compute standardized values */
```

```
proc probit;
```

```
  class satlife1;
  model satlife1=gender sleep newage newiq;
  output out=new p=pred;
run;

data new1; set new;

proc sort;
  by gender;
run;

proc means;
  class gender sleep;
  var pred;
  types gender*sleep;
run;
```

Example 3.8

SPSS Syntax

```
LOGISTIC REGRESSION VAR=volrelig
  /METHOD=ENTER gender age educate
  /SAVE PRED DEV
  /CRITERIA PIN(.05) POUT(.10) ITERATE(20) CUT(.5) .
EXECUTE .
```
**[Note: SPSS's SAVE command does not include ΔD_i] .

SAS Code

```
libname glm '[place data subdirectory here]';
data one; set glm.gss96;

proc logistic descending;
  model volrelig= gender age educate / expb rsq;
  output out=new
  pred=pred difdev=delta resdev=dev;
run;

data new1; set new;

proc univariate;
  var delta;
run;

proc logistic descending;
  where delta < 4;
  model volrelig= gender age educate / expb rsq;
run;
```

Chapter 4

Example 4.1

SPSS Syntax

```
CROSSTABS
  /TABLES=spanking BY gender
  /FORMAT= AVALUE TABLES
  /CELLS= COUNT .
EXECUTE .
```

SAS Code

```
libname glm '[place data subdirectory here]';
data one; set glm.gss96;

proc freq;
  tables spanking*gender;
run;
```

Exmple 4.2 (note that the gender coefficients are reversed in the SPSS and SAS outputs)

SPSS Syntax

```
PLUM
  spanking BY gender
  /CRITERIA = CIN(95) DELTA(0) LCONVERGE(0) MXITER(100) MXSTEP(5)
  PCONVERGE(1.0E-6) SINGULAR(1.0E-8)
  /LINK = LOGIT
  /PRINT = FIT PARAMETER SUMMARY TPARALLEL .
EXECUTE .
```

SAS Code

```
libname glm '[place data subdirectory here]';
data one; set glm.gss96;

proc logistic;
  model spanking=gender;
run;
```

Example 4.3

SPSS Syntax

```
RECODE
  spanking
  (1=1) (2=1) (3=1) (4=0) INTO spank1a .
```

EXECUTE .

RECODE
 spanking
 (1=1) (2=1) (3=0) (4=0) INTO spank2a .
EXECUTE .

RECODE
 spanking
 (1=1) (2=0) (3=0) (4=0) INTO spank3a .
EXECUTE .

COMPUTE spank1 = 1 - spank1a .
EXECUTE .
COMPUTE spank2 = 1 - spank2a .
EXECUTE .
COMPUTE spank3 = 1 - spank3a .
EXECUTE .

** We have recomputed these variables so that the SPSS output agrees with the Stata output .

LOGISTIC REGRESSION VAR=spank1
 /METHOD=ENTER gender
 /CRITERIA PIN(.05) POUT(.10) ITERATE(20) CUT(.5) .

LOGISTIC REGRESSION VAR=spank2
 /METHOD=ENTER gender
 /CRITERIA PIN(.05) POUT(.10) ITERATE(20) CUT(.5) .

LOGISTIC REGRESSION VAR=spank3
 /METHOD=ENTER gender
 /CRITERIA PIN(.05) POUT(.10) ITERATE(20) CUT(.5) .
EXECUTE .

SAS Code

```
libname glm '[place data subdirectory here]';
data one; set glm.gss96;

spank1=.;
if (spanking=1 or spanking=2 or spanking=3) then spank1=1;
if (spanking=4) then spank1=0;

spank2=.;
if (spanking=1 or spanking=2) then spank2=1;
if (spanking=3 or spanking=4) then spank2=0;

spank3=.;
if (spanking=1) then spank3=1;
if (spanking=2 or spanking=3 or spanking=4) then spank3=0;
```

```
proc logistic;
  model spank1=gender / expb;
run;

proc logistic;
  model spank2=gender / expb;
run;

proc logistic;
  model spank3=gender / expb;
run;
```

Example 4.4

SPSS Syntax

At the time of writing, SPSS did not offer an ordinal probit routine.

SAS Code (note that the cutpoints differ between SAS and Stata)

```
libname glm '[place data subdirectory here]';
data one; set glm.gss96;

/* recode gender to match the Stata output */
gender1=2-gender;

proc probit;
  class spanking;
  model spanking=gender1;
  output out=three prob=pred;
run;
```

(Examples using other software are not available at this time.)

Example 4.7

SPSS Syntax

```
PLUM
  spanking BY gender WITH educate polviews
  /CRITERIA = CIN(95) DELTA(0) LCONVERGE(0) MXITER(100) MXSTEP(5)
  PCONVERGE(1.0E-6) SINGULAR(1.0E-8)
  /LINK = LOGIT
  /PRINT = FIT PARAMETER SUMMARY TPARALLEL .
  /SAVE = PCPROB .
EXECUTE .
```

SAS Code

```
libname glm '[place data subdirectory here]';
data one; set glm.gss96;
```

```
proc logistic descending;
  model spanking=gender educate polviews;
run;
```

Example 4.8

SPSS Syntax

At the time of writing, SPSS did not offer an ordinal probit routine.

SAS Code

```
libname glm '[place data subdirectory here]';
data one; set glm.gss96;
```

```
/* recode spanking to match the Stata output */
spanking1=5-spanking;
```

```
proc probit;
  class spanking1;
  model spanking1=gender educate polviews;
  output out=five p=pred;
run;
```

Chapter 5

Example 5.1

SPSS Syntax

```
CROSSTABS
 /TABLES=polview1 BY race
 /FORMAT= AVALUE TABLES
 /CELLS= COUNT .
EXECUTE .
```

SAS Code

```
libname glm '[place data subdirectory here]';
data one; set glm.gss96;
```

```
polview1=.;
if (polview=1 or polview=2 or polview=3) then polview1=1;
if (polview=4) then polview1=2;
if (polview=5 or polview=6 or polview=7) then polview1=3;
```

```
proc freq;
  tables polview1*race;
run;
```

Example 5.2

SPSS Syntax

Note that SPSS fixes the base category to be the highest coded category. In order to make *moderate* the base category, recode *polview1* so that *moderate* is coded 3 and the other categories are coded 1 and 2.

```
NOMREG
  polview1 BY race
  /CRITERIA = CIN(95) DELTA(0) MXITER(100) MXSTEP(5) CHKSEP(20)
LCONVERGE(0)
  PCONVERGE(1.0E-6) SINGULAR(1.0E-8)
  /MODEL
  /INTERCEPT = INCLUDE
  /PRINT = CELLPROB PARAMETER SUMMARY LRT
  /SAVE = PCPROB .
EXECUTE .
```

SAS Code

Note that recoding is needed to set the base category to agree with the base category used by Stata.

```
libname glm '[place data subdirectory here]';
data one; set glm.gss96;

proc catmod;
  direct race;
  model polview1=race / pred=prob NOITER;
run;
```

Example 5.4

SPSS Syntax

Note that SPSS fixes the base category to be the highest coded category. In order to make *moderate* the base category, recode *polview1* so that *moderate* is coded 3 and the other categories are coded 1 and 2.

```
NOMREG
  polview1 BY gender WITH age educate
  /CRITERIA = CIN(95) DELTA(0) MXITER(100) MXSTEP(5) CHKSEP(20)
LCONVERGE(0)
  PCONVERGE(1.0E-6) SINGULAR(1.0E-8)
  /MODEL
  /INTERCEPT = INCLUDE
```

```
/PRINT = PARAMETER SUMMARY LRT .
EXECUTE .
```

SAS Code

Note that recoding is needed to set the base category to agree with the base category used by Stata.

```
libname glm '[place data subdirectory here]';
data one; set glm.gss96;

proc catmod;
  direct gender age educate;
  model polview1=gender age educate / NOITER;
run;
```

Example 5.6

SPSS Syntax

Note that SPSS fixes the base category to be the highest coded category. In order to make *moderate* the base category, recode *polview1* so that *moderate* is coded 3 and the other categories are coded 1 and 2.

```
NOMREG
  polview1 BY gender WITH zage zeducate
  /CRITERIA = CIN(95) DELTA(0) MXITER(100) MXSTEP(5) CHKSEP(20)
LCONVERGE(0)
  PCONVERGE(1.0E-6) SINGULAR(1.0E-8)
  /MODEL
  /INTERCEPT = INCLUDE
  /PRINT = CELLPROB PARAMETER SUMMARY LRT
  /SAVE = PCPROB .
EXECUTE .
```

SAS Code

Note that recoding is needed to set the base category to agree with the base category used by Stata.

```
libname glm '[place data subdirectory here]';
data one; set glm.gss96;

proc catmod;
  direct gender zage zeducate;
  model polview1=gender zage zeducate / pred=prob NOITER;
run;
```

Example 5.7 (partial only)

SPSS Syntax

```
RECODE
 polview1
 (1=1) (2=SYSMIS) (3=0) INTO conslib .
EXECUTE .

RECODE
 polview1
 (1=SYSMIS) (2=1) (3=0) INTO consmod .
EXECUTE .

LOGISTIC REGRESSION VAR=conslib
 /METHOD=ENTER gender age educate
 /SAVE PRED DEV
 /CRITERIA PIN(.05) POUT(.10) ITERATE(20) CUT(.5) .

LOGISTIC REGRESSION VAR=consmod
 /METHOD=ENTER gender age educate
 /SAVE PRED DEV
 /CRITERIA PIN(.05) POUT(.10) ITERATE(20) CUT(.5) .
EXECUTE .
```

SAS Code

```
libname glm '[place data subdirectory here]';
data one; set glm.gss96;

/* See the polview1 recodes under Example 5.1 */

conslib=.;
if polview1=1 then conslib=1;
if polview1=3 then conslib=0;

consmod=.;
if polview1=2 then consmod=1;
if polview1=3 then consmod=0;

proc logistic descending;
  model conslib=gender age educate;
  output out=predict
  pred=p1;
  resdev=dev1;
run;

proc logistic descending;
  model consmod=gender age educate;
```

```
    output out=predict2
    pred=p2;
    resdev=dev2
run;
```

Chapter 6

Example 6.1

Note that at the time of writing, SPSS did not offer a straightforward way to estimate Poisson or negative binomial models. Specialized syntax files are needed.

SAS Code

```
libname glm '[place data subdirectory here]';
data one; set glm.gss96;

proc freq;
  tables volteer;
run;
```

Example 6.2

SAS Code

```
libname glm '[place data subdirectory here]';
data one; set glm.gss96;

proc univariate;
  var volteer;
run;
```

Example 6.3

SAS Code

```
libname glm '[place data subdirectory here]';
data one; set glm.gss96;
proc sort;
  by gender;
run;

proc univariate;
  by gender;
  var volteer;
run;
```

Example 6.4

SAS Code

```
libname glm '[place data subdirectory here]';
data one; set glm.gss96;

proc genmod;
  model volteer=gender / dist=p;
run;
```

Example 6.5

SAS Code

```
libname glm '[place data subdirectory here]';
data one; set glm.gss96;

proc genmod;
  model volteer=gender race educate income / dist=p;
  output out=one p=volunt1;
run;

data two; set one;

proc sort;
  by gender;
run;

proc means;
  by gender;
  var volunt1;
run;

proc sort;
  by educ2;
run;

proc means;
  by educ2;
  var volunt1;
run;

proc genmod;
  model volteer=gender race educate zincome / dist=p;
  output out=three p=volunt2;
run;
```

Example 6.6

SAS Code

```
libname glm '[place data subdirectory here]';
data one; set glm.gss96;

proc genmod;
  model volteer=gender race educate income / dist=p pscale;
run;
```

Example 6.7

SAS Code

```
libname glm '[place data subdirectory here]';
data one; set glm.gss96;

proc genmod;
  model volteer=gender race educate income / Dist=nb;
  output out=one p=volunt3;
run;

data two; set one;
proc sort;
  by gender;
run;

proc means;
  by gender;
  var volunt3;
run;
```

Example 6.8

SAS Code

```
libname glm '[place data subdirectory here]';
data one; set glm.gss96;

proc genmod;
  model volteer=gender race educate income / Dist=p;
  output out=one p=count resdev=dev1;
run;

data two; set one;
```

```
scount=sqrt(count);
adjdev=dev1 + (1/(6*scount));

run;

proc gplot;
  plot dev1*count;
run;

/* Note that the figure based on this code is different from the */
/* Stata-generated figure because the deviance values are plotted */
/* on the y-axis rather than the x-axis */

proc capability noprint;
  probplot dev1 / cframe = ligr;
run;
```

Chapter 7

Examples 7.1–7.5

SPSS Syntax (partial only)

```
KM
  marriage /STATUS=marr1(1 THRU 1071)
  /PRINT TABLE MEAN
  /PLOT SURVIVAL
  /SAVE SURVIVAL HAZARD .


KM
  marriage BY cohab / STATUS=marr1(1 THRU 1071)
  /PRINT TABLE MEAN
  /PLOT SURVIVAL
  /SAVE SURVIVAL HAZARD .


KM
  marriage BY cohab / STATUS=marr1(1 THRU 1071)
  /PRINT TABLE MEAN
  /TEST LOGRANK
  /COMPARE OVERALL POOLED
  /SAVE SURVIVAL HAZARD .
EXECUTE .
```

SAS Code

```
libname glm '[place data subdirectory here]';
data one; set glm.event1;
```

```
proc lifetest plots=(s) graphics;
  time marriage;
  symbol v=none;
run;
```

```
proc lifetest plots=(s) graphics;
  time marriage;
  strata cohab;
  symbol1 v=none color=black line=1;
  symbol2 v=none color=black line=2;
run;
```

Example 7.6

Note that at the time of writing, SPSS did not offer a straightforward way to estimate parametric event history models.

SAS Code

```
libname glm '[place data subdirectory here]';
data one; set glm.event1;
```

```
proc lifereg;
  model marriage*evermarr(0)=educate age1sex attend14 cohab race / dist=lnormal;
run;
```

Example 7.7

SAS Code (note that the signs of the coefficients are reversed from the Stata example)

```
libname glm '[place data subdirectory here]';
data one; set glm.event2;
```

```
proc lifereg;
  model marriage*evermarr(0)=educate age1sex attend14 cohab race / dist=exponential;
run;
```

Example 7.8

SAS Code

```
libname glm '[place data subdirectory here]';
data one; set glm.event2;
proc lifereg;
  model marriage*evermarr(0)=educate age1sex attend14 cohab race / dist=weibull;
  output out=a cdf=f;
run;
```

```
data b;
  set a;
  e=-log(1-f);
run;
```

```
proc lifetest data=b plots=(ls) notable graphics;
  time e*evermarr(0);
  symbol v=none;
run;
```

Examples 7.9–7.10

SPSS Syntax (partial only)

```
COXREG
  marriage /STATUS=evermarr(1)
  /METHOD=ENTER educate age1sex attend14 cohab race
  /CRITERIA=PIN(.05) POUT(.10) ITERATE(20) .
EXECUTE .
```

```
COMPUTE wmarr = race * marriage .
EXECUTE .
```

```
COMPUTE cmarr = cohab * marriage .
EXECUTE .
```

```
COXREG
  marriage /STATUS=evermarr(1)
  /PATTERN BY cohab
  /CONTRAST (cohab)=Difference
  /METHOD=ENTER age1sex attend14 cohab race educate wmarr cmarr
  /PLOT SURVIVAL
  /CRITERIA=PIN(.05) POUT(.10) ITERATE(20) .
EXECUTE .
```

SAS Code (partial only; see Allison (1995) for more comprehensive SAS codes.)

```
libname glm '[place data subdirectory here]';
data one; set glm.event2;
```

```
proc phreg;
  model marriage*evermarr(0)=educate age1sex attend14 cohab race / ties=efron;
  output out=two ressch=schedu schage schatt schcoh schrace;
run;
```

```
proc print data=two;
run;
```

```
proc gplot data=two;
  plot schedu*marriage schage*marriage schatt*marriage schcoh*marriage
schrace*marriage;
```

```
symbol1 value=dot h=.02;
run;
```

Example 7.12

SPSS Syntax

```
** Note that, in contrast to the text, year four (rather than year one) is the reference.
** year or category. Thus, notice that the odds of first delinquent acts are higher.
** in early years than in later years.

LOGISTIC REGRESSION VAR=delinq1
  /METHOD=ENTER stress cohes year
  /CONTRAST (year)=Indicator
  /CRITERIA PIN(.05) POUT(.10) ITERATE(20) CUT(.5) .
EXECUTE .
```

SAS Code

Note that the year coefficients differ from those of the Stata output.

```
libname glm '[place data subdirectory here]';
data one; set glm.event3;

proc logistic descending;
  class year;
  model delinq1=stress cohes year;
run;
```

Example 7.13

SAS Code

```
libname glm '[place data subdirectory here]';
data one; set glm.event3;

proc phreg;
  model year*delinq1(0)=stress cohes sttime / ties=efron;
  sttime=stress*year;
  output out=two ressch=schstress schcohes;
run;

proc print data=two;
run;

proc gplot data=two;
  plot schstress*year cohes*year;
  symbol1 value=dot h=.02;
run;
```

Example 7.15

SPSS Syntax

```
LOGISTIC REGRESSION VAR=delinq
  /METHOD=ENTER stress cohes year
  /CONTRAST (year)=Indicator
  /CRITERIA PIN(.05) POUT(.10) ITERATE(20) CUT(.5) .
EXECUTE .
```

SAS Code (note that the year coefficients differ slightly)

```
libname glm '[place data subdirectory here]';
data one; set glm.event4;

proc logistic descending;
  class year;
  model delinq=stress cohes year;
run;
```

Example 7.16

SAS Code (note that the hazard ratios differ slightly)

```
libname glm '[place data subdirectory here]';
data one; set glm.event4;

proc phreg;
  model year*delinq(0)=stress cohes sttime / ties=efron;
  sttime=stress*year;
run;
```

Chapter 8

Example 8.1

Note that at the time of writing, SPSS did not include a GEE routine.

SAS Code

```
libname glm '[place data subdirectory here]';
data one; set glm.event4;

proc genmod descending;
  class year newid;
  model delinq = stress cohes / dist=bin;
  repeated subject=newid / type=ind covb corrw;
run;
```

Example 8.2

SAS Code

```
libname glm '[place data subdirectory here]';
data one; set glm.event4;

proc genmod descending;
  class year newid;
  model delinq stress cohes / dist=bin;
  repeated subject=newid / type=exch covb corrw;
run;
```

Example 8.3

SAS Code

```
libname glm '[place data subdirectory here]';
data one; set glm.event4;

proc genmod descending;
  class year newid;
  model delinq stress cohes / dist=bin;
  repeated subject=newid / type=ar(1) covb corrw;
run;
```

Example 8.4

SAS Code

```
libname glm '[place data subdirectory here]';
data one; set glm.event4;

proc genmod descending;
  class year newid;
  model delinq stress cohes / dist=bin;
  repeated subject=newid / type=unstr covb corrw;
run;
```

References

Agresti, Alan. 1990. Categorical Data Analysis. New York: Wiley.

Agresti, Alan. 1996. An Introduction to Categorical Data Analysis. New York: Wiley.

Agresti, Alan, and Ivy Liu. 2001. "Strategies for Modeling a Categorical Variable Allowing Multiple Category Choices." Sociological Methods and Research 29:403–434.

Aiken, Leona S., and Stephen G. West. 1991. Multiple Regression: Testing and Interpreting Interactions. Newbury Park, CA: Sage.

Allison, Paul D. 1990. "Change Scores as Dependent Variables in Regression Analysis." Pp.93–114 in Clifford C. Clogg (Ed.), Sociological Methodology. Washington, DC: American Sociological Association.

Allison, Paul D. 1995. Survival Analysis Using the SAS System: A Practical Guide. Cary, NC: SAS Institute.

Allison, Paul D. 1999. Multiple Regression: A Primer. Thousand Oaks, CA: Pine Forge Press.

Amemiya, Takeshi. 1985. Advanced Econometrics. Cambridge, MA: Harvard University Press.

Azen, Razia, David V. Budescu, and Benjamin Reiser. 2001. "Criticality of Predictors in Multiple Regression." British Journal of Mathematical and Statistical Psychology 54:201–225.

Beck, E.M., and Stewart E. Tolnay. 1995. "Analyzing Historical Count Data: Poisson and Negative Binomial Regression Models." Historical Methods 28:125–131.

Beck, Nathaniel, and Simon Jackman. 1998. "Beyond Linearity by Default: Generalized Additive Models." American Journal of Political Science 42:596–627.

Berry, William D. 1993. Understanding Regression Assumptions. Newbury Park, CA: Sage.

Bijleveld, Catrien C.J.H., and Leo J. Th. van der Kamp. 1998. Longitudinal Data Analysis: Designs, Models, and Methods. Thousand Oaks, CA: Sage.

Blossfeld, Hans–Peter, and Gotz Rohwer. 1995. Techniques of Event History Modeling: New Approaches to Causal Analysis. Mahwah, NJ: Lawrence Erlbaum Associates.

Bolks, Sean M., Diana Evans, and J.L. Polinard. 2000. "Core Beliefs and Abortion Attitudes: A Look at Latinos." Social Science Quarterly 81:253–260.

Borooah, Vani K. 2001. Logit and Probit: Ordered and Multinomial Models. Thousand Oaks, CA: Sage.

Bowerman, Bruce L., and Richard O'Connell. 1993. Forecasting and Time Series: An Applied Approach, 3rd Ed. Brooks/Cole Publishing.

Box-Steffensmeier, Janet M., and Bradford S. Jones. 1997. "Time is of the Essence: Event History Models in Political Science." American Journal of Political Science 41:1414–1426.

Bradstreet, Thomas E. 1996. "Teaching Introductory Statistics Courses So That Nonstatisticians Experience Statistical Reasoning." American Statistician 50:69–78.

Breen, Richard. 1996. Regression Models: Censored, Sample Selected, or Truncated Data. Thousand Oaks, CA: Sage.

Cameron, A. Colin, and Pravin K. Trivedi. 1998. Regression Analysis of Count Data. Cambridge: Cambridge University Press.

Carothers, Andew D., and Lynne Murray. 1990. "Estimating Psychiatric Morbidity by Logistic Regression: Application of Post-Natal Depression in a Community Sample." Psychological Medicine 20:695–702.

Chatterjee, Samprit, and Bertram Price. 1991. Regression Analysis by Example, 2nd Ed. New York: Wiley.

Chen, Zhen, and Lynn Kuo. 2001. "A Note on the Estimation of the Multinomial Logit Model with Random Effects." American Statistician 55:89–95.

Chilcoat, Howard D., and Christian G. Schultz. 1996. "Age-Specific Patterns of Hallucinogen Use in the US Population: An Analysis Using Generalized Additive Models." Drug and Alcohol Dependence 43:143–153.

Christensen, Ronald. 1990. Log-Linear Models. New York: Springer-Verlag.

Clark, Andrew, Andrew Oswald, and Peter Warr. 1996. "Is Job Satisfaction U-Shaped in Age?" Journal of Occupational and Organizational Psychology 69:57–81.

Cleveland, William S. 1993. Visualizing Data. Summit, NJ: Hobart Press.

Cleves, Mario, William Gould, and Roberto Gutierrez. 2002. An Introduction to Survival Analysis Using Stata. College Station, TX: Stata Press.

Clogg, Clifford C. 1995. "Latent Class Models." Pp.311–360 in Gerhard Arminger, Clifford C. Clogg, and Michael E. Sobel (Eds.), Handbook of Statistical Modeling in the Social and Behavioral Sciences. New York: Plenum Press.

Clogg, Clifford C., and Edward S. Shihadeh. 1994. Statistical Models for Ordinal Variables. Thousand Oaks, CA: Sage.

Coley, Rebekah Levine, and P. Lindsay Chase-Lansdale. 1999. "Stability and Change in Paternal Involvement Among Urban African-American Fathers." Journal of Family Psychology 13:416–435.

Crosnoe, Robert. 2001. "Parental Involvement in Education: The Influence of School and Neighborhood." Sociological Focus 34:417–434.

Cunradi, Carol B., Raul Caetano, and John Schafer. 2002. "Religious Affiliation, Denominational Homogamy, and Intimate Partner Violence Among U.S. Couples." Journal for the Scientific Study of Religion 41:139–151.

Danes, Sharon M., and Mary Winter. 1990. "The Impact of Employment of the Wife on the Achievement of Home Ownership." Journal of Consumer Affairs 24:148–169.

Davison, A.C., and A. Gigli. 1989. "Deviance Residuals and Normal Score Plots." Biometrika 76:211–221.

Diggle, Peter J., Kung-Yee Liang, and Scott L. Zeger. 1994. Analysis of Longitudinal Data. Oxford: Clarendon Press.

Dionne, Georges, Christian Gourieoux, and Charles Vanasse. 2001. "Testing for Evidence of Adverse Selection in the Automobile Insurance Market: A Comment." Journal of Political Economy 109:444–453.

Dispensa, Gary S. 1997. "Use Logistic Regression with Customer Satisfaction Data." Marketing News 31:13.

Dobson, Annette J. 1990. An Introduction to Generalized Linear Models. London: Chapman & Hall.

Dolsak, Nives. 2001. "Mitigating Global Climate Change: Why Are Some Countries More Committed Than Others?" Policy Studies Journal 29:414–433.

Draper, Norman R., and Harry Smith. 1998. Applied Regression Analysis, 3rd Ed. New York: Wiley.

Duncan, Terry E., Susan C. Duncan, Hyman Hops, and Mike Stoolmiller. 1995. "An Analysis of the Relationship between Parent and Adolescent Marijuana Use via Generalized Estimating Equation Methodology." Multivariate Behavioral Research 30:317–339.

Duncan, Terry E., Susan C. Duncan, Lisa A. Strycker, Fuzhong Li, and Anthony Alpert. 1999. An Introduction to Latent Variable Growth Curve Modeling: Concepts, Issues, and Applications. Mahwah, NJ: Lawrence Erlbaum Associates.

Duncombe, William, Mark Robbins, and Douglas A. Wolf. 2001. "Retire to Where? A Discrete Choice Model of Residential Location." International Journal of Population Geography 7:281–294.

Eliason, Scott R. 1992. Maximum Likelihood Estimation: Logic and Practice. Newbury Park, CA: Sage.

Finkel, Steven E. 1995. Causal Analysis with Panel Data. Thousand Oaks, CA: Sage.

Firebaugh, Glenn. 1997. Analyzing Repeated Surveys. Thousand Oaks, CA: Sage.

Flood, Lennart, and Urban Grasjo. 2001. "A Monte Carlo Simulation Study of Tobit Models." Applied Economic Letters 8:581–584.

Flowerdew, Robin, and Alistair Geddes. 1999. "Poisson Regression Analysis of Limiting Long-Term Illness Data for Parts of North-East England." Geographical and Environmental Modelling 3:63–82.

Fox, John. 1991. Regression Diagnostics. Newbury Park, CA: Sage.

Fox, John. 1997. Applied Regression Analysis, Linear Models, and Related Methods. Thousand Oaks, CA: Sage.

Fox, John. 2000. Multiple and Generalized Nonparametric Regression. Thousand Oaks, CA: Sage.

Fry, Tim R.L., and Mark N. Harris. 1998. "Testing for Independence of Irrelevant Alternatives: Some Empirical Results." Sociological Methods and Research 26:401–423.

Fry, Tim R.L., and Chris D. Orme. 1998. "Generalized Logistic Tobit Models." Journal of Quantitative Economics 14:23–32.

Gardner, William, Edward P. Mulvey, and Esther C. Shaw. 1995. "Regression Analyses of Counts and Rates: Poisson, Overdispersed Poisson, and Negative Binomial Models." Psychological Bulletin 118:392–404.

Gilbert, Janelle A., and Kenneth S. Shultz. 1998. "Multilevel Modeling in Industrial and Personnel Psychology." Current Psychology 17:287–300.

Gill, Jeff. 2000. Generalized Linear Models: A Unified Approach. Thousand Oaks, CA: Sage.

Goldberger, Arthur S., and Charles F. Manski. 1995. "Review Article: The Bell Curve by Herrnstein and Murray." Review of Economic Literature 33:762–776.

Goldstein, Harvey. 1995. Multilevel Statistical Models. London: Edward Arnold.

Graybill, Franklin A., and Harharan K. Iyer. 1994. Regression Analysis: Concepts and Applications, 2nd Ed. Belmont, CA: Duxbury Press.

Greene, William H. 2000. Econometric Analysis, 4th Ed. Upper Saddle River, NJ: Prentice Hall.

Hagenaars, Jacques A. 1993. Log-Linear Models with Latent Variables. Newbury Park, CA: Sage.

Hagle, Timothy M. 1993. "Strategic Retirements: A Political Model of Turnover on the United States Supreme Court." Political Behavior 15:25–48.

Hamerle, Alfred, and Gerd Ronning. 1995. "Panel Analysis for Qualitative Variables." Pp.401–451 in Gerhard Arminger, Clifford C. Clogg, and Michael E. Sobel (Eds.), Handbook of Statistical Modeling in the Social and Behavioral Sciences. New York: Plenum Press.

Hamilton, Lawrence C. 1999. Regression With Graphics: A Second Course in Applied Statistics. Pacific Grove, CA: Brooks/Cole.

Hardin, James, and Joseph Hilbe. 2001. Generalized Linear Models and Extensions. College Station, TX: Stata Press.

Hastie, Trevor J., and Robert J. Tibshirani. 1990. Generalized Additive Models. New York: Chapman and Hall.

Hausman, Jerry A., and Daniel McFadden. 1984. "Specification Tests for the Multinomial Logit Model." Econometrica 52:1219–1240.

Haynes, Stephen E., and David Jacobs. 1994. "Macroeconomics, Economic Stratification, and Partisanship: A Longitudinal Analysis of Contingent Shifts in Political Identification." American Journal of Sociology 100:70–103.

Heaton, Tim B., and Vaughn R.A. Call. 1995. "Modeling Family Dynamics with Event History Techniques." Journal of Marriage and the Family 57:1078–1090.

Hilbe, Joseph. 1994. "Generalized Linear Models." American Statistician 48:255–265.

Hill, Nancy Thorley, and Susan E. Perry. 1996. "Evaluating Firms in Financial Distress: An Event History Analysis." Journal of Applied Business Research 12:60–72.

Hoffmann, John P. 2002. "The Community Context of Family Structure and Adolescent Drug Use." Journal of Marriage and Family 64:314–330.

Hoffmann, John P. 2001. "Answering Old Questions: The Potential of Multilevel Models." Sociological Theory and Methods 16:61–74.

Hoffmann, John P., and Felicia Gray Cerbone. 1999. "Stressful Life Events and Delinquency Escalation in Early Adolescence." Criminology 37:343–374.

Hoffmann, John P., and Cindy L. Larison. 1999. "Worker Drug Use and Workplace Drug Testing Programs." Contemporary Drug Problems 26:331–354.

Holloway, Steven R. 1998. "Labor Demand, Metropolitan Context, and Male Youths' Activity Strategies." Urban Geography 19:591–612.

Horton, Nicholas J., and Stuart R. Lipsitz. 1999. "Review of Software to Fit Generalized Estimating Equation Regression Models." American Statistician 53:160–169.

Hoshino, Shimoi. 2001. "Multilevel Modeling of Farmland Distribution in Japan." Land Use Policy 18:75–90.

Hosmer, David W., and Stanley Lemeshow. 1989. Applied Logistic Regression. New York: Wiley.

Hsiao, Cheng. 1989. Analysis of Panel Data. Cambridge: Cambridge University Press.

Hsu, Louis M. 1980. "Determination of the Number of Items and Passing Score in a Mastery Test." Educational and Psychological Measurement 40:709–714.

Huet, Sylvie, Annie Bouvier, Marie-Anne Gruet, and Emmanuel Jolivet. 1996. Statistical Tools for Nonlinear Regression: A Practical Guide with S-PLUS Examples. New York: Springer.

Johnson, Daniel Carson. 1997. "Formal Education vs. Religious Belief: Soliciting New Evidence with Multinomial Logit Modeling." Journal for the Scientific Study of Religion 36:231–246.

Johnson, W. Wesley. 1996. "Transcarceration and Social Control Policy: The 1980s and Beyond." Crime & Delinquency 42:114–126.

Jones, Andrew P., and Stig H. Jorgensen. 2003. "The Use of Multilevel Models for the Prediction of Road Accident Outcomes." Accident Analysis and Prevention 35:59–69.

Jones, Kelvyn, and Neil Wrigley. 1995. "Generalized Additive Models, Graphical Diagnostics, and Logistic Regression." Geographical Analysis 27:1–21.

Kawachi, Ichiro, Bruce P. Kennedy, and Richard G. Wilkinson. 1999. "Crime: Social Disorganization and Relative Deprivation." Social Science and Medicine 48:719–731.

Kennedy, Peter. 1992. A Guide to Econometrics, 3rd Ed. Cambridge, MA: MIT Press.

Kleinbaum, David G. 1994. Logistic Regression: A Self-Teaching Text. New York: Springer.

Kleinbaum, David G. 1996. Survival Analysis: A Self-Teaching Text. New York: Springer.

Kleinbaum, David G., Lawrence L. Kupper, Keith D. Muller, and Azhar Nizam. 1998. Applied Regression Analysis and Other Multivariable Methods, 3rd Ed. Pacific Grove, CA: Duxbury Press.

Kline, Rex B. 1998. Principles and Practice of Structural Equation Modeling. New York: Guilford Press.

Knudsen, Daniel C. 1990. "A Dynamical Analysis of Interaction Data: US Rail Freight Flows, 1972–81." Geographical Analysis 22:259–269.

Knoke, David, and Peter J. Burke. 1980. Log-Linear Models. Beverly Hills, CA: Sage.

Land, Kenneth C. 1992. "Models of Criminal Careers: Some Suggestions for Moving Beyond the Current Debate." Criminology 30:149–155.

Land, Kenneth C., Patricia L. McCall, and Daniel S. Nagin. 1996. "A Comparison of Poisson, Negative Binomial, and Semiparametric Mixed Poisson Regression Models: With Empirical Applications to Criminal Careers." Sociological Methods and Research 24:387–442.

Lambert, David. 1992. "Zero Inflated Poisson Regression with an Application to Defects in Manufacturing." Technometrics 34:1–14.

Lee, Elisa T. 1992. Statistical Methods for Survival Data Analysis. New York: Wiley.

Lee, Jong-Tae, Ho Kim, Yun-Chul Hong, Ho-Jang Kwon, Joel Schwartz, and David C. Christian.

2000. "Air Pollution and Daily Mortality in Seven Major Cities of Korea, 1991–1997." Environmental Research 84:247–254.

Lehmann, Erich L. 1998. Nonparametrics: Statistical Methods Based on Ranks. Upper Saddle River, NJ: Prentice Hall.

Leiter, Jeffrey, and Matthew C. Johnsen. 1997. "Child Maltreatment and School Performance Declines: An Event-History Analysis." American Educational Research Journal 34:563–589.

Liao, Tim Futing. 2000. "Estimated Precision for Predictions from Generalized Linear Models in Sociological Research." Quality and Quantity 34:137–152.

Lindsey, James K. 1995. Introductory Statistics: A Modelling Approach. Oxford: Clarendon Press.

Lindsey, James K. 1997. Applying Generalized Linear Models. New York: Springer.

Littell, Ramon C., George A. Milliken, Walter W. Stroupe, and Russell D. Wolfinger. 1996. SAS System for Mixed Models. Cary, NC: SAS Institute.

Lloyd, Chris J. 1999. Statistical Analysis of Categorical Data. New York: Wiley.

Loehlin, John C. 1992. Latent Variable Models: An Introduction to Factor, Path and Structural Analysis, 2nd Ed. Hillsdale, NJ: Lawrence Erlbaum Associates.

Long, J. Scott. 1997. Regression Models for Categorical and Limited Dependent Variables. Thousand Oaks, CA: Sage.

Long, J. Scott, and Laurie H. Ervin. 2000. "Using Heteroscedasticity Consistent Standard Errors in the Linear Regression Model." American Statistician 54:217–224.

Long, J. Scott, and Jeremy Freese. 2001. Regression Models for Categorical Dependent Variables in Stata. College Station, TX: Stata Press.

Lowery, David, and Virginia Gray. 1998. "The Dominance of Institutions in Interest Representation: A Test of Seven Explanations." American Journal of Political Science 42:231–255.

Luke, Douglas A., and Sharon M. Homan. 1998. "Time and Change: Using Survival Analysis in Clinical Assessment and Treatment Evaluation." Psychological Assessment 10:360–378.

Manski, Charles F. 1995. Identification Problems in the Social Sciences. Cambridge, MA: Harvard University Press.

McCullagh, P., and J.A. Nelder. 1989. Generalized Linear Models, 2nd Ed. New York: Chapman & Hall.

Montgomery, Douglas C., Elizabeth A. Peck, and G. Geoffrey Vining. 2001. Introduction to Linear Regression Analysis, 3rd Ed. New York: Wiley.

Muthen, Bengt. 2001. "Second-Generation Structural Equation Modeling with a Combination of Categorical and Continuous Latent Variables." Pp. 291–322 in Linda M. Collins and Aline G. Sayer (Eds.), New Methods for the Analysis of Change, Washington, DC: American Psychological Association Press.

Myers, Raymond H., Douglas C. Montgomery, and G. Geoffrey Vining. 2002. Generalized Linear Models: With Applications to Engineering and the Sciences. New York: Wiley.

Neeley, Grant W., and Lillard E. Richardson. 2001. "Who is Early Voting? An Individual Level Examination." Social Science Journal 38:381–392.

Nownes, Anthony J. "Primaries, General Elections, and Voter Turnout: A Multinomial Logit Model of the Decision to Vote." American Politics Quarterly 20:205–226.

Pagan, Jose A., and Alberto Davila. 1997. "Obesity, Occupational Attainment, and Earnings." Social Science Quarterly 78:756–770.

Park, Kang H., and Peter M. Kerr. 1990. "Determinants of Academic Performance: A Multinomial Logit Approach." Journal of Economics Education 21:101–111.

Peel, Michael J., and Mark M. Goode. 1998. "Estimating Consumer Satisfaction: OLS Versus Ordered Probability Models." International Journal of Commerce & Management 8:75–85.

Pierce, Donald A., and Daniel W. Schafer. 1986. "Residuals in Generalized Linear Models." Journal of the American Statistical Association 81:977–986.

Plewis, Ian. 1997. Statistics in Education. London: Arnold Publishers.

Poole, Charles. 1987. "Beyond the Confidence Interval." American Journal of Public Health 77:195–199.

Powell, Richard J. 2000. "The Impact of Term Limits on the Candidacy Decisions of State Legislators in U.S. House Elections." Legislative Studies Quarterly 25:645–661.

Powers, Daniel A., and Yu Xie. 2000. Statistical Methods for Categorical Data Analysis. San Diego, CA: Academic Press.

Raftery, Adrian E. 1995. "Bayesian Model Selection in Social Research (with Discussion)." Sociological Methodology 25:111–163.

Ramamurti, Ravi. 2000. "A Multilevel Model of Privatization in Emerging Economies." Academy of Management Review 25:525–550.

Rasler, Karen. 1996. "Concessions, Repression, and Political Protest in the Iranian Revolution." American Sociological Review 61:132–152.

Retherford, Robert D., and Minja Kim Choe. 1993. Statistical Models for Causal Analysis. New York: Wiley.

Rhea, Anisa, and Luther B. Otto. 2001. "Mothers' Influences on Adolescents' Educational Outcome Beliefs." Journal of Adolescent Research 16:491–510.

Ringdal, Kristen. 1992. "Methods of Multilevel Analysis." Acta Sociologica 25:235–243.

Roncek, Dennis W. 1992. "Learning More From Tobit Coefficients: Extending a Comparative Analysis of Political Protest." American Sociological Review 57:503–507.

Rose, Nicholas J. (Ed.). 1988. Mathematical Maxims and Minims. Raleigh, NC: Rome Press.

Ross, Sheldon. 1994. A First Course in Probability, 4th Ed. New York: Macmillan.

Rountree, Pamela Wilcox, and Kenneth C. Land. 1996. "Burglary Victimization, Perceptions of Crime Risk, and Routine Activities: A Multilevel Analysis Across Seattle Neighborhoods and Census Tracts." Journal of Research in Crime and Delinquency 33:147–180.

Rowell, R. Kevin. 1996. "Partitioning Predicted Variance into Constituent Parts: How to Conduct Regression Commonality Analysis." Advances in Social Science Methodology 4:33–43.

Rumberger, Russell W. 1995. "Dropping Out of Middle School: A Multilevel Analysis of Students and Schools." American Educational Research Journal 32:583–625.

Schwartz, Eduardo S., and Walter N. Torous. 1993. "Mortgage Prepayment and Default Decisions: A Poisson Regression Approach." Journal of the American Real Estate and Urban Economics Association 21:431–449.

Sherer, Peter D., and Kyungmook Lee. 2002. "Institutional Change in Large Law Firms: A Resource Dependency and Institutional Perspective." Academy of Management Journal 45:102–115.

Sherkat, Darren E. 2000. "'That They Be Keepers of the Home': The Effects of Conservative Religion on Early and Late Transitions into Housewifery." Review of Religious Research 41:344–358.

Shpayer-Makov, Haia. 1991. "Measuring Labor Turnover in Historical Research." Historical Methods 24:25–34.

Sigelman, Lee, Paul Wahlbeck, and Emmett H. Buell. 1997. "Vote Choice and the Preference for Divided Government: Lessons of 1992." American Journal of Political Science 41:879–894.

Singer, Judith D. 1998. "Using SAS PROC MIXED to Fit Multilevel Models, Hierarchical Models, and Individual Growth Models." Journal of Educational and Behavioral Statistics 24:323–355.

Smith, Richard L., Joel W. Ager, and David L. Williams. 1992. "Suppressor Variables in Multiple Regression/Correlation." Educational and Psychological Measurement 52:17–29.

Snell, Marilyn N., Brent Mallinckrodt, Robert D. Hill, and Michael J. Lambert. 2001. "Predicting Counseling Center Clients' Response to Counseling: A 1-Year Follow-Up." Journal of Counseling Psychology 48:463–473.

Sobel, Michael E. 1995. "The Analysis of Contingency Tables." Pp. 251–310 in Gerhard Arminger, Clifford C. Clogg, and Michael E. Sobel (Eds.), Handbook of Statistical Modeling in the Social and Behavioral Sciences. New York: Plenum Press.

SPSS, Inc. 2002. SPSS 11.0 Advanced Models. Chicago: Author.

Steenbergen, Marco R., and Bradford S. Jones. 2002. "Modeling Multilevel Data Structures." American Journal of Political Science 46:218–237.

Stigler, Stephen M. 1986. The History of Statistics: The Measurement of Uncertainty before 1900. Cambridge, MA: Harvard University Press.

Stokes, Maura E., Charles S. Davis, and Gary G. Koch. 2000. Categorical Data Analysis Using the SAS System, 2nd Ed. Cary, NC: SAS Institute.

Stolzenberg, Ross M., and Daniel A. Relles. 1997. "Tools for Intuition About Sample Selection Bias and Its Correction." American Sociological Review 62:494–507.

Tansey, Richard, Michael White, and Rebecca G. Long. 1996. "A Comparison of Loglinear Modeling and Logistic Regression in Management Research." Journal of Management 22:339–358.

Therneau, Terry M., and Patricia M. Grambsch. 2000. Modeling Survival Data: Extending the Cox Model. New York: Springer-Verlag.

Therneau, Terry M., Patricia M. Grambsch, and Thomas R. Fleming. 1990. "Martingale-Based Residuals for Survival Models." Biometrika 77:147–160.

Tolnay, Stewart E., Glenn Deane, and E.M. Beck. 1996. "Vicarious Violence: Spatial Effects on Southern Lynchings. 1890–1919." American Journal of Sociology 102:788–815.

Wayman, Jeffrey C. 2002. "The Utility of Educational Resilience for Studying Degree Attainment in School Dropouts." Journal of Educational Research 95:167–178.

Weiler, William C. 1987. "An Application of the Nested Multinomial Logit Model to Enrollment Choice Behavior." Research in Higher Education 27:273–282.

Willett, John B., and Judith D. Singer. 1993. "Investigating Onset, Cessation, Relapse, and Recovery: Why You Should, and How You Can, Use Discrete-Time Survival Analysis to Examine Event Occurrences." Journal of Consulting and Clinical Psychology 61:952–965.

Winship, Christopher, and Robert D. Mare. 1992. "Models for Sample Selection Bias." Annual Review of Sociology 18:327–350.

Woolson, Robert F., and Joel C. Kleinman. 1989. "Perspectives on Statistical Significance Testing." Annual Review of Public Health 10:423–440.

Xiang, Dong. 2002. "Fitting Generalized Additive Models with the GAM Procedure." SAS Paper P256–26. Cary, NC: SAS Institute.

Yamaguchi, Kazuo. 1991. Event History Analysis. Newbury Park, CA: Sage.

Yatchew, Adonis. 1998. "Nonparametric Regression Techniques in Economics." Review of Economic Literature 36:669–721.

Zhou, Xiao-Hua, and Anthony J. Perkins. 1999. "Comparisons of Software Packages for Generalized Linear Multilevel Models." American Statistician 53:282–290.

Zorn, Christopher W. 1998. "An Analytic and Empirical Examination of Zero-Inflated and Hurdle Poisson Specifications." Sociological Methods and Research 26:368–400.

Zucchini, Walter. 2000. "An Introduction to Model Selection." Journal of Mathematical Psychology 44:41–61.

Index